COMMUNICATION AND PERSONAL RELATIONSHIPS

Edited by

KATHRYN DINDIA AND STEVE DUCK

JOHN WILEY & SONS, LTD

Chichester · New York · Weinheim · Brisbane · Singapore · Toronto

Other Wiley Editorial Offices

John Wiley & Sons, Inc., 605 Third Avenue,
New York, NY 10158-0012, USA

Jacaranda Wiley Ltd, 33 Park Road, Milton,
Queensland 4064, Australia

John Wiley & Sons (Canada) Ltd, 22 Worcester Road,
Rexdale, Ontario M9W 1L1, Canada

John Wiley & Sons (Asia) Pte Ltd, 2 Clementi Loop #02-01,
Jin Xing Distripark, Singapore 129809

Library of Congress Cataloging-in-Publication Data

Communication and personal relationships : edited by Steve Duck and Kathryn Dindia.
     p. cm.
   Includes bibliographical references and indexes.
   ISBN 0-471-49133-0
     1. Interpersonal communication. 2. Interpersonal relations. I. Duck, Steve. II. Dindia, Kathryn.

   HM1116.C65 2000
   302.3′4—dc21

                                                                        00-021833

British Library Cataloguing in Publication Data

A catalogue record for this book is available from the British Library

ISBN 0-471-49133-0

Typeset in 10/12pt Times by Saxon Graphics Ltd, Derby
Printed and bound in Great Britain by Antony Rowe Ltd, Chippenham, Wilts
This book is printed on acid-free paper responsibly manufactured from sustainable forestry, in which at
least two trees are planted for each one used for paper production.

CONTENTS

ABOUT THE EDITORS

Kathryn Dindia is Professor and Chair of the Department of Communication at the University of Wisconsin, Milwaukee. She has published articles on self-disclosure, relationship maintenance, and sex-differences in journals in communication, psychology and personal relationships. She was Associate Editor of the *Journal of Social and Personal Relationships*, President of the International Network on Personal Relationships, and Section Editor of the second *Handbook on Personal Relationships*. She recently co-edited (with Dan Canary) the boook, *Sex differences and similarities in Communication.*

Steve Duck is the Daniel and Amy Starch Distinguished Research Professor at the University of Iowa and has been a keen promoter of the field of personal relationships research since it was formed. He co-founded the first International Conference on Personal Relationships in 1982, and was founder and first editor of the *Journal of Social and Personal Relationships,* first President of the International Network on Personal Relationships, the professional organization for the research field, and Editor of the first edition of the *Handbook of Personal Relationships.* The Steve Duck New Scholar Award was endowed and named in his honor by a group of independent scholars to recognize his promotion of the work of younger professionals and his dedication to developing the field.

ABOUT THE AUTHORS

Leslie A. Baxter, Professor of Communication Studies at the University of Iowa, has published widely in the area of communication in personal relationships. Her theoretical interests focus on the role of contradictions in relating.

Arthur P. Bochner is Professor of Communication and Co-Director of the Institute for Interpretive Human Studies in the Department of Communication, University of South Florida. He has published more than 40 monographs and research articles on interpersonal relationships, communication theory, and narrative. His currrent projects focus on local narratives that show how couples jointly construct relationship meanings, and on auto-ethnographies of relationship life.

Christine L. Carson (MA, Illinois State University, 1999) is a doctoral student in the Department of Communication Arts at The University of Wisconsin—Madison. Her research interests include criticism in close relationships, applications of face management theory to close relationships, cognitive influences in the communication of emotion, and interpersonal aspects of health communication.

William R. Cupach (PhD, University of Southern California, 1981) is Professor of Communication at Illinois State University. His research focuses on the dynamics of problematic interactions in social and personal relationships (including such contexts as embarrassing predicaments, relational trangressions, interpersonal conflict and criticism, sexual communication, and obsessive relational pursuit). His publications appear in a diversity of academic journals and books. Previously he served as Associate Editor for Communication for the *Journal of Social and Personal Relationships.*

Carolyn Ellis is Professor of Communication and Sociology and Co-Director of the Institute for Interpretive Human Studies at the University of South Florida. She is the author of *Final Negotiations: A Story of Love, Loss and Chronic Illness* (Temple University Press), *Fisher Folk: Two Communities on Chesapeake Bay* (University Press of Kentucky), and Co-Editor of *Investigating Subjectivity: Research on Lived Experience* (Sage), as well as other edited collections and articles on qualitative methods and emotions. Her current work focuses on narrative, auto-ethnography, and emotional experience.

Sandra Metts (PhD, University of Iowa, 1983) is a Professor in the Department of Communication at Illinois State University, where she teaches interpersonal communication, intercultural communication, language, and research methods. Her research interests focus on the management of problematic social and relational episodes, including embarrassment, relationship disengagement, deception, social support, and sexual communication. Her books include *Self Disclosure* (with Val Derlega, Sandra Petronio, and Stephen Mangulis) and *Facework* (with William Cupach). Her work appears in a variety of journals, as well as in edited volumes. She has served as the President of the Central States Communication Association, as Editor of *Communication Reports*, and Associate Editor of *Personal Relationships*.

Barbara M. Montgomery is Dean of Humanities and Social Sciences at Millersville University of Pennsylvania. She has taught and written extensively about communication in personal relationships, and has co-authored *Relating: Dialogues and Dialectics* and co-edited *Dialectical Approaches to Studying Personal Relationships*, both with Leslie Baxter. Dr Montgomery is a former Associate Editor of the *Journal of Social and Personal Relationships*.

Malcolm R. Parks (PhD, Michigan State University, 1976) is Associate Professor of Speech Communication at the University of Washington. His research focuses primarily on the development of interpersonal relationships and personal networks. He has conducted studies on the development of a variety of personal relationships and relationships in work settings. He also conducts research on the social uses of the Internet and the development of social relations in computer-mediated settings. He is currently Assistant Vice-Provost for Research at the University of Washington.

Chris Segrin (PhD, University of Wisconsin, 1990) is Associate Professor of Communication and Adjunct Professor of Psychology at the University of Arizona. His research focuses on the role of interpersonal communication and relationships in mental health problems. He has published this research in communication and psychology journals, and recent works can be found in *Human Communication Research, Journal of Social and Personal Relationships,* and *Clinical Psychology Review*. Recently he has served on the editorial board of Personal Relationships and Communication Studies.

Brian H. Spitzberg (PhD 1981, University of Southern California) is currently Professor in the School of Communication at San Diego State University. His areas of research are interpersonal competence, conflict, jealousy, courtship violence, sexual coercion, and stalking. He has co-authored *Interpersonal Communication Competence* (1984), *Handbook of Interpersonal Competence Research* (1989), co-edited *The Dark Side of Interpersonal Communication* (1994), and *The Dark Side of Close Relationships* (1998), and authored or co-authored numerous chapters in scholarly texts. He is author or co-author of over 50 scholarly publications and over

100 scholarly conference papers, including eight "top-ranked" papers. He also serves in an advisory capacity for the San Diego City Attorney's Domestic Violence unit and the San Diego District Attorney's intergovernmental Stalking Strike Force, and is a member of the Association of Threat Assessment Professionals.

Lisa M. Tillmann-Healy is an Assistant Professor in the Department of Communication at Rollins College. Her areas of emphasis include close relationships, interpretive and qualitative methodology, health communication, friendship and sexual identity. Her PhD dissertation focused on friendships between heterosexuals and gay men.

Lise VanderVoort is a doctoral student in the department of Communication Studies at the University of Iowa, and winner of a Jakob Javits Fellowship. Her areas of interest include interpersonal relationships, intercultural communication, narrative, and the philosophy of social science.

Kathy J. Werking received her doctorate from Purdue University in 1992. She is an Assistant Professor at Eastern Kentucky University. She has published a book about cross-sex friendship entitled, *We're Just Good Friends*. Her current writing project articulates a Buddhist perspective on communication in close relationships.

PREFACE

In the opening chapter of this volume, "Talking about 'Relationships': Variations on a theme", *VanderVoort and Duck* answer the question, "What is a personal relationship?", with the response that it depends on who is answering the question, the occasion of the answer, and the audience for the answer. They argue that there is a rhetorical framework implicit in all descriptions of relationships, both scholarly and lay. The speaker always frames the description of the relationship in ways that suit the speaker's goals on a particular occasion to a particular audience. VanderVoort and Duck also argue that descriptions of relationships are not, and never can be, permanent or objective. Personal relationships are always subjectively experienced and are always in the process of "becoming". Although a particular description of a relationship may sound objective and final, it never is because relationships are not objective or static.

VanderVoort and Duck's chapter, as well as all subsequent chapters in this volume, can therefore be viewed as descriptions of relationships given by particular scholars in the field of communication, on a particular occasion (some of these chapters were originally written for the second edition of the *Handbook on Personal Relationships*; others were added to expand the breadth of this volume), for a particular audience (professors and students in communication and other disciplines who study personal relationships). All the chapter authors have the goal of elaborating a particular perspective, their theoretical perspective, on communication and personal relationships.

The descriptions and explanations of communication and personal relationships represented in these chapters are not permanent or objective (as can be witnessed in Dindia's chapter, which is changed from the original chapter in the *Handbook* because Dindia's perspective has changed). All the authors in this volume study communication and personal relationships, but our approaches differ, focusing on different aspects of relationships, explaining them in different ways because we are all enmeshed in our different theoretical perspectives as well as our own personal relationships. None of our descriptions and explanations of communication and personal relationships are objective. Similarly, because relationships are unfinished business, so too is theory and research on communication and personal relationships. Thus, this volume represents these authors' (and not others') views of communication and personal relationships at this particular point in time for this particular audience. Given these assumptions, let's preview the rest of the chapters in this volume.

Following closely in the theme elaborated in VanderVoort and Duck, *Bochner, Ellis, and Tillman-Healy* address an aspect of real persons' relationships that has been largely overlooked in the personal relationships literature—the stories people tell about their relationships. Their chapter focuses on narrative modes of investigating and representing interpersonal relationships. Specifically, they argue that we create and understand our relationships in the form of stories, and we reveal our understandings of our relationships to others by telling them our relationship stories. Relationships are given shape and meaning by the stories that form and inform their enactment. The authors discuss canonical and popular stories and their influence on personal stories. They review three narrative approaches to personal relationships: accounts, storied lives, and evocative narratives. In sum, these authors argue persuasively for a narrative approach, rather than the traditional social scientific approach, to personal relationships.

Baxter and Montgomery present a dialectical view of communication and personal relationships. They discuss the commonly shared assumptions of a dialectical perspective, major scholarly research programs emerging from a dialectical perspective, and directions for future research based on Bakhtin's dialogic perspective. Dialectical perspectives address several of the issues raised in VanderVoort's and Duck chapter. According to a dialectical perspective, relationships are not static but rather dynamic, involving contradiction, change, interdependence, and contextual embeddedness. Further, from a dialogic view, individuals are not contained, pre-formed, intact, stable, and sovereign selves; rather, individuals are fluid, social, open-ended, unstable, and changing. Selves are constructed in relationships. Similar to VanderVoort and Duck, Baxter and Montgomery argue that relationships exist in a social and cultural context that affects the meaning of dialectical tensions in relationships, and that context influences the exigencies of contradictions in relationships.

Parks also addresses the issue of context of personal relationships by discussing the social networks in which relationships are situated. Parks argues that relationships and networks are connected from relationship beginning to end. To develop his argument, Parks first discusses the dimensions of relationship development and deterioration, and second discusses the features of communication networks that are most relevant for relationships. Parks then reviews the research linking the development of personal relationships with the partners' surrounding social networks and advances a theoretical perspective for understanding these linkages. The social contextual perspective advocated by Parks fills a theoretic void in the interpersonal communication literature by explaining how personal relationships are situated in the larger social network and how participants' social networks affect, and are affected by, the process of relationship development and deterioration.

Metts discusses the role of facework in personal relationships. Metts argues that one of the most pervasive, yet seldom studied, aspects of personal relationships is the degree to which partners enhance, preserve, or diminish each other's desired identity, or face. In the chapter Metts demonstrates the utility of a face perspective for the study of personal relationships. Metts begins the chapter with a discussion of "face" and "facework", based on the writings of Goffman, and illustrates the contribution of Goffman's perspective to personal relationships by discussing the management of relational transgressions, the management of conflict, and the management of a couple's joint identity in public. Metts then moves to a discussion of face and facework, as elaborated by Brown and Levinson in politeness theory, and illustrates the contributions of this perspective to the study of personal relationship by discussing the role of positive politeness in the provision of social support and relationship disengagement. Metts's chapter addresses the process nature of relationships in that she clearly indicates that partners' identities (and couples' joint identity) are not pre-formed and stable but are continuously affected by partners' facework.

Segrin's chapter illustrates how the speaker's perspective and the intended audience can greatly influence the description of mental health problems as well as communication and personal relationships. Segrin describes and explains mental health problems as relational and communication problems, rather than as psychological problems. Segrin reviews theory and research indicating that mental health problems are correlated with communication and relationship variables, indicating that mental health problems are the cause of, or are caused by, disrupted and distressed interpersonal relationships, or, more likely, that there is a reflexive relationship where mental health problems and distressed relationships are in a vicious cycle. Specifically, Segrin reviews theory and research on depression, social anxiety, schizophrenia, eating disorders, personality disorders and somatoform disorders, and a common correlate, dysfunctional interpersonal relationships. Segrin argues that interpersonal relationships play a central role in the development, course, and outcome of these mental health problems.

Werking goes outside the description of traditional relationships (heterosexual romantic relationships) by describing cross-sex friendship. Werking conducts a critical examination of the existing cross-sex friendship literature and, in particular, addresses the ideological assumptions underlying research conducted in the area of cross-sex friendship. Werking argues that the selection of research topics in the area of cross-sex friendship reflects an ideological stance and that existing studies privilege an individualistic and heterosexist view of cross-sex friendship. Although her observations and recommendations are directed toward the cross-sex friendship literature, they are useful to the larger audience of personal relationships researchers in general, because the ideological assumptions of which she speaks are found in traditional descriptions of personal relationships (scholarly and lay).

Cupach, Spitzberg and Carson extend the boundaries of the description of personal relationships even farther than Werking. Their past efforts to examine "the dark side of relationships" (Cupach and Spitzberg, 1994, 1998) are continued in this chapter. Cupach et al. describe obsessive relational intrusion (ORI) and stalking. ORI is defined as "repeated and unwanted pursuit and invasion of one's sense of physical or symbolic privacy by another person, either stranger or acquaintance, who desires and/or presumes an intimate relationships" (Cupach & Spitzberg, 1998, pp. 234–235). ORI is a form of relationship in which the two parties are fundamentally opposed to each other in their desire to have a relationship; "one party desires a type of relationship that the other party clearly does not want" (Cupach et al., this volume, first page of their chapter). Cupach et al. provide evidence that ORI is a relatively common occurrence and thus in need of being described and understood. They provide their description of this phenomenon, which differs considerably from clinical orientations, which locate stalking and ORI in the realm of "abnormality". Cupach et al. describe ORI and stalking within the realm of normality, that is, "in the ordinary and often mundane experience of managing potential and actual personal relationships" (Cupach et al., this volume). The authors describe the process in which normal and acceptable pursuit becomes obsessive. In particular, they describe three interrelated cognitive processes that transform normal relationship-seeking behavior into obsessive intrusion and stalking: rumination, emotional flooding and rationalization.

Returning to a more traditional area of study in the field of communication and personal relationships, *Dindia* describes the process of self-disclosure in the final chapter in this volume. However, to do so, she departs from traditional descriptions of self-disclosure, having recently adopted a dialectical point of view of self-disclosure. Similar to VanderVoort and Duck, Dindia too describes relationships as not being static containers of two stable individuals. In particular, she argues that self-disclosure is not a dichotomous event, (i.e. either a person has disclosed; or has not disclosed; a person is out of the closet or is not out of the closet). Rather, in real relationships, self-disclosure is an ongoing process that is inherently dialectical in nature. Individuals in relationships disclose on the same topics over time, revealing, then concealing, then revealing … Full or total disclosure is impossible from a dialectical perspective because individuals are always changing. In particular, the ongoing processes of individual identity and relationship development mutually affect and are affected by the ongoing process of self-disclosure.

VanderVoort and Duck urge us to remember that there is a rhetorical framework implicit in all descriptions of relationships. The chapters in this volume do not represent the only or the last word on communication and personal relationships. They represent the descriptions of communication and relationships given by a particular group of authors at a particular point in time for this particular volume. Individuals and relationships are unfinished business. So too is theory and research on personal relationships.

KATHRYN DINDIA AND STEVE DUCK

Chapter 1

Talking about "Relationships": Variations on a Theme

Lise VanderVoort and Steve Duck

University of Iowa, Iowa City, IA, USA

The question "What is a personal relationship?" has been offered at least twice over the last 25 years as the central issue facing personal relationship research (Kelley, 1979; Duck, 1990). Some responses to this question have highlighted the role of communication as a means of expressing a relationship (Planalp & Garvin-Doxas, 1994), as vitally constitutive of the relationship itself (Shotter, 1992), or as both an instrumental medium for and the essential substance of the relationship (Duck & Pond, 1989). Scholars have also asked important questions about relational partners' talk about relationships (Acitelli, 1988) and about researchers' own discourse about relationships (Baxter & Montgomery, 1996; Duck, 1994a). When Duck, West, and Acitelli (1997) asked, "Whose personal relationship is the personal relationship literature talking about—the researchers' or that of the ordinary person going about a real life?"—they pointed to the fact that the question "What is a personal relationship?" cannot really be treated as a single, simple question. The question entails a range of concurrent and essentially contingent questions, including "Whose relationship?", "Whom does one ask?", "To whom does one answer?", and "Under what circumstances and for what purposes does one attempt a response?". Duck et al. (1997) are pointing to the fact that any response to the question or any description of a relationship represents the inherent suppositions, theories, or beliefs about that relationship held by that speaker at that time.

Communication and Personal Relationships
Edited by Kathryn Dindia and Steve Duck. © 2000 John Wiley & Sons Ltd.

Given the complexity of daily life experience in any relationship, these related questions alert us to the possibility that speakers attend to that which is most salient to their present concerns, report selectively, privilege one perspective on a relationship over another, and for any discussion of "a relationship" reify the relationship (which may itself be a form of privileging a perspective). Accordingly, this chapter makes three points: (1) There is a rhetorical framework implicit in the description of a relationship offered by a given speaker on a given occasion. By this we mean that any speaker frames the presumed essentials of the thing described in ways that suit the speaker's goals in relation to the present audience. Simply put, descriptions of relationships are not universally true: they suit needs and occasions and are variations on a theme. (2) This rhetorical framework is even more important to examine when it is also noted that most of the "doing" of relationships occurs at the daily level of trivial and haphazard behavior. It does not occur at the level of certainty or focus that is occasioned within (or amenable to) an experimental paradigm and controlled conditions. People are faced with a variety of predictable and unpredictable experiences that amount to the unfinished business of relating (Duck, 1990), and such open-endedness is not well-captured in single measures or reports of relationship activity. We will argue that the vicissitudes of experience are precisely why the rhetorical framework is significant: people are not reporting on one uniform set of experiences but are selecting or being asked to select from a variety of behaviors, emotions and interpretations. (3) Rhetorical concerns pertain to *what* is said and *how* it is said, but also to *where* and *when* it is said. Reports on the variability or continuity of relationships occur in a particular situation and at a particular time, whose particularity can be subsequently effaced so that the report may take on an appearance of stasis and objectivity. In sum, our notion of "rhetorical framework" entails explicit consideration of the speaker, the audience, the purpose and the occasions for communication about a relationship, whether the speaker is a relational participant or a relational researcher, and whether the report sounds like an objective description of a definite, static entity or like a subjective description of a protean, dynamic experience.

These are the themes of the present chapter, each of which will now be reviewed at greater length.

RELATIONSHIPS IN EVERYDAY LIFE

The question "What is a relationship?" is one that requires consideration of the ways in which relaters communicate with one another, how they explain their relationship to each other and to third parties, and how researchers explain relationships to relaters, to each other and to a wider audience. In this chapter, relational communication is any communication by partners about a relationship, although we also extend that here to include the discussions of researchers concerning relationships. We seek to build on the point made by Watzlawick, Beavin, and Jackson (1967), that messages have not only content but relational implications—they convey not only a literal message but also information about the relationship between speaker and audience. They also convey the present (presumed) beliefs of the speaker, be it partner or researcher, about a particular relationship or relationships in general. Relational communication reflects the speaker's needs, desires, purposes, and frameworks of understanding, but in the context of perceived audience and cultural norms about the acceptability of certain descriptions of relationships, relating and relational partnering.

Many scholars have pointed to the importance of the commonplace circumstances and activities of daily life that actually serve *as* the conduct of relationships (e.g., Fitch, 1998). Such scholars remind us that *everyday* communication is the means by which emotions are conveyed, cognitions are represented, behaviors are performed and explained, and thus relationships are conducted—indeed, brought into existence. Yet, what is "everyday" communication? In one sense, it is contrasted with exceptional and extraordinary relational and communicative events, such as instances of intimate self-disclosure, sharp conflictive arguments, or turning points which, by their very nature, are neither typical nor representative of that relationship's ordinary daily conduct. Significant, dramatic and, as it turns out, rare behaviors are well researched, as for example is intimate self-disclosure, something that happens only 2% of the time in daily life (Dindia, 1994). Everyday conversation is more likely to be trivial, task-focused, gossipy, jocular, playful or light than it is to be heavy with significant intimacy, conflict, or deep connection of minds—and yet it does important relational work (Duck, Rutt, Hurst, & Strejc, 1991).

In another sense, "everyday communication" points to the range of positive and negative relational and communicative experiences that people have every day all the time. These experiences include not only the positive side of relationships (Andersen, 1993; Berger, 1988, 1993; Berscheid, 1994; Fehr, 1993; Fincham & Bradbury, 1987; Fletcher & Fitness, 1993; Honeycutt, 1993; Kelley et al., 1983) but also the negative or difficult, such as embarrassment (Miller, 1996), shame and anger (Retzinger, 1995), daily hassles (Bolger & Kelleher, 1993), or the dark side of relationships (Cupach & Spitzberg, 1994; Duck, 1994b). Thus, a focus on the everyday experiences of relational communication entails attention not only to routine and trivial activities on the one hand, but also to the complex mixture of good and bad experiences that are matched and managed and, indeed, incorporated into the overall composition of "a relationship" described by someone on a given occasion.

Just as everyday life is complex by reason of its various *types* of experience, so is there also variability of experience within a given type and within the same aspect of a relationship. Unfortunately, the noun "relationship" tends to reify and consolidate that which is, in reality, an open-ended range of experiences—the unfinished business of relating. It is all too easy for the term "our relationship" to be used as if there were only one appropriate way to represent a relationship, that is equally useful to all people equivalently, or to both partners identically, or to each person consistently at all times. Some authors (e.g., Baxter & Montgomery, 1996) have criticized attempts to measure intimacy or "the state of a relationship" for this reason. Relationships are not stable, consistent experiences of given dimensions or features. Measures of individual psychological states tend to obfuscate the fact that within any element—be it feelings towards partner, degree of commitment, or level of satisfaction—there are experiential variations from positive to negative, fluctuations resulting from mood or daily experience, and fluidity reflecting life's ups and downs generally. Accordingly, communication about these psychological states should likewise be expected to show range and variance. "Our relationship" can be experienced as a collection of positive and negative sentiments and expressed in a variety of ways to different audiences selectively on different occasions. However, people in life and in research studies are often made to choose particular relational roles or aspects of the relationship as topics for apparently representative reports (Duck, 1994a, b; Duck & Wood, 1995). These reports may be treated not as momentary temperature readings but as an essential representation of the relationship, both by ordinary folks and by researchers. Yet in many ways the circumstances surrounding a relationship can momentarily change in a way that provokes not only a different description or a different form of communicative behavior but also differences in other behaviors. For example, central to the understanding of personal relationships and social support is the issue of how particular circumstances warrant different psychological reconstructions of the same relationship between people. A sudden disaster evokes different facets of relational obligations and duties from those facets regarded as normal at other times (Kaniasty & Norris, 1997), and so warrants their being stressed in reports of the relationship at that time. Whereas friends are normally expected to do such paradigmatically friendly things as confiding in one another, disclosing, talking, having fun together, and showing intimacy (Davis & Todd, 1985), the occurrence of a disaster may warrant switches from confiding to physical support, from playfulness to emotional assistance, and from intimate disclosure to self-sacrifice and perhaps physical effort (Hobfoll, 1996). Dindia (this volume) supports the same analysis with her example showing that self-disclosure is an ongoing transactional process that "occurs in the context of individual lives and personal relationships and should be studied as such" (see p. 150). She further argues that "self-disclosure transforms the nature of the relationship and the relationship transforms the meaning and consequences of self-disclosure" (see p. 151). Moreover, Bochner, Ellis, and Tillman-Healy (this volume) advocate the study of *narrative construction* of relationship history by the partners, as do Veroff and colleagues (1993, 1997). Finally, as Acitelli (e.g., 1993) has taught us, talking about the relationship is not the same as talking about self in the relationship, even if the talk about self is intimate, revealing and tending to increase closeness or mutual knowledge.

Even amid the mundane exigencies of everyday life, relationships are therefore motley, not monochromatic, experiences. Friends do not sit and confide intensely all day long, day after day. Rather they play (Baxter, 1992), swear and gossip (Winters & Duck, 2000), have small talks (Spencer, 1994), argue (Wood, 1995), go shopping or play sports or have coffee or mend cars (Wood, 1993) ... and so on. Experiences of, activities in, and reports about relationships are richly variegated in real life—reports about relationships are like variations on a theme, and should be so regarded by researchers. Neither standardized scales designed to measure the state of a relationship nor enduring labels in everyday talk are sufficient to represent this rich variability, especially as it is shaped by the circumstances in which people report about their lives to researchers and to each other. For example, Werking (this volume) demonstrates how cross-sex friendship involves ongoing conversational negotiation of both the internal nature of the friendship and the external explanation of it to other people. In short, cross-sex friendships cannot be unproblematically enjoyed: they must be accounted for often in a context of the suspicion and disbelief on the part of the audience, e.g. "Oh, so you are *really just* good friends?". Expectations of suspicion and disbelief therefore frame the ways in which partners report about their relationship in such circumstances to such audiences. This talk reveals implicit relationship ideologies reproduced or questioned by partners, particularly the need to counter the typical assumption by others that any cross-sex friendship is probably a concealed sexual liaison. Werking also points out the ideological assumptions of research of cross-sex friendships and shows how researchers can illuminate these assumptions by observing, tape-recording, and transcribing the conversations of cross-sex friends. Werking thus stresses the importance of considering the situatedness of discussions of relationships—whether by participants or researchers—in terms of rhetorical concerns (e.g., audience, occasion) and within the history of the relationship (or research on relationships).

Once we recognize the importance of studying relationships in all their variability and circumstantial alternatives, we necessarily also recognize variability in relational communication. Duck, Rutt, Hurst, and Strejc (1991) mapped out daily conversations and found, for example, consistent differences between conversations held on different days of the week, and Cirstea, VanderVoort, and Duck (in preparation) similarly have found differences according to time of day. Thus, individual reports of relationships should not be regarded as necessarily consistent with or representative of other reports gathered at different times within "the same" relationship. Relational partners may consider some conversations less important than others and may judge conversations differently, depending on the situation. Likewise, researchers must recall that samples of relational communication chosen for study should be not treated equally if researchers wish to gain relevant insight into "the meaning" of a given communication in a given relationship at a given time. Surveys can be filled out, interviews can be conducted, and talk can be recorded in the wake of a vicious argument, a romantic dinner, or a mundane trip to the supermarket, leaving us with interesting, if unrepresentative (depending on what we aim to represent), reports of relational communication.

When studying partners' accounts of relationships, researchers must therefore carefully consider not only the particularities of the account-giving situation, but also the fact that the recounted relational experiences may not be "typical" of the relationship. Complex, variable, and open-ended relationships are tricky things to describe. Reports often suffer from gross simplification (in the manners described above), not only by participants but also by researchers. All relationships necessarily include both bonds and binds (Wiseman, 1986), all have darkness and light in them (Duck, 1994b), and all have hassles and irritations that have to be not merely experienced but also managed in daily life (Bolger & Kelleher, 1993). Some dialectical theorists argue that it is the simultaneity of contradictory needs which characterize experience in relationships (Altman, Vinsel, & Brown, 1981; Baxter, 1988, 1993; Conville, 1988; Baxter & Montgomery, this volume). A number of scholars have noted that relational experiences can be described in different ways from different personal vantage points (Duck & Sants, 1983; Surra & Ridley, 1991) and that relational "facts" are really someone's interpretations, whether the partners' or the researchers'. For instance, as the passage of time brings new perspectives, so a seemingly negative aspect of a relationship can be transformed into a positive or neutral feature (e.g., the case where something negative like a conflict can be resolved in ways that are perceived to be ultimately beneficial to the relationship; Lloyd & Cate, 1985; Wood, Dendy, Dordek, Germany, & Varallo, 1994), or a seeming positive feature can be reconstrued as a negative one (e.g., when a trait like "reliability" can be reconstrued as "boringness"; Felmlee, 1995), depending on the reporter's present state of mind. So also can the *absence* of a remark, its tone, its context, and the inflection, timing, placement, sound, and force of a remark carry interpretive weight. Positive and negative interpretations of present and absent communication can change significantly over time and in different contexts, making generalizations from single reports a dubious enterprise at best.

RELATIONSHIPS IN RESEARCH REPORTS

How could the above comments apply to *researchers'* reports about relationships? All researchers know that data can be rendered less "authentic" by the data-collecting situation itself and will thus try to reduce demand characteristics in an effort to capture what the participants would have done or said had they not been aware of being studied. The "Limitations" sections of journal papers also remind us that the results can be influenced by the specific research setting, and that generalizability is limited to the population sampled. Happily, the scientific method has taught us to be fastidious about reliability and validity. Unhappily, research on the situatedness and variability of participants' experiences in and of themselves is still in the minority, if perhaps a growing one. Until quite recently it was more typical to treat variation as a limitation on reliability, validity, or generalizability rather than as a fundamental part of the experience being researched. In order to make generalizations, researchers look for (and thus usually find) commonalities across situations; but this is not excep- tional—in our non-research lives we necessarily presume and rely on many sorts of commonalities in order to get on with our lives. Yet there are countless times when generalizing across situations in our ordinary lives does not yield the expected outcomes, and indeed, many of life's most important experiences occur only once or rarely in our lives, even if they are expected or hoped for (marriage, birth of children, first big NIH grant, graduation, first publication in a journal...). Sometimes, when we aim to predict and control what happens in our lives, unexpected outcomes are maddening; at other times we may welcome them as the proverbial spice of life. Published scientific research is traditionally of a decidedly gentle palate, however. A delicate white sauce of predicted and controlled outcomes, remarkable in their simi- larity across situations, is savored—and rightfully so, except that it is consistently the similarity and not the situations that get all the attention, at least in the final published version (see Acitelli, 1997, for a cogent account of the ways in which reports do or do not reflect actual processes of research). As Fine and Demo (2000) further note, such styles of reporting and interpretations of data are themselves reflective of the expec- tations that researchers hold about the situations and topics which they study.

It might seem natural for research examining people's variegated and situated everyday experiences to celebrate individuals in their individuality, i.e., in the glory of their unique and distinctive experiences. After all, to consider individuals and situations in their fullness is eventually to see them as less generalizable and more distinctively individual. But too narrow a focus on the individual risks myopia, to the extent that it neglects the social and cultural frames in which those individuals or groups of individuals conduct their lives. When researchers treat relationships as internally-driven products of individual or dyadic actions, or thoughts that are separate from the evolving social situations, they run the risk of overlooking changes in expectations represented by the surrounding standards of judgment about conduct acceptable for relationships (Prusank, Duran, & DeLillo, 1993). Yet individuals are constantly exposed to such standards through the cultural products of media (Kidd, 1975; McCall, 1988) and researchers, likewise, through the norms of their own discipline (Bazerman, 1987). Both everyday folk and researchers also frequently encounter such standards through conversations with network members who do not judge the appropriateness of a relationship solely by its own internal standards, but perforce attach to it judgments of quality and legitimacy provided by the culture at that time (Montgomery, 1988). Other humans, both far (media) and near (networks), participate in a dyad's relationship insofar as they provide examples of, or pronounce judgments on, appropriate and inappropriate ways of relating and communicating (or, in the case of journals and scholarly societies, pronounce on ways in which to conduct and report on research on relationships). In everyday conversations with friends and family, for example, a person is likely to confront a specific sort of rhetorical context: the need (or opportunity) to account for relational behavior that may feel "private" and to face advice, approval, or reprimand based on the account offered (Antaki 1987; Antaki & Rapley, 1999)—or no reaction at all to the extent that what is produced is also what is expected. Similarly, in scholarly writing about their research, scholars are normally attentive to the audience for their research, adopting publication norms and speaking styles suited for particular journals or spectators.

Cultural norms expressed in the media or expectations communicated from one person to another are rendered so familiar as to be essentially invisible and taken for granted. They are "common sense"—defined by Linde (1993, p. 222) as ...

> the set of beliefs and relations between beliefs that speakers may assume are known and shared by all competent members of the culture. As a system, common sense is transparent within its culture: it consists of beliefs that purport not to be beliefs, but to be a natural reflection of the way things really are.

Because research itself is culturally situated, commonsense beliefs imbue researchers' interpretations of actions in subtle ways, just as research can shape commonsense beliefs [cf., for example, the resonance of Deborah Tannen's (1990) and John Gray's (1992) books, with mass audiences]. In research on relationships, commonsense beliefs are reflected in the built-in assumptions about what can be taken as normal experience, what sorts of relationship types and forms are acceptable, what may be taken as the right and proper expression of emotion, and what kinds of questions about relationships can be asked. In using particular measures of relationships, researchers inevitably encode those assumptions into research. For example, Western research accepts as "understandable" (and even expected) that romantic partners will display affection by holding hands, and may use this tie-sign as an operational measure of closeness in research (Rubin, 1973). By contrast, some Eastern cultures condemn such behavior as altogether inappropriate in public, so its occurrence at all would communicate not simple affection but defiance of norms and authority. Nonetheless, Western scholarship often theorizes about distinctly Western cultural constructs such as autonomy, individuality, empathy, support, face, sociality, and communality as though they were universals of human experience and thought, experienced and thought about in uniform ways. Researchers need to consider not only the local contexts for the relationships that they study but also the broader situatedness of the concepts that they use to theorize about relationships.

AUDIENCE AND OCCASION FOR COMMUNICATION

Just as relationships are complex entities inextricable from their situations of enactment, so too is relational communication responsive to the audience, occasion, and medium for communication, whether this communication is to a partner or to a researcher. Communication is an everyday embodiment or enactment of processes that may be analyzed simultaneously at psychological, sociological, and cultural levels. Emphasizing not the personal characteristics revealed (and discovered) through self-disclosure but the process of interpreting them, Harré (1995) argues that the intended action of a discloser achieves its force as an act in a relationship only from the response of the partner, so that intent in the discloser may differ from the interpretation of the perceiver and affect the partners in the relationship differently. Other important forms of situation, variability, and communication are noted by Hendrick and Hendrick (1993). They observe that it is more likely that researchers would focus on the different types of love as absolute and relatively constant, rather than on the variety of ways in which "the same" love could be expressed in different contexts or to different audiences (e.g., to a researcher, in writing, to parents, to a priest, or to a sexual partner). We could add to knowledge about love by exploring the various manners in which the same person can talk about or express love to the same partner as a function of situation or perceived appropriateness to the occasion, e.g., in proposing marriage, on their honeymoon, or during a request for support (Duck, 1994a). In these cases the audience, and perhaps even some of the words, are the same but the situation is different.

To study the different ways in which people describe relationships of course requires consideration of the significance of the audience for the telling; it also importantly requires consideration of the acceptable and expected ways of telling a story. Certain principles of structural coherence must be followed in order for the story to be acceptable—for example, people from Western cultures expect tellers to indicate chronological order through a sequence of past-tense clauses, provide occasional evaluative statements about the events reported, give an adequate indication of causality, and ensure continuity between events (Linde, 1993). More specifically, a culture includes models of prototypical relationships that are expected to be confirmed or refuted in a given narrative about a relationship. The described path of a relationship is ultimately a narrative imposed on a number of events and occurrences perceived within a particular social context as a reasonable path. For instance, "We met and fell in love and got married" is more acceptable in North America than "It is a good match for both families", which is more acceptable in many other parts of the world. Account-making, in some form or another, is perhaps a universal human communicative practice, but the acceptable forms for accounts, as well as the acceptable forms for the relationships being accounted for, are culturally relative. A further form of coherence, however, is situational coherence: a well-constructed story about falling in love is situationally inappropriate at most funerals, as a response to a question about one's financial investments, or in the context of a faculty retreat. In sum, the depiction of relationships must follow a number of rules for coherence in order to be culturally and socially acceptable to the audience at that time.

As with all social practices, the description of relationships can either reinforce or subvert the privileged beliefs about both relationships and narratives. While living their lives, individuals (at least Western ones) surely do not perceive themselves as simply responding to some social dictates about their relationship, but see themselves as exercising relational choice. Yet they not only produce their own relationship in their behaviors but also perpetuate the social form and its emotional tone, familiar topics, and associated styles of relating. They reproduce as well as draw upon that social form (e.g., "friendship," "marriage") by invoking socially acceptable and unacceptable explanations of relationships in relational talk. For example, accounts (as well as theories) of relationship dissolution often use one or a number of culturally acceptable reasons for break-up, including pre-existing doom ("It was destined to fail; we were so different from the start"), mechanical failure ("He was impossible to live with"), process loss ("We just didn't communicate enough"), and sudden death ("I found out she was cheating on me") (Duck, 1982). It is important to recall that, although accounts such as "We both hated the opera" or "My car broke down" do not currently count as culturally adequate explanations of dissolution, one day they might. Not long ago in this culture, "He didn't love me" was not considered a wholly acceptable reason for leaving a marriage, but as long as it continues to be invoked, the cultural belief that love is an important ingredient of marriage will perdure.

SO WHAT (IS A PERSONAL RELATIONSHIP)?

While traditionally the goals of social science have been prediction and control, an alternative goal is to understand the meaning of human behaviors and experiences. The question then becomes, "The meaning for whom, on what occasion, for which audience?" Research on personal relationships involves multiple meaning systems (acknowledged or not): cultural meanings, familial meanings, symbolic meanings generally, the meaning systems constructed between two people, and the meaning systems that researchers themselves bring to their enterprise of observation. Whose meanings are we interested in? Speech Act Theory (Searle, 1969) suggests that to understand an utterance is to understand what the speaker "meant to say". Thus, a true understanding requires that we grasp our interlocutors' meanings by getting inside their heads and seeing what they intended to express. An alternative approach to meaning is one described by anthropologist Alessandro Duranti (1988), in his study of Samoans who interpret utterances more in terms of their consequences for social relationships than in terms of what an individual "meant to say". Whether we regard interpretation of meaning as an attempt at mind reading, as an analysis of relational consequences, or as a different process altogether, it is clear that understanding of meaning depends on the people involved and the situation of interpretation. So when we, as researchers, ask "Meaning for whom?" we must consider whose meaning systems we engage and whose we wish to inform. For example, the construction of form for a relationship is a matter of coordination of one's own behavior, not only with that of the partner but also with the network and the wider social group (Milardo, 1984; Parks & Eggert, 1991; Milardo & Wellman, 1992; Parks, this volume). All such constructions are essentially manipulations of meaning systems that involve the sharing and coordination of meaning (cf. Pearce & Cronen, 1980)— or, rather more particularly, the coordination of meanings embodies expectations for one's own and others' behavior, whether these others are relational partners, network members, or colleagues in the research field. A problem with conventional views of a relationship as the product of two individuals alone has been the correlated assumption of simple communality of expectations—that is, the assumption that the meanings associated with particular acts are commonly shared, uniformly agreed upon in particular cultures of study, and removable from contexts as absolute examples of behaviors that are typical of a given sort of relationship (see, e.g., Davis & Todd, 1985, who listed commonly assumed absolute characteristics of friendship, such as "loyalty" and "trust"). By contrast, we point to the fundamental negotia-bility—in talk—of meanings for acts as a function of different relational reference groups and individual action.

Such negotiation of meanings between partners is not just limited to clarifying the differences between a compliment vs. a sexual proposition or an insult vs. teasing (Masheter & Harris, 1986), but includes the particular ways in which partners nego-tiate intimacy in interactions (e.g., Harris & Sadeghi, 1987; Hopper, Knapp, & Scott, 1981) and the things that are taken for granted in interactions between partners. These "taken-for-granteds" (TFGs, as Hopper, 1981, describes them) provide the glue of continuity in relationships, other instances of which (such as "future talk" about the relationship) are proposed by Sigman (1991) and Knapp and Vangelisti (1992). In the process of negotiating the meaning of acts within a relationship, partners develop a specifically interpersonal set of meanings that often differ from the socially familiar and culturally common set of meanings (Montgomery, 1988; Wood, 1995). They may even negotiate unique but shared understandings of their relationships (Acitelli, 1993). To the extent that each person interprets information in accordance with a personal meaning system (Andersen, 1993), any piece of information can mean something different to two persons unless they reach agreement on meaning, either by active negotiation or by passive adoption of cultural interpretations. The relational art is to create a symbiosis, and ultimately a fusion, of personal meaning systems through communication, so that interpretations of information, self-disclosure, historical context, and so forth, have similar meanings for all parties in a relationship (Planalp & Garvin-Doxas, 1994). If researchers hope to understand how partners come to create meaning for themselves, they must investigate the communicative process of negotiating meaning in talk. Note that we are not intending here to limit the notion of such meaning creation only to the content of the spoken words, even though these are a primary source of relevant data. Given this, we believe that an energetic theorist could extend our argument about principles of situational form as a meta-feature of relational communication in ways that would blend social psychological work on non-verbal communication with analysis of interpersonal communication, speech acts, and pragmatic linguistics.

These issues can all be subsumed under a global question: "What is it in relational talk that represents, indicates, or embodies the relationship?" One obvious place to look for an answer is in content of talk but, for example, changes in style of talk can themselves represent changes in the form of relationship. The form as well as the content of relational talk can be significant (Norton, 1988). We suggest, for example, that people can communicate change in relationship in much the same way that they can communicate anxiety, not only by asking anxious questions but by changing rates of speech and other paralinguistic features of their communicative behaviors, broadly construed. Some communication about relationships is likely "leaked" in talk and not addressed directly as such.

Our general point is further exemplified by other topics in communication. Although some branches of research on accounts and narratives have a long history (e.g., Bochner, 1984; Burnett, 1984; Gergen & Gergen, 1987), other forms of everyday talk about the experience of living are newer additions. Gossip, for example, is a form of talk by which we learn that (and how) people formulate loose generalizations about human motivation (Bergmann, 1993), but we also learn about particular people and consider what we would do in their circumstances (Collins, 1994). When other people ask us about our own experiences we often consider how to offer relational descriptions (in light of the fact that the performance itself could become the subject of gossip!): we probably describe the same experience differently to a spouse, to a child, to a colleague, to a parent, to a client; we may describe it differently on the phone and in person; we may give a new version three weeks later; we may give a different slant when we're tired, or sick of telling the story over and over; we probably tell it quite distinctly when a researcher asks us to relate it for a scholarly study of relationships.

By focusing strongly on relationship experiences within the mundane activities and speech of everyday life, scholars will encounter new challenges surrounding the ever-present existence of choice among (descriptions of) activities that could have been chosen instead. The intrusive permeation of a living social environment, the chatter of playfulness, the not-so-small talk that weaves lives together, the live murmur of human interaction, and the complexities of personal interpretations are not merely busy; they are occasions for *selection* of response, action, emotion, description, attribution, and reaction in situations. We stress that, in real life, relating occurs in a variety of situations that are experienced as dynamic processes, not as static structures, that relational communication in turn transforms the tenor of these situations, and that choice is a key aspect—and a dynamic aspect—of lived relational experience. Thus, we recommend that relationship researchers not only ask individuals about their relationships while taking into account their situatedness, ask those partners probingly about their relationship in a search for narrative themes, and take across-time assessments of what people report doing in relationships, but also use techniques sensitive to time and style of response to such issues in the everyday flow of experience and alternative choices. For example, representation of "a relationship" should include temporality and the variance of experience that we note above; thus, repeated measures of any "relational state" should be collected and not then averaged out to describe the "true state" but presented as an essential aspect of relational experience. Single means of the intimacy of a relationship are, we suggest, inherently suspect. Although there is a theme to relating, much of the relating is variation around a central theme.

In the broader sense, then, to tackle the opening question "What is a personal relationship?" is to consider a range of questions concerning the audience, purpose, and occasion for the question. We have argued that the discourse of both relaters and researchers talking in and about relationships is permeated by these rhetorical elements that generate variation around a theme. Careful examination of these elements permits us to recognize that static characterization of the "state" of a relationship can be mistaken for a stable "truth" about it. This is because everyday relational experiences are variegated and multifaceted restatements of the theme. Furthermore, reports of relational experiences are themselves situated at a particular time and place and are reflective of the speaker's concerns at that moment. Standard one-shot measurement scales are poorly adapted to address the variation in relational experiences. Instead of attempting to get at only the theme of the relationship behind relational talk, we have suggested that researchers study the talk itself, seeking to understand the meanings embedded there and to grasp the narrative coherence of accounts. In such a way we hope that researchers' everyday talk about relationships may more fully represent the talk that relaters themselves carry out.

ACKNOWLEDGMENTS

We are grateful to Linda Acitelli, Kathryn Dindia and Kristine Fitch for their helpful comments on this chapter.

Chapter 2

Relationships as Stories: Accounts, Storied Lives, Evocative Narratives

Arthur P. Bochner, Carolyn Ellis

University of South Florida,

and

Lisa M. Tillmann-Healy

Rollins College

We are born into a world of stories. Our births mark the beginning of a distinctive story in which each of us assumes a leading part. Our deaths end our unique stories, which live on in the minds and hearts of our survivors. Between birth and death, we rely on stories circulating through our culture to make sense of our everyday lives and guide our actions. Much of who we are and what we do originates in the tales passed down to us and the stories we take on as our own. As Robert Coles (1989, p. 24) says, "Few would deny that we all have stories in us which are a compelling part of our psychological and ideological make-up". Barbara Myerhoff (1978, p. 272) refers to human beings as "*Homo narrans*", a term that places narrative and storytelling at the core of human existence. Undoubtedly narrative plays a crucial role in understanding and organizing human experience.

Nevertheless, social scientists are just beginning to appreciate the profound significance of narrative in the lived experience of personal relationships. The first edition

Communication and Personal Relationships
Edited by Kathryn Dindia and Steve Duck. © 2000 John Wiley & Sons Ltd.

of *The Handbook of Personal Relationships* (Duck, 1988b) gave no systematic attention to the connections between narrative and relationship development. Accounts written in diaries were discussed briefly by Harvey, Hendrick, and Tucker (1988) in a chapter on "self-report methods". The authors emphasized subjective thoughts and feelings associated with personal relationships and complained that "[s]ocial science has formalized the process of researching personal relationships but often without 'touching' us in the process" (Harvey, Hendrick, & Tucker, 1988, p. 113). In a chapter on "rules, scripts, and prototypes", Ginsburg (1988) also mentioned the potential significance of studying accounts, calling attention to the "words and phrases" (but not the stories) interactants use to justify their involvement in personal relationships. The terms "narrative" and "storytelling", however, were not included in the index of *The Handbook* (Duck, 1988b).

TOWARD MEANING

Over the past 10 years, interest in narrative among other social scientists has mushroomed. Scholars in several disciplines have inaugurated new journals promoting the narrative study of lives (Josselson & Lieblich, 1993; McCabe, 1993), encouraged storied versions of interpersonal events (Denzin & Lincoln, 1994; Harvey, 1996), and published an extensive corpus of books and monographs reflecting a shift from analytic to narrative modes of investigating and representing interpersonal life (see: Baumeister & Newman, 1994; Bochner, 1994; 1997; Bochner & Ellis, 1992, 1995; Bochner, Ellis, & Tillmann-Healy, 1998; Bochner & Waugh, 1995; Brody, 1987; Butler & Rosenblum, 1991; Bruner, 1986, 1990; Coles, 1989; Denzin 1989a, 1989b, 1993. 1997; Ellis, 1993, 1995a, 1995b, 1996; Ellis & Bochner, 1996, in press; Fisher, 1987; Frank, 1991, 1993, 1995; M. Gergen, 1992; Gergen & Gergen, 1986, 1987; Gergen & Walter, 1998; Harvey, Flanery, & Morgan, 1986; Harvey, Orbuch & Weber, 1990; Kerby, 1991; Linden, 1993; Maines, 1993; McIntyre, 1981; Mishler, 1986, 1995; Mukaia, 1989; Paget, 1993; Parry, 1991; Parry & Doan, 1994; Polkinghorne, 1988; Ronai, 1992, 1994; Richardson, 1990; Riessman, 1990, 1992; Rosaldo, 1984; Rosenwald & Ochberg, 1992; Sarbin, 1986; Stone, 1988; Swados, 1991; Yalom, 1989; Yalom & Elkin, 1974; Zola, 1982a, 1982b). Collectively, these works underscore the significance of narrative as both a way of knowing about and a way of participating in the social world. The turn toward narrative promoted by these works coincides with two related developments influencing research on personal relationships: (1) the turn away from orthodox approaches to scientific representation; and (2) the turn toward interpretive perspectives that focus on human sense-making.

The Crisis of Representation

Postmodernist and poststructuralist writers have seriously challenged some of our most venerable assumptions about scientific knowledge and truth (Denzin, 1992; Dickens & Fontana, 1991; Foucault, 1970; Kuhn, 1970; Lyotard, 1984; Rorty, 1979; Rosenau, 1992). In particular, these writers have impeached the theory of language on which orthodox approaches to scientific inquiry are based. The correspondence theory of knowledge, which is the foundation of scientific method, attributes significance to language scientifically only insofar as language can achieve its denotative and referential function of describing objects in a world out there, apart from and independent of language users (Bochner & Waugh, 1995; Rorty, 1967, 1982, 1989). Accordingly, the language used in scientific theories implicitly assumes that words represent *the* world, rather than specifying *a* world, and can denote what is *out there* in the world apart from, or prior to, the interpretations of language users. Conforming to this view, orthodox communication theory, for example, treats messages and meanings as "things" or "objects" that are merely *transferred* from one person to another, reducing what is problematic in communicative experience to metaphors such as *information processing, social exchange, transmission*, or *attributional errors*. Communication thus becomes a kind of *external object*, a commodity to be packaged and exchanged (Bochner & Waugh, 1995).

The history and philosophy of science since Kuhn (1970) shows that we should understand language as not simply a tool for mirroring what is discoverable about reality, but as an ongoing and constitutive part of reality (Bochner & Waugh, 1995). The assumption that language is a neutral medium of communication has been displaced by a deeper understanding of the ways we use language to deal with the world (Kerby, 1991). What we can say in language about the world inevitably involves the indistinguishable provocations of the world and the interventions of language by which we make claims about it (Bochner & Waugh, 1995; Rorty, 1982). The world we seek to describe as social scientists does not exist in the form of the sentences we write when theorizing about it (Rorty, 1989).

As the model of language underlying social science research practices necessarily shifts from the presumption of neutral description to engaged communication, from language as a tool to language as a means of coping, the focus of social science research shifts accordingly from the goal of describing a pre-existing world of stable objects to the goals of understanding how, as social scientists, we are part of the world we investigate and the ways we human beings use language to make and change it (Bochner & Waugh, 1995; Steier, 1991). Our focus becomes showing how meaning is performed and negotiated by speakers and interpreters (Bochner & Waugh, 1995), a decidedly narrative endeavor. Although academic disciplines deeply entrenched in the correspondence theory of knowledge, such as mainstream psychology and sociology, have been slow to respond to the challenges of postmodernism, a new generation of social scientists who understand and appreciate language as a way of dealing with the world are drawn increasingly to a narrative approach to inquiry.

The Interpretive Turn

Interpretive approaches to social science focusing on human sense-making have gained wider acceptance and legitimation. If language cannot be differentiated from the world and we cannot remove language from our lives, then our understanding of the empirical world and our hope for coping with the world must originate in something other than modes of representation presumed to mirror the world. By showing that all knowledge claims rely on contingencies of language and, however "objective" or "scientific," inevitably involve "attaching significance" by interpreting (K. Gergen, 1973, 1982; Maturana, 1991; Rabinow & Sullivan, 1987; Schutz, 1971; Steedman, 1991; Taylor, 1977), writers championing the causes of phenomenology (Berger & Luckmann, 1966, Schutz, 1971), hermeneutics (Bleicher, 1980; Gadamer, 1989; Taylor, 1977), social construction (K. Gergen, 1973; Gergen & Davis, 1985; Shotter & Gergen, 1989), sociology of knowledge (Berger & Luckmann, 1966), and interpretive interactionism (Denzin, 1989a, b) gradually inspired a wider acceptance of alternative ways of understanding the empirical world and displaying its possible meanings. Particularly in the human disciplines, where we are inside what we are studying, there is only and always interpretation (Denzin, 1993; Taylor, 1977).

As attention turned toward what it means to live in a mediated world, writers across the divides of the human sciences concentrated on the issue of how people use language to make sense of their lived experiences. Geertz (1973, p. 5) portrays anthropology as "not an experimental science in search of law, but an interpretive one in search of meaning". Defining psychology as an interpretive discipline, Bruner (1990, p. 2) refers to meaning as "the central concept of psychology". Harvey and his associates (Harvey, Orbuch, Weber, Merbach, & Alt, 1992; Weber & Harvey, 1994) suggest that persons are "inexorably driven to search for meaning", and successful coping with stressful turning points in life is dependent on one's ability to construct meanings. Bochner (1994) argues that displaying how people do things together in the process of "making meanings" should be a central focus in the study of interpersonal communication; and Duck and Pittman (1994, p. 683) maintain that "the construction of relationships is part of a wider tendency to co-construct meaning with others…"

MEANINGS THROUGH STORIES

The interpretive turn in social science research shifts the focus of inquiry from objects to meanings (Rabinow & Sullivan, 1987). Of particular interest is the interactive and conversational work of constructing meanings, the process of making sense of experiences by situating them in an intelligible frame. "The primary human mechanism for attaching meaning to human experiences", writes Brody (1987, p. 5), "is to tell stories about them". Narrative—the stories people tell about their lives—is both a means of "knowing" and a way of "telling" about the social world (Richardson, 1990). By framing our experiences in the form of stories, we investigate what they mean to us, and we make what we understand about our experiences accessible to others by telling them our stories. As Stone (1988, p. 244) concluded at the end of her detailed study of family stories, "our meanings are almost always inseparable from stories, in all realms of life".

Storytelling is not only the way we understand our relationships, but also the means by which our relationships are fashioned. A personal relationship, in this sense, is a work of art, something made rather than given (Weinstein, 1988). Co-created by the joint actions of two people, a personal relationship lives as a contingent sequence of intertwined experiences, given shape and meaning by the stories that form and inform its enactments. To have or be in a relationship is to have or be in a story and, usually, to want to tell about it. When we tell others about our relationships, we portray events in the form and language of stories: who did what to whom, where, when, and why. These "acts of meaning", as Bruner (1990) calls them, give content to our relationships. Through the signifying practices of narration, the abstract construct we refer to as "relationship" assumes concrete meaning and value. Thus, a personal relationship may be construed as the conversational work through which two people negotiate, co-construct, and story the meanings and values of essentially incomplete experiences (Duck, 1994a). All couples face the sense-making problem of transforming vague experiences into stories.

The precise connection between experience and story is hotly contested among narrative theorists. Is life narratively structured or is human narration an *ad hoc* grafting of story onto experience? Some writers allege that humans impose narrative structures on their experiences. Louis Mink (1969–1970), for example, argues that life is not lived as a story. Instead, stories are projected onto experience after the fact. Accordingly, the meanings of experience are not given by or inherent in the experience itself. As Hayden White (1980, p. 8) observes: "It is because real events do not offer themselves as stories that their narrativization is so difficult". When we form stories out of lived events, we give them structure and meaning which, as Shotter (1987, p. 235) suggests, "they do not in themselves possess but which none the less they will afford or allow".

Other writers, however, dispute the idea that stories arbitrarily impose a narrative structure on memories. They argue that experience seems to call forth narration, not only because humans feel a need to tell stories about their lives but also because "consciousness is itself an incipient story" (Crites, 1971, p. 297). Storytelling is a direct and obvious form of recollecting memories, because the modalities of experience are temporal and the images preserved in memory are cinematic, transient episodes that gain significance and continuity by being situated in a story (Crites, 1971). Alasdair McIntyre (1981, p. 197) opposes the idea that experience can be severed from narrative because "…we all live out narratives in our lives and…we understand our lives in terms of the narratives that we live out…." McIntyre's sentiments are echoed by Kerby (1991, p. 42), who argues that "our unexamined life is already a quasi-narrative, and that lived time is already a drama of sorts". Accordingly, the prenarrative level of experience constitutes what Ricoeur (1983) called "a demand for narrative". Life anticipates narrative.

The dispute over the connection between lives and stories about them revolves mainly around the question of whether stories falsify experience. What is the truth value of a story that depicts meanings attached to one's lived experiences? To say that stories are imposed on experience is to suggest that narrative gives experience a structure it does not have, that stories fictionalize life. Shotter (1987) expresses this point of view when he laments the distortions introduced by plot structures of stories. Stories can have the effect of giving a determinate ordering to indeterminate and incomplete experiences. Because stories about relationships are based on details that often are vague and uncertain, that is, open to many interpretations, Shotter (1987) seeks an alternative to narratives that would be more grounded in facts and less prone to distortion. The alternative he chooses is a lexicon of tropes along the lines advanced by Barthes' *A Lover's Discourse* (1983), because Barthes' "dictionary" does not promote the illusion of completeness or order implied by many stories.

Shotter's (1987) concern about the distortions of narratives, however, runs the risk of limiting the ground claimed by narrative to that of a mirrored retrieval of the past. He is correct to say that narratives cannot depict the way things are or were, and this is precisely the point. Narrative truth seeks to keep the past alive in the present; through narrative we learn to understand the meanings and significance of the past as incomplete, tentative, and revisable according to contingencies of present life circumstances. The factual distortions that may arise from contingencies of narrative emplotment are worrisome only if one sees narrative interpretation as a neutral attempt to mirror the facts of one's life, to recover already constituted meanings. But it is not the "facts" themselves that one tries to redeem through narrative tellings, but rather an articulation of the significance and meaning of one's experiences; it is within the frame of a story that "facts" gain their importance. Life stories are thus based on "facts" but not determined by them. "Facts" achieve significance and intelligibility contextually by being articulated within a temporal frame that considers what came before and what comes after. Stories that address the meanings of a life always seek a way of extending them into the future (Rosenwald, 1992).

The kind of truth narrative seeks is not akin to correspondence with prior meanings assumed to be constituted in prenarrative experience. Scholars need not assume that narratives aim to represent lives correctly, only that narrators believe they are doing so. One narrative interpretation of events can be judged against another, but there is no standard by which to measure any narrative against the meaning of events themselves, because the meaning of prenarrative experience is constituted in its narrative expression. Life and narrative are inextricably and dialectically connected. Life both anticipates telling and draws meaning from it. Narrative is both about living and part of it.

To eschew human storytelling because of its possible distortions is to miss or ignore the interpretive importance of narrative for understanding and accepting life's contingencies. We are not scientists seeking laws that govern our behavior; we are storytellers seeking meanings that help us cope with our circumstances. Our stories must be adequate for the situations with which we must deal. Even if we wanted to, we could not turn off our narrative sensibilities. As adults we have lost any semblance of narrative innocence by being socialized into a narrative realm of consciousness. We use language, and we have seen, heard, read, and interpreted stories; we are already embedded in a story, and we are committed to a life imbued with meaning (Kerby, 1991). We tell our stories in a particular style, for a particular purpose, at a particular time. Often our purpose is to foster a story of the past that helps us function effectively in the present. Our tellings rework, refigure, and remake our past in accordance with a future onto which we project our possibilities. Thus, narrative truth is pragmatic truth (Spence, 1982). The question is not whether narratives convey the way things actually were, but rather what narratives do, what consequences they have, to what uses they can be put.

NARRATIVE AND TIME

A relationship is an historical process; time is the medium of relationship; change its constant. The dynamic, temporal qualities of relationships are, at once, the most obvious and most frustrating aspects of relationship life with which researchers must cope. It is one thing to say that relationships are developmental, that they evolve over time. It is considerably more difficult, however, to know how to incorporate time meaningfully in research on relationships. Narrative is the way people express a continuity of experience over time (Crites, 1971, 1986). Moreover, to the extent we, as social scientists, seek to represent relationship life as dynamic process, we must use the resources of narrative to express the movement and modalities of change over time. We must not only understand how couples use narrative as a means of coping with contingencies of time and order, but we must also use it ourselves as a form of writing that expresses the ebb and flow of lives lived together over time. As Crites (1971, pp. 303, 306) tells it: "Narrative alone can contain the full temporality of experience in a unity of form...Only narrative form can contain the tensions, the surprises, the disappointments and reversals and achievements of actual temporal experience."

Personal relationships are lived within the tensions constituted by memories of the past and anticipations of the future. Our personal identities seem largely contingent on how well we can bridge the remembered past with the anticipated future to provide a continuity of meaningful experience across time. The narrative challenge to which many stories are put is a desire for a continuity of experience over time (Crites, 1986). The stories we tell are remembrances of the past situated in connection to the present moment in which they are recollected and projected toward an anticipated but uncertain future. "The present of things past and the present of things future", says Crites (1971, p. 302) "are the tension of every moment of experience, both united in that present and qualitatively differentiated by it". Thus, our storied accounts of past lived experiences appropriate the past in the interest of the future (Crites, 1986). It is not uncommon to recognize the changes and revisions we make as we edit the stories we tell about our past, in part because the moment of telling has changed and in part because our vision of the future has been altered. Storytelling thus promotes "a continuous life of experience", forging coherence from the stream of experience flowing across the temporal coordinates of one's life.

CANONICAL, POPULAR, AND PERSONAL STORIES

Narrative interpretation is a method of negotiating and renegotiating meanings in a world of others. Any storied account of an event is subject to the evaluation of others—its audience—and thus must draw on situated narrative conventions and cultural typifications to achieve intelligibility. Models of intelligibility endemic to our culture constrain both how we tell our stories and what stories we can tell. In particular, narratives that become culturally "normative" function to legitimate dominant forms of understanding and organizing reality and subsequently operate as a form of social control (Langellier & Peterson, 1993).

Canonical forms are stories that represent the generally accepted version in a particular culture, the "right story" which, on the whole, is taken for granted as the way things are supposed to work (Bruner, 1990; Yerby, Buerkel-Rothfuss, & Bochner, 1995). Elizabeth Stone (1988, p. 50) suggests that families have a special interest in promoting canonical tales: "The fact is that the family, any family, has a major stake in perpetuating itself, and in order to do so it must unrelentingly push the institutions that preserve it—the institution of marriage especially, but also the institution of heterosexual romantic love, which, if all goes the way the family would have it go, culminates in marriage, children, and enhanced family stability".

Canonical stories express the boundaries of acceptable relationship and family practices against which alternative stories are judged. When a person's actions deviate from the canonical story, the person may feel a strong need to explain, justify, excuse, or legitimize these actions (Scott & Lyman, 1968). For example, Riessman (1990) observes that individuals whose marriages end in divorce go to great lengths to explain why they are divorced; the canonical story sets the expectation, after all, that married persons will live "happily ever after", together until death. As Riessman (1990) notes, the divorced person typically feels the need to convince other people that it was right to leave the marriage, because in our culture it is taken for granted that marriage is "a desired and honored state; one cannot walk away from it lightly" (Riessman, 1990, p. 78). On such painful occasions, the work of narrative accounts is not only to provide a meaningful defense and justification for one's actions, but also to provide a means for surviving separation and loss (Harvey, Flanery, & Morgan, 1986; Weber, Harvey, & Stanley, 1987; Weiss, 1975). These accounts respond to the canonical stories against which they must be measured. Gay and lesbian families, interracial marriages, single-parent families, families with adopted children, and childless couples, to name a few notable cases, are recognizable examples of relationship stories lived out against a background of "official" canonical stories, that silence, closet, or otherwise marginalize these forms of lived relationship life.

Many of the stories that are crucial to the development of interpersonal relationships emphasize personal troubles and existential dilemmas (Denzin, 1989a, b). Our storytelling is an effort to make sense of epiphanies, what Denzin (1993) refers to as "existential turning points", which may include such personal traumas as incest, alcoholism, family violence, unexpected death, chronic illness, abortion, adultery, and betrayal. Tales about such experiences emphasize both the crisis and the recovery. Denzin (1991, 1993, 1995) sees these existential narratives as stories embedded in meaning systems made available or forced upon us by our culture and its textual representations. These personal narratives are drawn from popular forms of communication—music, television, and film—that shape the meaning and values we attach not only to epiphanies but also to the quotidian experiences of romance, love, intimacy, and sexuality.

Portraying humans as voyeurs adrift in a sea of visual and aural symbols, Denzin (1991, 1993, 1995) argues that the images and meanings that flow through cinema, television, and music teach us ways of seeing, feeling, talking, and thinking. Thus, we live in a second-hand world of consciousness (Mills, 1963), mediated, commodified, and dispatched by mass communications. Accordingly, stories transmitted by popular culture are received passively and eventually become part of what we take for granted in performing our relationships. Thus, many of the meanings we think we make and live ourselves may actually be chosen for us, not by us. Our dreams and crises are screened for us by the cinematic world through which our consciousness is mediated. As a consequence, writes Denzin (1993, p. 5), "we become storied versions of somebody else's version of who we should be".

Although Denzin's argument exaggerates the degree to which our own experiences are manipulated and replaced by the fictions staged by popular culture, the attention he draws to the ways everyday social life interacts with the productions of popular culture raises important issues for narrative research. Undoubtedly, we need to study the ways in which cinema and personal relationships interact with and mutually inform each other. In Denzin's terms, we need to become "the projectors that screen for ourselves the very histories we come to call our own" (1993, p. 10); hidden assumptions become exposed when we are able to retell the course by which our stories were secured, the stories about our stories (Rosenwald, 1992). If we are to become authors rather than carriers of our own stories, we need to understand better why we talk the way we do about our crises and their resolutions, as well as what options exist for reframing or inventing new terms for understanding and articulating the meanings of these epiphanies. Human beings are not condemned entirely to live out the stories passed on through cultural productions and family traditions. Often we seek to define ourselves and our lives by stories of our own making, stories that conflict with or deviate from the expected, usual, or conventional. Much of the work of personal narrative involves mitigating the constraints of canonical and cultural conventions. As Bruner (1990, p. 68) indicates, the power of narrative rests not only on an ability to understand what is culturally canonical but also "to account for deviations that can be incorporated in narrative". Many personal narratives attempt to authorize and/or legitimate marginalized, exceptional, or particular experiences. These narratives function as oppositional stories that seek to reform or transform canonical ones. Personal and relational development are facilitated not by strict compliance of stories to conventions, but by the tensions and conflicts between them (Rosenwald, 1992). If our stories did not thwart or contest received and canonical stories, we would have no expectation of change, no account for conflict, no reason for diversity, no real demand to account for our actions, no sense of agency. We would be locked forever within the walls of normative stories.

One problem with Denzin's cultural production thesis is simply that stories are underdetermined by narrative conventions. Social actors continually remake and remystify the meanings of their social worlds despite, or perhaps because of, the power culture brandishes against them. It is precisely the workings of these meaning-centered negotiations between people and cultural productions that is missed, slighted, or overlooked by an insistence on the imperial control of culture (Sherwood, Smith, & Alexander, 1993). When we look at how people articulate and use personal narratives, we learn that cultural forces are not sovereign in the realm of human subjectivity (Rosenwald, 1992). Culture may establish the routine parameters of experience, but it does not fill in all permutations. Humans have a dazzling capacity to conceive optional ways of reforming or reframing the meaning of their actions (Bruner, 1990). Moreover, socialization is rarely successful in consigning human desire to the demands of culture. As Rosenwald points out, there is always an uncomfortable tension between restless desire and stabilizing conventions (Rosenwald, 1992). Culture's grip is not unbreakable. Surely, we reap certain rewards by abiding by rules and conventions, but just as surely we may recognize, however momentarily, the potential tyranny and numbing effect of blindly succumbing to them. Regarding family stories, Stone (1988, p. 195) acknowledges that often we learn that they are "… not at all what we wanted, but a burden we either live with uncomfortably or struggle later on to get rid of".

Many people come to a decisive moment in their lives when they feel a need to take charge of their stories, subverting the constraints of received and inherited stories by "drawing alternatives out of the vast realm of unremembered, neglected, minimized, and even repudiated events" (Parry, 1991, p. 53). This point may be particularly significant for the course of a personal relationship because, as Parry observes, in deconstructing and re-forming received stories, we learn to see our own stories as connected to the stories of significant others:

> While each of us is the central character in our own stories, we are also characters in the stories of all those others with whom we are connected, whether by marriage, family, friendship, or simply by being an inhabitant of the earth [Parry's emphasis] (Parry, 1991, p. 45).

This feature gives personal narratives a relational quality.

We expect other people involved in our lives to play certain roles and be certain characters within the plot of our lives. Other people also have a place for us in their stories; they assume we will play certain parts in their stories. Who we are in their stories and who they are in ours presumably are meshed. When they are not meshed, we introduce the possibility of confusion, misunderstanding, mystification, or betrayal (Goffman, 1959, 1967; Laing, 1969). Normally, some degree of mutuality and agreement on the script is expected; the supportive roles we play in one another's stories help us maintain a stake in each other's lives—albeit a fragile one. In examining any particular relationship between people, one can ask: who is he expected to be as a character in her story? What role does she want him to play in hers?

Within a marriage, however, it may be necessary to do more than simply coordinate individual stories. Usually, there is a desire for a collective story, "our story", the couple's story (Parry, 1991). The two stories of the individuals may be retained, but there is a need, if not a demand, to underscore the couple's togetherness by negotiating a co-authored or co-constructed story (Bochner and Ellis, 1995; Ellis and Bochner, 1992) that can become a shared story of their life together. The two individuals become characters in a single story of "us", rather than merely role players in each other's separate stories, which may, of course, still be retained.

Bochner and Ellis (1992, 1995) conceive *narrative co-construction* as an active method to create stories that address turning points in relationships. They provide procedures for comparing and synthesizing partner's perceptions, expectations, and aspirations for a given relationship. These procedures can function effectively in both therapeutic and research situations, encouraging each member of a family or relationship to have a voice and play a part in plotting the course of their relationship.

NARRATIVES OF PERSONAL RELATIONSHIPS

All research on personal relationships can be considered narrative insofar as it tries to make sense of relationship life by placing it within an intelligible frame of reference. We may call what we do "theorizing", but the theories we spin are never free from interpretations that rely on certain conventions for turning "knowing" into "telling" (White, 1980). And no matter how hard we try to make our tellings neutral and data-based, our research promotes a normative plotline that risks turning "is" into "ought" (Montgomery, 1988). Social science research consists of hundreds of studies of attraction, courtship, love, marriage, parenting, and family life that, taken collectively, advances a story line, whether intentional or not, about the "natural" course of personal relationships. These studies provide a discourse on personal relationships that may unwittingly pass on the logic of the culture, both the culture of causal social scientists (Shotter, 1987) and the larger interests of the society in which social science is deeply entrenched (K. Gergen, 1973, 1982; Lannamann, 1991). In our view, there has been far too little interest in examining closely the attitudes and values our research transmits to the public, but for our purposes here we need only make the point that social science is itself a canonical discourse on relationship life that promotes ways of thinking and talking about this subject.

Narrative approaches to personal relationships show how people breach canonical conventions and expectations, how they cope with exceptional, difficult, and transformative relationship crises, how they invent new ways of speaking when old ways fail them, how they make the absurd sensible and the disastrous manageable, and how they turn calamities into gifts. What is special and important about a storied approach to personal relationships, and what may make it so appallingly difficult to digest for more orthodox relationship researchers, is its oppositional stance. Stories activate subjectivity and compel emotional response; stories long to be used, rather than analyzed; to be told and retold, rather than theorized and settled; to offer lessons for further conversation, rather than truths without any rivals; and stories promise the companionship of intimate details as a substitute for the loneliness of abstracted facts. Thus, stories not only breach ordinary and canonical inscriptions about living, but ideally they challenge norms of writing and research, forcing us to reconsider the goals of our research, the forms we use for expressing relationship experience, and the divisions we accept and enforce that separate literature from social science. Below we briefly review three narrative approaches to personal relationships: (1) accounts; (2) storied lives; and (3) evocative narratives. Collectively, these approaches represent an attempt to use personal narratives to show, tell, and analyze the lived experiences of personal relationships.

Accounts

Scott and Lyman (1968) introduced the term "account" into sociological research to emphasize how talk is used to repair and/or restore order when relational expectations have been violated. Inspired by accounts of loss presented in Weiss's (1975) landmark work on marital separation, Harvey and his associates (see, e.g., Harvey,

Agostinelli, and Weber, 1989; Harvey, Orbuch, Weber, 1990, 1992; Harvey et al., 1992; Harvey, Weber, and Orbuch, 1990; Harvey, Wells, and Alvarez, 1978; Harvey and Uematsu, 1995) broadened the concept of account beyond its earlier microsociological application. They developed a storied version of the account-making process, and initiated a program of research on relationship loss that focuses on empirical analyses of the motivations, content, and functions of accounts. Although they grant that accounts apply to positive as well as negative experiences, Harvey and his associates centered their research on account-making as a narrative strategy for working through relationship loss (Weber and Harvey, 1994).

Using interviews, diaries, archival materials, and other non-reactive procedures for producing accounts, Harvey and his colleagues portray how people deal effectively with different kinds of losses in their lives, ranging from separation and divorce to death of a spouse and loss of home and possessions in natural disasters (Harvey and Uematsu, 1995; Weber and Harvey, 1994). Although important qualitative differences distinguish relationship break-ups from death of a spouse, these researchers emphasize needs that cut across different forms of loss: the need to construct meanings, to reach completion, and to learn a lesson that can be passed on to successive generations. In their view, the grieving process associated with loss involves both the subjective process of chronicling, confirming, and translating strong emotions and memories into symbolic images accessible for communication with others *and* the opportunity to confide the story of loss to others on a personal level. Recovery from loss appears to be contingent on both the private experience of formulating an account and the public experience of disclosing it to others (Weber and Harvey, 1994; Harvey and Uematsu, 1995). Their discussion of the private and public levels of account-making may leave the impression that accounts are formulated privately, then disclosed publicly, although the process undoubtedly is more reflexive and interactive; that is, the formulation of one's story may be significantly influenced by the activity of telling it to others. After telling a story to a confidant, one may be inspired to rethink its meanings and to search for different and more satisfying ways of communicating the story to others.

Until recently, most research on accounts has relied on data-reduction techniques and conventional styles of reporting. Individual cases have rarely, if ever, been presented in their entirety or in a comprehensive, evocative style. Instead, case materials have been conventionally summarized or cut down to snippets to illustrate conceptual arguments. Recently, Harvey and Uematsu (1995) have shown interest in the merits of presenting more extended narrations of accounts of loss (Uematsu, 1996).

Storied Lives

Rosenwald and Ochberg (1992) have developed a critical-cultural perspective for investigating the stories people tell about their lives. While conceding that "all stories are told and that all self-understanding takes place within the narrative frame each culture provides its members" (Rosenwald and Ochberg, 1992, p. 2), these writers are concerned, nonetheless, with the tensions between personal narratives and the conventions from which they achieve intelligibility. Storied lives become interesting when they push beyond conventions and canonical forms and thus become a site for critique and innovation. The stories people tell contribute significantly to the identities they create, perform, and live. Stories also provide access to interpretations and critical evaluations of cultural conditions that constrain and may oppress the way people live and what they can tell. Narrating one's life history provides opportunities for self-renewal over time as a person objectifies life experiences in stories, evaluates their successive accounts, and generates new cycles of lived experience and new accounts of it. Storied lives often take on a relational focus, first, because the story defines who one is in relation to others, and second, because self-accounts normally attempt to achieve harmony with accounts that significant others give of the narrator and of themselves (Rosenwald and Ochberg, 1992).

Three essays published in *Storied Lives* (Rosenwald and Ochberg, 1992) are relevant to the study of personal relationships particularly from a critical–cultural perspective. Rosenberg, Rosenberg, and Farrell (1992) use marital conversations with a single family, initially contacted in the early 1970s and interviewed again in 1984, to interrogate Berger and Kellner's (1964) contention that the family is where people turn for a sense of self and satisfaction. They present vignettes from the 1984 interviews, in which the family discussed their changes over the 12 years and each family member individually narrated an account of family and personal history. Although the narratives show the family trying hard to interpret troubling events in ways that protect the esteem of the family, their stories also present a painful and complicated portrayal of the ideological intricacies with which marital and family conversation must cope. The family conversation painfully reveals "ambivalence and confusion about how merged they sometimes feel with an entangling familial mass of emotion, beliefs, and values" (Rosenberg, Rosenberg, and Farrell, 1992, p. 50). While the authors seem too intent on tearing down the wall of security promoted by Berger and Kellner's (1964) romanticized ideal of family stability, the accounts they analyze show that relationships can never totally satiate desire. The irony promoted by cycles of mismatched expectations and unequal power among family members is that "each needs the other to liberate him or her by granting a self that feels fulfilling, yet each resents and fights the possibility of the other's owning his or her life in this way" (Rosenberg, Rosenberg, and Farrell, 1992, p. 58).

Addressing the question of what cultural forces inspire such high expectations for the experience of parenting, Walkover (1992) discusses accounts provided by interviews with 15 young couples unable to conceive. These couples struggle with a split consciousness in which, on the one hand, parenting is viewed as an experience that provides "a richness and depth otherwise unattainable" while, on the other hand, child-rearing is considered potentially restricting, oppressive, and alienating (Walkover, 1992, p. 180). In terms of their marriage, these couples see the transition to parenting as an inspiration for deeper love, but also as "a wedge that could drive them apart" (Walkover, 1992, p.180). Moreover, the cultural discourse of reproduction encourages couples to personalize their ambivalence and remain unconscious of the moral impositions of cultural definitions of the meaning of parenting. The anxieties they express in their stories revolve around hidden moral assumptions, both about the importance of conceiving children and about the proper ways of raising them. The insidious cultural rhetoric on which their expectations are grounded promotes moral expectations that parents should care "perfectly" for their children and should consider a child's actions as a reflection exclusively on the parent(s) (Walkover, 1992).

Riessman (1992) analyzes the story of Tess, a 23 year-old white woman who justifies her decision to divorce her husband on the grounds of marital rape. Attempting "to heal wounds that only narrative can heal" (Riessman, 1992, p. 247), Tess creates a heroic portrait of her painful life as a victim of her husband's sexual abuse. Her narrative reveals the power of language to make a difference in a person's life. Applying "marital rape" as a metaphor for expressing her husband's savage behavior, Tess is able to escape a violent and abusive marriage and offer publicly acceptable terms for ending it. The vocabulary of sexual abuse—a relatively new public discourse—offers Tess an intelligible means of interpreting and communicating her story in ways previously unavailable to women.

Evocative Narratives

Whereas research on accounts and storied lives tends to conform to rational/analytical conventions of social science reporting, evocative narratives break away from these traditions. In evocative narratives, the author often writes in the first person, making herself the object of research and thus breaching the separation of researcher and subjects (Jackson, 1989); the story usually focuses on a single case, and thus breaches the traditional concerns of research from generalization across cases to generalization within a case (Geertz, 1973); the mode of storytelling is more akin to the novel or biography, and thus fractures the boundaries that normally separate social science from literature; the disclosure of hidden details of private life highlights emotional experience and thus challenges the rational actor model of social performance that dominates social science; and the episodic portrayal of the ebb and flow of relationship experience dramatizes the motion of connected lives across the curve of time, and thus resists the standard practice of portraying a relationship as a snapshot.

Space permits only a selective review of the wide range of evocative narratives relevant to the study of personal relationships. Below we discuss four recent works that display distinctly different styles of expressing lived experiences in personal relationships. The four we have chosen focus on the course of a single relationship over an extended period of time ranging from several months to nine years.

Patrimony is the "true story" of novelist Philip Roth's (1991) intimate bond with his elderly father during the last few months of his father's life. Forced to reassess his appraisal of his father in light of the father's old age and chronic illness, Roth achieves an empathic understanding that reframes his father's most offensive characteristics as merely what it took to survive for 86 years. Told in the first person, this unmistakably autobiographical account plunges readers into the emotional trauma many people experience when they become parents to their parents. Recognizing that "if not in my books or in my life, at least in my dream I would live perennially as his little son, just as he would remain alive there not only as my father but as *the* father sitting in judgment of what I do" (pp. 237–238), Roth nevertheless musters the courage to take charge of the man who had terrorized him as a boy, ushering in "the end of one era, the dawn of another" (p. 83). Roth's narrative paints a rare portrait of an ambivalent son trying to "do it right" for his father, coming to grips with "the over-powering force of bloodbonds", the workings of a mind seeking to detach itself from "the agonizing isolation of a man at the edge of oblivion", in order to find comfort as a member of a clan, and the dissonance arising from the necessity of uniting into a single father the fierce and vigorous father of his childhood and the fragile and stricken father of the present moment.

In *Cancer in Two Voices*, Sandra Butler and Barbara Rosenblum (1991) use journal entries and personal letters to tell their story of what it was like to live with terminal cancer, and what it was like to be the partner who survives. Beginning to write within a few days of Barbara's diagnosis of advanced breast cancer, Butler and Rosenblum define their narrative as "a story of loss and the gifts it brings" (p. 1). In Barbara's voice we hear a candid assessment of what she did to mobilize the help and love of her friends to help her cope with the fear of this scary disease; of her feelings about the war being waged inside her body; of her growing recognition that the cancer spreading inside her was *hers* not theirs, and that she ultimately would have to fight it alone; of how she and Sandra "closed ranks" to face their crisis together; of how her friend of so many words silently withdrew as they became trapped in their own terror and were unable to reach each other; of what it was like to face the "if only" days after mastectomy and to want desperately to squeeze life out of every minute of the day; of the changing images of her concept of a future and the meanings of money, sexuality, and love; of the ironies of being kept alive with poisons that cause fatigue and depression; of her hope for miracles and the aloneness of one who faces death squarely within a finite body that is changing radically every day; and finally, of being too weak to speak, or interact, or care.

In Sandy's voice, we hear her tell of a fear of losing herself in her partner's needs; of trying to stay calm in the face of her partner's terror; of sometimes being angry at Barbara for getting cancer and ruining their lives together, then wanting to protect her from the cancer; of her growing feelings of disengagement and loneliness; of beginning to imagine a life without the person she wanted to grow old with; of their fight for meaning and for maintaining connection; of her longing for the way things used to be; of how Barbara's body became *the* body in their lives, and how she became only an extension of Barbara's physical capacities; and then, at the end, of the guilt of survival and comparison.

Written with an ethnographer's commitment to tell a story that coheres with details of memories, field notes, and systematic introspection (Ellis, 1991), *Final Negotiations* presents Carolyn Ellis' (1995a) detailed personal account of her nine-year intimate relationship with Gene Weinstein, a sociologist 20 years older than she, who died of emphysema in 1985. Told through her perceptions and emphasizing her feelings and coping strategies, Carolyn takes the measure of herself as a sociologist and as a romantic partner caught in the grip of attachment and loss, as she and Gene wage their insatiable appetite for life against the relentless progression of his disease. In *Final Negotiations,* conversation is shown not only as the means for endowing a relationship with meaning but also as a writing method for bringing the flux and flow of connected lives to life with immediacy and vitality. Splicing concrete, ethno-graphic details regarding the entrapment of chronic illness onto the liberating effects of a relationship devoted to conversation and negotiation at all costs, their story is a reminder of how untidy, ambiguous, and menacing relationships can be. Offering her work as "comfort and companionship [and] … when your time comes … a point of comparison" (p. 335), she uses literary strategies of writing to make the reader a participant in emotional episodes of jealousy, rage, depression, embarrassment, fear, and pain, as she and Gene negotiate a balance between hovering and making space, denial and acceptance, arguing and making up, and feeling and blocking out pain.

Dan Franck's *Separation* (Franck, 1993) is a daily chronicle of a man's obsessive attempt to understand and prevent the dissolution of his marriage. Using a third-person narrative style, the main character, presumably Dan, keeps detailed notes of his conversations with friends and records, in micro-detail, observations of his wife's behavior in his presence as she enters into a relationship with another man. Written "to purge himself, to give some direction to his excavation of his own feelings, and perhaps to win her back" (pp. 58–59), *Separation* is not only about the demise of a relationship but part of it: "his children and his wife were like characters getting ready to walk out of his book" (p. 52). Chilling in his anguished yet coolly detached obser-vations of betrayal, mistrust, and obsession, the main character highlights in aston-ishing detail the observable nuances of relational performances—what happens when one person decides to give up the act while the other plays on. *Separation* delivers a believably stark account of the frightening consequences of asymmetrical attachment—"a meadow turned to weeds"—and shows convincingly that no matter how deep one's longing, the loving course of a relationship must be jointly authored.

These four books, and others of the same genre (see Frank, 1991; Haskell, 1990; Kiesinger, 1995; Mairs, 1989; Mukaia, 1989; Neugeboren, 1997; Ronai, 1992, 1994; Sexton, 1994; Swados, 1991; Tillmann-Healy, 1998; Yalom, 1989; Zola, 1982a) should appeal to students of personal relationships who prefer experience-near depic-tions of relationship life and are willing to abandon established conventions of social science writing that promote the illusion of distance and detachment. As evocative narratives, these "true" accounts provoke emotional absorption; they invite readers to connect their own experiences to those of the author; they inspire serious attention to matters of choice and commitment, and arouse understanding of life's contingencies and uncertainty; they mention the unmentionables of everyday life, revealing the flaws and warts of human character as well as human decency and virtue; they reach our minds and our hearts, showing us that our intellects can never be fully cut off from our emotions; they display life's details, reminding readers of past experiences and shaping future dreams and expectations; and they make it clear that the most compelling issues of relationship life are moral questions, struggles to decide the right way to act in concert with others (Coles, 1989).

CONCLUSION

We can do nothing to prevent the entropic march of time. Personal relationships change over time and so must the study of personal relationships. As scholars approaching the next generation of work on personal relationships, we face vexing questions about the inspiration, purposes, and significance of our work (Bochner, 1997). What Richardson (1994) said about much of academic sociology applies—our work is underread; undergraduates find many of our publications boring; graduate students often say our scholarship is dry and inaccessible; seasoned scholars confess they don't finish half of what they start reading; and the public hardly knows we exist. Should we care? Can we do anything about it?

Narrative inquiry is not necessarily a solution, but it is clearly an alternative. To embrace narrative inquiry is to desire works that may be more author-centered and, at the same time, more inviting to readers. Narratives ask readers to feel their "truth" and thus to become fully engaged—morally, aesthetically, emotionally, and intellectually. If we can accept this vision of our work, one that opens the study of personal relationships to the storied particulars of lived experience in their diverse moral, cultural, emotional, and intellectual dimensions, we may be able to touch people where they live and make our work linger in their minds. Whether we trust stories or not, they remain one of the few human resources capable of telling us what we do not hear and showing us what we fail to see.

Chapter 3

Rethinking Communication in Personal Relationships from a Dialectical Perspective

Leslie A. Baxter

University of Iowa, Iowa City, IA, USA

and

Barbara M. Montgomery

Millersville University, Millersville, PA, USA

A dialectical perspective on communication in personal relationships was presented in the 1988 edition of the *Handbook of Personal Relationships* (Baxter, 1988). Since then, substantial empirical and theoretical work has appeared in which the term "dialectical" has been invoked. Rather than simply updating the 1988 chapter, we think it is more useful to offer a fresh articulation of this perspective, organized around three themes: (1) the commonly shared assumptions of a dialectical perspective; (2) major scholarly research programs emanating from a dialectical perspective; and (3) directions for future research. Our motive for addressing "shared assumptions" is to advance criteria by which a perspective can rightfully be described as dialectical; our observation is that the term "dialectical" has been invoked too loosely by some to describe work that is not fully dialectical in nature. Our motives

Communication and Personal Relationships
Edited by Kathryn Dindia and Steve Duck. © 2000 John Wiley & Sons Ltd.

for summarizing the major scholarly research programs are twofold: first, we want to give the reader bibliographic guidance to the major programmatic approaches that adopt a dialectical perspective; and second, we want to emphasize that each of the major dialectical scholars contributes something unique to the study of communication in personal relationships. Several excellent pieces of dialectically-oriented research have been conducted outside the framework of the research programs which we will be summarizing, and we refer the reader elsewhere for more comprehensive reviews of this work (Baxter & Montgomery, 1996; Montgomery & Baxter, 1998; Werner & Baxter, 1994). We reserve the bulk of the chapter to a discussion of directions for future research based on our reading of the dialogic perspective articulated by the Russian scholar Mikhail Bakhtin.

SHARED ASSUMPTIONS OF A DIALECTICAL PERSPECTIVE

Dialectics is not a theory in the traditional sense. It lacks the structural intricacies of formal theories of prediction and explanation; it offers no extensive hierarchical array of axiomatic or propositional arguments. It does not represent a single, unitary statement of generalizable predictions. Dialectics describes, instead, a family of theoretical perspectives with a shared set of conceptual assumptions (Baxter & Montgomery, 1998). Those assumptions, which revolve around the notions of contradiction, change, praxis and totality, constitute what is better thought of as a meta-theoretical perspective (Benson, 1977; Buss, 1979; Cornforth, 1968, Murphy, 1971; Rawlins, 1989; Rychlak, 1976).

Contradiction

From a dialectical perspective, contradictions are inherent in social life and are the basic "drivers" of change and vitality in any social system. The term "contradiction" holds a technical meaning to dialectical theorists and refers to "the dynamic interplay between unified opposites".

In general terms, tendencies or features of a phenomenon are "opposites" if they are incompatible and mutually negate one another. Not all oppositions are alike, however. A logically defined, or "negative", opposition takes the form "X and not X". That is, an opposition consists of some feature and its absence; for instance, stable vs. not stable, autonomous vs. not autonomous, and loving vs. not loving are logically defined contradictions in personal relationships. By contrast, functionally-defined, or "positive", oppositions take the form "X and Y", where both "X" and "Y" are distinct features that function in incompatible ways, such that each negates the other. Examples include stable vs. fluid, autonomous vs. connected, and loving vs. hateful. In practice, functionally defined oppositions are easier to study than logically defined contradictions, simply because both oppositional poles are more explicitly referenced phenomena (Adler, 1927, 1952; Altman, Vinsel & Brown, 1981; Georgoudi, 1983; Israel, 1979).

But functionally defined oppositions have their own complications. First, because the researcher does not have the luxury of logical negation (i.e., "X" and "not X") as the basis of defining an opposition, he/she bears the burden of demonstrating that "X" and "Y" are functionally opposite, that is, that the totality of one precludes the other. What constitutes a functional opposition in one context, culture, or time period might not generalize to another.

A second complication of functionally defined oppositions is that they are likely to be more complicated than a simple binary pair; that is, many oppstions, not just one, are likely to exist in relation to a given feature. For example, the researcher interested in examining the feature of "certainty" from a dialectical perspective might identify several dialectical oppositions that could co-exist: certainty–unpredictability, certainty–novelty, certainty–mystery, certainty–excitement, etc. The complete dialectical understanding of "certainty" rests on the researcher's ability to understand the complexity of multiple oppositions of which "certainty" is an element.

Opposition is a necessary but not sufficient condition for contradiction. In addition, the opposites must simultaneously be unified or interdependent with one another, a concept often referred to as "the unity of opposites". Dialectical unity can occur in two basic ways (Altman, Vinsel & Brown, 1981). First, each oppositional tendency presupposes the existence of the other for its very meaning; this is a unity of identity. The concept of "certainty", for example, is meaningful only because we have an understanding of its logical and/or functional opposites; without knowledge of "uncertainty", "chaos", "unpredictability" and so forth, the concept of "certainty" would be meaningless.

Second, the oppositional tendencies are unified as interdependent parts of a larger whole; this is interdependent unity. For example, in the context of personal relationships, individual autonomy and relational connection are unified opposites. The two tendencies form a functional opposition in that the total autonomy of parties precludes their relational connection, just as total connection between parties precludes their individual autonomy. However, individual autonomy and relational connection form an interdependent unity, as well. Connection with others is necessary in the construction of a person's identity as an autonomous individual (e.g., Askham, 1976; Mead, 1934; Zicklin, 1969), just as the ever-changing nature of a relational connection is predicated on the existence of the parties' unique identities (e.g., Askham, 1976; Karpel, 1976; Kernberg, 1974; L'Abate & L'Abate, 1979; Ryder & Bartle, 1991). Thus, in a contradiction, opposites negate one another. Unity is the basis of the "both/and" quality of contradictions.

Third, a requisite condition for a contradiction is dynamic interplay or tension between the unified opposites. Within the dialectical perspective, the concept of tension carries no negative connotations; instead, the term simply refers to the ongoing, ever-changing interaction between unified oppositions. This interplay is what distinguishes a dialectical perspective from a dualistic one. It is easy to confuse dialectics with dualism, because both perspectives emphasize the presence of opposites. In dualism, however, opposites are conceived as more or less static and isolated phenomena that coexist in parallel fashion. For example, research exists on self-disclosure and on its binary opposite, privacy regulation. However, this research is dualistic so long as each phenomenon is conceived to be definitionally, developmentally, and practically independent. By contrast, a dialectical perspective emphasizes how parties manage the simultaneous but ever-changing exigence for both disclosure and privacy in their relationships and, especially, how the "both/and"-ness of disclosure and privacy is patterned through their mutual influence across the developmental course of a relationship. In short, dualism emphasizes opposites in parallel, whereas dialectics emphasizes the interplay of opposites.

Dialectical Change

The interplay of unified opposites means that all social systems experience the dynamic tension between stability and change. Although all dialectical approaches presume that change is an inherent feature of dialectical contradiction, differences of emphasis can be identified with respect to two underlying issues related to change: (1) the position taken with respect to causation, that is, the relative weighting given to Aristotle's "efficient cause" and "formal cause"; and (2) whether change is regarded as fundamentally indeterminate or teleological.

Aristotle's "efficient cause" refers to linear antecedent–consequent relations, that is, the familiar cause–effect relation, whether this relation is one-way (X is a cause of Y) or reciprocal (X and Y cause and are caused by one another) (Rychlak, 1988). By contrast, Aristotle's "formal cause" refers to the patterned relations among phenomena, that is, the "pattern, shape, outline, or recognizable organization in the flow of events or in the way that objects are constituted" (Rychlak, 1988, pp. 5–6). Unlike an emphasis on one-way or reciprocal cause–effect relations, formal cause focuses on how phenomena mutually define one another in patterned ways, how events flow and unfold over time, and how patterns shift and change; from the perspective of formal cause, none of the component phenomena is "caused" by any prior occurrence of another phenomena. Dialectical theorists differ in their emphasis on efficient causation and formal causation, as we illustrate later in the chapter.

A second issue around which dialectical theorists differ is whether the change process is presumed to be fundamentally indeterminate or teleological in nature. A teleological approach to change presumes that change is the servant of ideal end-states or goals; phenomena are more or less "pulled" toward an ideal outcome. By contrast, indeterminacy presumes that change is not directed toward some necessary or ideal end-state; rather, change involves ongoing quantitative and qualitative shifts that simply move a system to a different place. Some dialectical theorists endorse a teleological view of change, in which contradictions are transcended in a thesis–antithesis–synthesis dynamic. At a given point in time, one pole or aspect of a given contradiction is dominant (the so-called "thesis"), which in turn sets in motion a qualitative change that leads to the salience at a second point in time of the opposing aspect or pole (the so-called "antithesis"), after which a transformative change occurs in which the original opposition of poles is somehow transcended, such that the contradiction no longer exists (the so-called "synthesis").

Other dialectical theorists reject the teleological goal of transcendent change or synthesis, endorsing instead a model of indeterminacy in which two opposing tendencies simply continue their ongoing interplay (Rychlak, 1976). This indeterminate interplay of opposites can involve both cyclical change and linear change. That is, change can be characterized by a repeating patter (cyclical) and/or a series of changes representing progression from one state to another (linear). Cyclical change occurs when the interplay of oppositions takes on a back-and-forth flavor, with relationship parties emphasizing first one oppositional tendency and then the other in an ongoing ebb-and-flow pattern. Visually and theoretically, such an ebb-and-flow pattern would look like repeating sine waves; in actuality, the cycles are characterized by varying amplitudes and rhythms through time, rather than by the uniformity and regularity of sine waves (Altman, Vinsel & Brown, 1981). In contrast, linear change involves a series of non-repeating changes in which the system never returns to a previous state. Further, these two types of change can be combined into linear, cyclic change, or what Werner and Baxter (1994) refer to as "spiraling change". Strictly speaking, cyclicity assumes that phenomena recur in identical form. A spiral, by contrast, involves recurrence but recognizes that phenomena never repeat in identical form; a spiral thus combines elements of both cyclical change (recurrence) and linear change (the absence of identical repetition). Because cyclicity in its strict sense is counter to most conceptualizations of social interaction, spiraling change is probably a more accurate characterization of indeterminate change.

The ebb-and-flow nature of indeterminate, spiraling change often leads people mistakenly to conclude that the teleological goal of homeostasis or equilibrium "drives" this form of dialectical change (e.g., Stafford, 1994). Just the opposite is the case. What propels a spiral to shift toward the other pole(s) is not homeostasis but neglect of that pole. As Bopp and Weeks (1984) observed, the concept of homeostatic equilibrium privileges permanence and stability, thereby ignoring the pervasive dialectic tension between stability and change. Attempts to categorize dialectics as an equilibrium theory fail to recognize its core presumption that spiraling is "driven" by the nature of contradiction, which assumes that some aspect of the opposition is *always* left wanting.

Praxis

The third tenet of dialectics is that people are at once both actors and objects of their own actions, a quality dialectical theorists have termed "praxis" (e.g., Benson, 1977; Israel, 1979; Rawlins, 1989). People function proactively by making communicative choices. Simultaneously, however, they are reactive, because their actions become reified in a variety of normative and institutionalized practices that establish the boundaries of subsequent communicative choices. People are actors in giving communicative life to the contradictions that organize their social life, but these contradictions, in turn, affect their subsequent communicative actions. Every interaction event is a unique moment at the same time that each is informed by the history of prior interaction events and informs future events.

Praxis is an abstract and empty construct without consideration of the concrete practices by which social actors produce the future out of the past in their everyday lives. Dialectical theorists situate praxis in various domains of social life, depending on their particular interests. Marxist dialectical materialists, for example, center their study of contradiction in the material resources of production and consumption by the proletariat and bourgeoisie classes in capitalist societies. By contrast, dialectical theorists who study communication in relationships situate the interplay of opposing tendencies in the symbolic, not material, practices of relationship parties. They emphasize communication as a symbolic resource through which meanings are produced and reproduced. Through their jointly enacted communicative choices, relationship parties react to dialectical exigencies that have been produced from their past interactional history together. At the same time, the communicative choices of the moment alter the dialectical circumstances that the pair will face in future interactions together. Many possible patterns of dialectical change result from a pair's communicative choices (Baxter, 1988; Baxter & Montgomery, 1996), and we will return to this point later.

Totality

The fourth and final core concept of dialectics is "totality"; that is, the assumption that phenomena can be understood only in relation to other phenomena (Benson, 1977; Israel, 1979; Mirkovic, 1980; Rawlins, 1989). From a dialectical perspective, the notion of totality does not mean "completeness" in the sense of producing a total portrait of a phenomenon; the world is an unfinalizable process in which we can point, at best, to fleeting and fluid patterns of the moment. Totality, from a dialectical perspective, is a way to think about the world as a process of relations or interdependencies. On its face, the concept of totality appears to be the same as any number of other theoretical orientations that emphasize such holistic notions as contextuality or relatedness. Put simply, dialectics is one form of holism but not all holistic theories are dialectical; the criterion that distinguishes dialectical holism from other holistic perspectives is the focus on contradictions as the unit of analysis. Dialectical totality, in turn, implicates three issues: where contradictions are located, interdependencies among contradictions, and contextualization of contradictory interplay.

The Location of Contradictions

The first important implication of the dialectical emphasis on the whole is that the tension of opposing dialectical forces is conceptually located *within* the interpersonal relationship, not necessarily as antagonisms *between* individual partners. That is, dialectical attention is directed away from the individual as the unit of analysis and toward the dilemmas and tensions that inhere in relating. Dialectical tensions are played out, relational force against relational force rather than relational partner against relational partner (Montgomery, 1993). As people come together in any social union, they create a host of dialectical forces. Although partners are aware of many of the dialectical dilemmas they face (e.g., Baxter, 1990), a dialectical tension does not need to be consciously felt or expressed. Dialectical interplay may work "backstage" beyond partners' mindful awareness, nonetheless contributing to relational change.

Dialectical tension is thus jointly "owned" by the relationship parties by the very fact of their partnership. But joint ownership does not translate to perfect synchrony in the parties' perceptions; often there is little commonality in partners' experiences of relational contradictions. As Giddens (1979) has noted, dialectical interplay may surface as interpersonal conflict between parties if they are "out of sync" in their momentary experience of a contradiction, such that one person aligns his/her interests with one pole and the other person aligns his/her interests with the other pole. For example, one relationship party may want greater independence between the two of the partners, while the other may want less independence. Mao (1965, p. 48) refers to this asynchrony as antagonistic struggle. Thus, interpersonal conflict is not the equivalent of dialectical tension although, under special circumstances, dialectical tension may be manifested in interpersonal conflict between the parties.

Interdependencies among Contradictions

A system usually contains not one but many contradictions; Cornforth (1968, p. 111) describes this as the "knot of contradictions" that coexist and change in relation to one another over time. In analytically disentangling this dialectical "knot", dialectical theorists have introduced two basic distinctions in types of contradictions. The first, between principal and secondary contradictions, hierarchically organizes contradictions with respect to their impact on or centrality to the dialectical knot. Primary contradictions are those which are more central or salient to a dialectical system at a given point in time. For example, the interplay between autonomy and interdependence has often been identified by dialectical theorists as the most central of all relational contradictions, organizing the pattern of interdependencies among such secondary contradictions as openness and closedness (e.g., Baxter, 1988).

The second distinction is between internal contradictions and external contradictions (Ball, 1979; Cornforth, 1968; Israel, 1979; Mao, 1965; Riegel, 1976). As the term "internal" might suggest, an internal contradiction is constituted within the boundaries of the system under study, whereas an external contradiction is constituted at the nexus of the system with the larger system in which it is embedded. Within the context of personal relationships, internal contradictions are those oppositional forces that function within the boundaries of the dyad and which are inherent to dyadic relating; for example, how the partners can be open and expressive at the same time that they sustain privacy and protectiveness. By contrast, external contradictions are those inherent oppositional forces that operate at the nexus of the dyad and its external environment; for instance, how partners can both conform to society's conventions for relating at the same time that they construct a unique relational bond. External contradictions underscore that relationships are inherently social entities. That is, couples and society sustain a relationship, and in so doing they engage inherent contradictions of such relationships. From a dialectical perspective, internal and external contradictions are presumed to interrelate in dynamic ways. For example, society's conventions for self-disclosure in relationships no doubt are associated with a given couple's experience of their internal dilemma between openness and closedness.

Contextualization of Contradictory Interplay

As Mao (1965) observed, the fact of contradiction is universal but the particulars of the contradicting process vary from one context to another. Dialectical scholars are thus obliged to study contradictions in situ at both universal and particular levels, in contrast to efforts which might seek to reduce contradictions to abstractions stripped of their localized particularities. Social phenomena encompass concrete environmental, situational and interperpersonal factors which are integrally related with issues of praxis and the nature of dialectical change.

MAJOR DIALECTICAL RESEARCH PROGRAMS IN THE STUDY OF COMMUNICATION IN PERSONAL RELATIONSHIPS

A number of perspectives on communication in personal relationships echo with dialectical reverberations, some quite strongly (e.g., Altman, 1993; Conville, 1991; Rawlins, 1992), and others more faintly (e.g., Billig, 1987; Shotter, 1993). We cannot provide an exhaustive summary of this work here (see Baxter & Montgomery, 1996), but we hope to give a flavor of the contributions currently being made to a dialectical understanding of communication in personal relationships.

Bochner's Work on the Dialectics of Family Systems

Bochner (1984) articulated an early dialectical framework for understanding communication in personal relationships, which has been developed more recently in studies of family systems (Bochner & Eisenberg, 1987; Cissna, Cox, & Bochner, 1990; Ellis & Bochner, 1992; Yerby, Buerkel-Rothfuss, & Bochner, 1995). Bochner and his colleagues emphasize three particular functional contradictions in social interaction: (1) how partners are both expressive, revealing, and vulnerable (open) and, simultaneously, discrete, concealing, and protective (closed) with each other; (2) how family members sustain unique individual identities and behave independently (differentiation), while at the same time sharing a family identity and behaving in interdependent ways (integration); and (3) how the family system manages to be both stable (stability) yet adaptive to fluctuating demands placed on it (change).

Bochner is interested in formal cause, not efficient cause, and he argues that scholars should not "confuse predictive efficiency with an understanding of developmental processes" (Bochner, 1984, p. 580). He suggests that the contradictions that organize social life are ongoing throughout a relationship's life cycle, a position that implies indeterminate change rather than teleological change. He also calls for developing a research language of process and change that would recognize incremental variations but also temporally complex "turning points" and momentum reversions. In this recent work (e.g., Ellis & Bochner, 1992), Bochner has emphasized the "lived experience" of contradictory dilemmas as they are concretely and subjectively felt by relationship parties. Bochner's empirically-oriented work is interpretive and particularly emphasizes the study of narratives (Bochner, 1994).

The work of Bochner and his colleagues builds productively on a tradition of dialectical approaches to family systems that goes back as much as three decades.

Family therapists, for example, have long been intrigued by contradictions, paradox, disequilibrium and inconsistencies (e.g., Haley, 1963; Selvini-Palazzoli et al., 1978; Watzlawick, Weakland, & Fisch, 1974). In addition, the conceptual ground in family studies was fertile for nurturing the seeds of dialectics in the 1970s and 1980s, and many dialectical perspectives were produced (e.g., Bopp & Weeks, 1984; Hoffman, 1981; Kempler, 1981; Minuchin, 1974; Wynne, 1984).

Altman's Transactional World View

Over the past 20 years, Irwin Altman and his colleagues have contributed significantly to scholarly discourse about such topics as relationship development (Altman & Taylor, 1973, Altman, Vinsel & Brown, 1981), privacy regulation (Altman, 1977), cross-cultural relationship rituals and practices (Altman et al., 1992; Werner et al., 1993), and social psychological implications of the home environment (Altman & Gauvain, 1981). This body of work stems from a particular theoretical perspective, which Altman (1990, 1993) refers to as "a transactional world view". Altman uniquely couples transactionalism with dialectics to explore phenomena particularly salient to personal relationships. The mainstay of this work is a holistic integration of interpersonal processes (e.g., intimacy, self-disclosure), physical and social environments (e.g., the home, the culture) and temporal qualities (e.g., pace and rhythm of change) to understand social phenomena. Transactional dialectics thus gives particular emphasis to dialectical totality. Phenomena are not viewed in antecedent–consequent relations, but instead are seen as embedded in a continuing and dynamic process of patterned interplay. Altman and his colleagues contend that these coherent patterns of change and fluidity (i.e., formal causation) maintain a "transactional unity" among the elements of processes, environments and time.

Altman and his colleagues view dialectical contradiction as an intrinsic aspect of social existence. They have focused especially on the functional oppositions of openness and closedness, stability and change (Altman, Vinsel & Brown, 1981), and individuality and communality (Altman & Gauvain, 1981) as specific manifestations of social dialectics. Some of their work examines these basic contradictions with the individual as the unit of analysis; for example, how individuals both open themselves up to interaction with others yet maintain a boundary of privacy (e.g., Altman, Vinsel & Brown, 1981). Other work examines larger social units, including couples, families, neighborhoods, and cultures; for example, how couples within different cultures are integrated into the social networks of their families and friends while, at the same time, are differentiated as separate social entities (e.g. Altman & Ginat, 1996).

Temporally-oriented descriptions of change are paramount in Altman's work. He and his colleagues view the focus on change "as a necessary antidote to the proliferation of social psychological approaches that emphasized stability, consistency, or homeostasis as relational goals to the exclusion of needs for change, growth, and movement" (Brown, Altman, & Werner, 1992, p. 510). Collaborations with Werner and others (Werner, Altman, & Oxley, 1985; Werner et al., 1987, 1988) have produced a conceptual framework of temporal qualities like pace, rhythm and duration, which have been used to describe the changing qualities of relationships, home environments and cultural practices.

One of the strongest themes in the Altman et al. work is its multi-method orientation. Multiple sources of data (e.g., interviews, observations, archival data) are emphasized in order to represent different perspectives on events. "Methodological eclecticism" is valued with respect to research designs, procedures and measures (Brown, Werner & Altman, 1998).

Rawlins' View of Friendship over the Life Course

Like Altman, Rawlins (1983a, 1983b, 1989, 1992, 1994a, 1998; Rawlins & Holl, 1987, 1988) stresses totality by incorporating dialectics into what could be called a transactional view, although Rawlins limits his study to platonic friendships. To Rawlins (1992, p. 273), "A dialectical perspective calls for investigating and situating enactment of friendships in their concrete social conditions over time". The concrete social conditions of friendships which are most salient in Rawlins' studies are work, marriage, family, retirement and personal crisis. Time, for Rawlins, is defined predominantly by the life stages of childhood, adolescence, young adulthood, adulthood and later adulthood.

Rawlins has relied on the interpretive analysis of interviews with people of all ages to gain a dialectical perspective on a number of functionally defined contradictions, which he calls the "pulse" of friendships. He identifies two fundamental types. "Contextual dialectics" represent contradictions in culture-based notions, norms and expectations that frame the way any particular friendship is experienced or enacted. These include the tension between public and private enactments of friendship and the tension between abstract ideals and actual realities of friendship. "Interactional dialectics" represent the contradictions involved as friends manage and sustain their relationship on an ongoing, everyday basis. These "communicative predicaments of friendships" include the dialectics of exercising the freedoms to be independent and dependent, caring for a friend as a means-to-an-end (instrumentality) and as an end-in-itself (affection), offering evaluative judgements and offering unconditional acceptance, and, finally, being open and expressive and also being strategic and protective. While Rawlins focuses most on these six contextual and interactional contradictions, he has introduced others through his analyses, like the tension between historical perspectives and present experiences, a dialectic found to be particularly evident in adolescents' interactions with parents and friends (e.g., Rawlins & Holl, 1988).

Rawlins implicates both efficient cause and formal cause in his elucidation of dialectical change. Much of his empirical work seeks to describe the complex, patterned interplay among contradictions indicative of formal causation. However, in total, his extensive analyses construct an argument for efficient cause in that variations in the manifestations of dialectical tensions are due to types and degrees of friendship, cultural constraints, and individual characteristics, especially age and gender. Indeed, change and flux are represented most strongly in the transitions between life stages and not in day-to-day interaction. Rawlins appears to suggest that an individual's age is the antecedent causal variable that results in particular manifestations of given contradictions. Thus, both adolescents and older persons experience the dialectical interplay of independence and interdependence, but these two developmental stages lead people to experience this interplay differently.

Rawlins recognizes both teleological change and indeterminate change. Teleological change, or what Rawlins (1989) calls the "dialectic of transcendence", occurs when friends resolve contradictions and, in so doing, create new ones through the process of thesis–antithesis–synthesis. Rawlins also evokes a kind of indeterminate change when he talks about the "dialectic of encapsulation", which represents relatively closed, regulated and narrowly circumscribed change. While Rawlins' (1989) conceptual discussion of encapsulation focuses most on patterns that reflect the selecting and sustaining of a dominant polarity over a secondary one, his descriptive data about actual behavioral practices emphasize indeterminate changes represented in cycles and spirals between fairly equally weighted polarities (Rawlins, 1983a, 1983b, 1992).

Conville's Relational Transitions Model

Conville (1983, 1988, 1991, 1998) integrates dialectical notions into a structural approach to understand the development of personal relationships. Specifically, Conville argues that during the process of resolving dialectical contradictions, partners are "out of kilter". This imbalance propels relationships through transitions, which link the times when partners are "in kilter", i.e., feel comfortable, occupy complementary roles and coordinate their actions. Moreover these periods of "in kilter" security are but one phase of a recursive process, driven by dialectical oppositions. Security is followed sequentially by the phases of disintegration, alienation and resynthesis to a new pattern of security.

These teleologically defined, relational transitions occur throughout the relationship course, which Conville likens to a spiral or helix. He stresses that the helix represents the recurrence of "second-order" or qualitative changes, which result in the restructuring of the social realities of a relationship, creating new grounds for relating. Conville contrasts this with first-order change, which is change within the context of the given grounds for interaction. For instance, partners deciding to spend more (or less) time together is a first-order change; partners redefining a relationship from "a romantic fling" to "a long-term romance" is a second-order change. According to Conville, partners can cycle through the second-order change process and security–disintegration–alienation–resynthesis many times over the course of their relationship's history, qualitatively transforming the definition of their relationship with the completion of each four-period cycle. In this way, Conville's model underscores the functionality of relationship crisis, which signifies the disintegration of an old relational state.

Conville's conception of contradiction stresses efficient causation. The structural constraint of sequenced episodes leading, always, from security to disintegration, to alienation, to resynthesis and to a new security, represents the assumption of standard, directional changes in relating. Additionally, Conville defines two "meta-dialectics" in this sequence, formed in the juxtapositions of security–alienation and of disintegration–resynthesis. These primary contradictions set the relational stage for the playing out of the secondary contradictions associated with the themes of time (i.e., past–future), intimacy (i.e., close–distant) and affect (i.e., positive–negative).

Conville has applied his structural model to understand a variety of relationship case studies, ranging from the friendship of Helen Keller and Anne Sullivan to the romantic and marital relationships of ordinary persons. His method is a form of interpretive structural analysis.

Baxter's and Montgomery's Dialectical Work

Until recently, each of us has contributed independently to the literature on dialectics in personal relationships. Baxter's work has involved both quantitative and qualitative studies of contradictions in friendships (Bridge & Baxter, 1992), romantic relationships (e.g., Baxter, 1988, 1990; Baxter et al., 1997; Baxter & Widenmann, 1993), marital couples (Baxter & Simon, 1993; Braithwaite & Baxter, 1995) and family relationships (Braithwaite, Baxter & Harper, 1998). Six internal and external contradictions have received attention in this work: the internal contradictions of autonomy–connection, predictability–novelty, and openness–closedness; and the external contradictions of separation–integration, conventionality– uniqueness, and revelation–non-revelation (Baxter, 1993, 1994). Montgomery's work (1984, 1992, 1993) has been characterized by its theoretical orientation, building up on the work of Bateson (1972, 1979) in articulating the ongoing flux of both internal and external contradictions experienced by relationship parties. We have both emphasized the praxis of contradiction; that is, how contradictions are created and sustained through communicative practices.

Most recently, however, we have collaborated in an articulation of ways to rethink the dialectical study of communication in personal relationships (Baxter & Montgomery, 1996). This recent articulation reflects a shift in our previous dialectical work and raises new possibilities for the dialectically-oriented work of others. In particular, we have been influenced by one specific variant of dialectical thinking, Bakhtin's dialogism. Despite variability in recent understandings of dialogism, scholarly opinion seems to be coalescing on the centrality of the "dialogue" to Bakhtin's lifelong intellectual work (Clark & Holquist, 1984; Holquist, 1990; Morson & Emerson, 1990; Todorov, 1984). Bakhtin was critical of the "monologization" of the human experience that he perceived in the dominant linguistic, literary, philosophical and political theories of his time. His intellectual project was a critique of theories that reduced the unfinalizable, open and heterogeneous nature of social life to determinate, closed, totalizing concepts (Bakhtin, 1965/1984, 1981, 1984, 1986; Voloshinov/Bakhtin, 1973[1]). To Bakhtin, social life was a "dialogue", not a "monologue". The essence of dialogue is a simultaneous differentiation from, yet

---

[1] "Some scholars believe that Bakhtin, not Voloshinov, wrote *Marxism and the Philosophy of Language*. The most recent discussion of Bakhtin's authorship is Bocharov (1994). We will refer to "Voloshinov/Bakhtin" throughout.

fusion with, another. To enact dialogue, the parties need to fuse their perspectives while maintaining the uniqueness of their individual perspectives; the parties form a unity in conversation but only through two clearly differentiated voices. Dialogue, unlike monologue, is multivocal; that is, it is characterized by the presence of at least two distinct voices. Just as a dialogue is invoked by and also invokes unity and difference, Bakhtin (1981, p. 272) regarded all social processes as the product of "a contradiction-ridden, tension-filled unity of two embattled tendencies", the centripetal (i.e., forces of unity) and the centrifugal (i.e., forces of difference).

The implications of Bakhtin's work are substantial for moving dialectical work beyond efforts to date, which have tended to emphasize the task of identifying and categorizing binary contradictions in a variety of kinds of relationships. Page limitations do not permit a comprehensive discussion of the implications of dialogically-oriented dialectics, but we can sample some of the more interesting and significant ones in the space that remains (for a more complete discussion, see Baxter & Montgomery, 1996).

SOME IMPLICATIONS OF DIALOGIC DIALECTICS FOR FUTURE RESEARCH

Rethinking the Sovereign Self

A dialogic perspective is predicated on a view of the self as social, in contrast to existing dialectically-oriented research (including much of our own prior work), which is predicated largely on the notion of a contained, sovereign self. To argue that the self is social is to say that communication precedes and is the foundation for psychological or mental states. Further, communication is essential not only for the acquisition of mental states but also in the lifelong enterprise of sustaining and changing them. This is not a new idea, and many have creatively explored its relational implications (e.g., Buber, 1937; Mead, 1934; Sullivan, 1953; Vygotsky, 1986). Few, however, have accorded it as unqualified a rendering as Bakhtin, who saw the boundaries of our selves reaching far beyond the casings of our brains and bodies, encompassing *all* those with whom we interact. As Bakhtin indicated, "I become myself only ... through another and with another's help" (in Todorov, 1984, p. 96). This dialogic self is one that is much more of the moment and fluid than more traditional notions, which assume kinds of stable "mental reservoirs" from which all actions spring.

A view of the self as social challenges us to rethink two contradictions that have garnered much attention among dialectical scholars: openness–closedness (e.g., the tension between disclosive expression and its opposites) and autonomy-connection (e.g., the tension between interdependence with another and independence from another).

Rethinking the Openness–Closedness Contradiction

Existing work tends to view the self as pre-formed and intact before relating; the process of interacting in relationships, thus, is one of revealing the sovereign self.

From the perspective that presumes a sovereign self, relationships are problematic because of the risk and danger entailed in revelation. Self-disclosure is "owned" by the sovereign self and functions as an "access gate" that opens or closes one's self-territory to another's gaze. The theme of risk and danger appears throughout the dialectical work, especially in discussions of the openness–closedness contradiction. For example, Rawlins (1983b) refers to the dilemma between candor and discretion, with vulnerability serving as the arbiter of just how disclosive a person will be with another. Other dialectically-oriented scholars have similarly framed openness and closedness in terms of the vulnerabilities of disclosure (e.g., Altman, Vinsel, & Brown, 1981; Baxter, 1988; Dindia, 1994).

By contrast, a dialogic perspective shifts emphasis from the revelation of sovereign self to the emergent co-construction of self. Self-disclosure is not a decision made by a contained self but a kind of utterance that gives voice to self-as-becoming. From a Bakhtinian perspective, an utterance is more complex than the individuated act of an autonomous speaker. As Voloshinov/Bakhtin (1973, p. 86) put it:

> ...word is a two-sided act. It is determined equally by whose word it is and for whom it is meant. As word, it is precisely the product of the reciprocal relationship between speaker and listener, addresser and addressee. Each and every word expresses the "one" in relation to the "other" ... A word is a bridge thrown between myself and another.

This relational view of a "word", including words about the self, discourages the limiting juxtaposition of openness–closedness as it is currently conceptualized around the assumption of a contained, already defined, self. Rather, understanding communication that is relevant to the continually emerging and social self requires focusing on three additional contradictions (Bakhtin, 1986): the contradiction between *the said and the unsaid*, or the dialectical interplay between meaning encoded in verbalized language and meaning carried in the context; the contradiction between *freedom* and *constraint*, or the dialectical interplay between the "given" that is inherited by any inter-action and the "new" that is created in any interaction; and the contradiction between *inner speech* and *outer speech*, or the dialectical interplay between personal meaning and social meaning, out of which individual consciousness constantly re-emerges. From a dialogic perspective, then, it is too simplistic to ask whether a person is open or closed with respect to his/her "true self". Such a question ignores the complexity of contradictions underlying any utterance. A dialogically-based dialectics, thus, requires scholars to rethink the openness–closedness dialectic, complicating it with a multivocal set of contradictions that center around the process of co-constructing self-as-becoming.

Rethinking the Autonomy–Connection Contradiction

Just as the openness–closedness contradiction in existing dialectical research is conceived from the perspective of a sovereign self, so is the autonomy–connection contradiction. Rawlins (1983a), for example, discusses this contradiction as a matter of individual rights and responsibilities; the contained self grants to himself/herself the right of freedom of action, but the contained self also assumes a responsibility to be there when called on to fulfill the other's needs. Other dialectical scholars similarly conceptualize the autonomy–connection dialectic as an individually-centered tension between the desire to be autonomous or independent and the desire to be interdependent with another (e.g., Altman, et al., 1988; Baxter, 1988, Bochner, 1984). From the perspective of a sovereign self, interdependence is something the individual trades off against individual independence; independence is sacrificed to achieve interdependence. The social-exchange logic that undergirds this conception of the autonomy–connection dialectic is clear: sovereign selves enter relationships with their respective reward–cost structures as guides, and they experience both costs and rewards in independence (the loss of other's assistance and freedom of action, respectively) and both costs and rewards in interdependence (loss of freedom of action and reliance on other's assistance, respectively).

A dialogic perspective offers an alternative conception of autonomy and connection and so challenges the social exchange simplicities. A relationship is conceived as a dialogue, and as such, implicates both the differentiation and fusion of relationship parties. Just as a dialogue is the ongoing, joint coordination of two distinct voices, a relationship is an improvised, fluid boundary of unity and difference. An individual relationship partner does not "negotiate away" his/her independence in the other's dependence. Instead, relating is a joint dialogue of the two parties in which both connectedness and autonomy are inherent. Party B has a relational interest, not only in Party A's responsibility for interdependence, but a relational interest as well in Party A's independence, and vice versa. Both differentiation (autonomy or independence of the parties) and unity (connectedness or interdependence of the parties) are critical to relationship vitality and inherent in the very process of relating. Thus, from the perspective of a social self, the autonomy–connection contradiction is not centered in the individual but in the relationship between parties.

Rethinking Binary Contradictions

Existing dialectically-oriented scholarship has tended to conceive of contradictions as binary oppositions, for example, independence–interdependence, openness–closedness, and so forth. By contrast, a dialogic dialectics urges a more complex view in which multiple voices of opposition function at once, a phenomenon we call "multivocal contradiction".

By way of illustrating the implications of a shift from binary to multivocal contradictions, let us again reconsider the autonomy–connection contradiction. Existing dialectical work tends to conceive this contradiction narrowly in terms of behavioral independence and interdependence. From a dialogic perspective, this single binary pair is too limiting. The relationship dialogue is about unity and difference in many simultaneous manifestations including, but not limited to, behavioral independence–interdependence. For example, relationship partners can grapple with tensions between autonomy and co-dependence, autonomy and domination, autonomy and dependence, and autonomy and intimacy and many of these struggles can be engaged simultaneously. Additionally, partners can engage these struggles relative to many different levels of social existence implicated in personal relationships, including values, attitudes, beliefs, and ideal and actual behavioral practices (see, e.g., Duck, 1994a; Wood et al., 1994).

The multivocality of autonomy–connection becomes even more complex when we recognize that relationship parties are situated locally. Bakhtin (1981) refers to this situatedness as a "chronotope", that is, a time–space location, observing that "every entry into the sphere of meaning is accomplished only through the gates of the chronotope" (p. 258). Relationship parties are always relating from the time–space horizons of the moment, which hold the potential for multiple meanings of autonomy and connection. Goldsmith (1990), for example, found five qualitatively different meanings of "connection" and "autonomy" for parties reporting on the different developmental moments of their respective romantic relationships. Similarly, Stamp & Banski (1992) have reported qualitative shifts in what married partners mean by connection and autonomy upon the birth of the first child. Masheter's work with post-divorce couples has found that the connection–autonomy contradiction takes on a different meaning to partners before and after the divorce (Masheter, 1991, 1994; Masheter & Harris, 1986). In short, the autonomy–connection contradiction has multiple radiants of meaning which are dynamically chronotopic. By limiting this and other contradictions to single radiants anchored at either end by polar opposites, dialectical scholars have operated as if contradictions were simple binary pairs rather than complex webs of oppositions, all of whose elements are in simultaneous interplay with one another.

Rethinking Relationship Development

Linear progress is the dominant conception of relationship development in existing research and theory. That is, relationships are thought to move in a unidirectional manner from states of less to more on several key dimensions: less to more interde-pendence, less to more openness, less to more certainty, and so forth. Once some tele-ological end-state is achieved (typically marriage), the relationship shifts to homeostatic maintenance. Relationship deterioration and break-up is envisioned as the reverse developmental course: that is, moreness to lessness on the key underlying dimensions. In the Baxter (1988) Handbook essay, the process of contradictory change was rendered compatible with the dominant view of relationship development in that the essay discussed a movement from autonomy to connection, to a synthesis of autonomy with connection, to the return of autonomy in break-up. By contrast, a dialogic perspective views relationship change as an indeterminate process with no clear end-states and no necessary paths of change. Relationship change involves both centripetal and centrifugal movement, rather than centripetal unidirectionality alone. Relationships move both "upwards" and "downwards", both "toward" and "away from", both "forwards" and "backwards". However, in this approach, terms such as "upwards" and "downwards" are stripped of their connotations of progress and regression, respectively. Relationship change is conceived as dialogically complex, that is, simultaneously characterized as both independent and interdependent, both intimate and non-intimate, both open and closed, both certain and uncertain, both separated from the social order and integrated with the social order, and so forth. The ongoing interplay of contradictory forces opens up the playing field of change to encompass more than bidirectional movement; the very nature of the playing field is likely to change in qualitative ways which allow the relationship parties to change in new directions that are emergent in dialogic interplay. Thus, dialogic change is conceived as multivocal, both quantitatively and qualitatively.

A dialogic perspective adds a different perspective to the scholarly conversation on relationship beginnings, middles and endings. From the monologic stance of progress, a relationship begins when parties shift from strangers to acquaintances and ends when the parties cease to function interdependently. From a dialogic perspective, a relationship begins with the interplay of contradictory voices representing different forces that must be addressed by virtue of the two people being together. A relationship ends in dialogic silence when contradictions are no longer present. As Masheter's (1991, 1994; Masheter & Harris, 1986) work demonstrates, this does not occur at traditional ending markers like divorce, because "ex's" usually continue to grapple with a host of dialectical tensions around such themes as autonomy and connection and openness and closedness. Thus, a relationship is constituted solely in and through the dialogues of its multivocal contradictions.

The reconceptualization of relationship "middles" is predicated on the notion that a relationship is not teleologically oriented toward some idealized destination or outcome. Such relationship types as acquaintance, friendship, and romantic attachment are not viewed as less developed "way-stations" along the road of courtship; rather, these types stand conceptually on their own ground (Delia, 1980). Acquaintanceship, for example, is not merely an undeveloped relationship but rather a relationship form in its own right that should be studied for its dialogic complexities. In abandoning the notion of some idealized destination for relationships, a dialogic perspective positions scholars to be more responsive to what Stacey (1990) has called the postmodern relationships that characterize late twentieth century Western culture, relationships that are "inhabite[d] uneasily and reconstitute[d] frequently in response to changing personal and occupational circumstances" (p. 17). Bridge and Baxter (1992) join Stacey in suggesting the prevalence in modern society of "blended relationships", that is, those that cross the boundary between role-based and personally-based elements. Blended relationships, such as friendships at work and mentor–protégé relationships, are not easily understood from the traditional monologue of developmental progress. Rather than marginalizing these relationships that are simultaneously impersonal and personal in structure, a dialogic perspective would have us examine them each in its own right for its dialogic complexities.

The progress orientation of existing research and theory on relationship "middles" emphasizes homeostatic equilibrium once the relationship's destination is reached. Dialogic dialectics positions us to view differently the "maintenance" of relationships (Montgomery, 1993). Because there is no destination in a dialogic system, there is no homeostatic goal whose steady state is sought through adaptive change. Relationships are not homeostatically organized around a stable point of "equilibrium", neither are they developmental organisms whose evolution is marked by progressive "moreness". Thus, the very concept of "relationship maintenance" is seen to privilege one pole only of the ongoing and ever-present dialectic between stability and change. For these reasons, we prefer to think of partners "sustaining" a relationship rather than "maintaining" it. Relationships are sustained to the extent that dialogic complexity is given voice.

In short, a dialogic perspective conceives of relationship development as fundamentally indeterminate, slippery, and fuzzy. Relationship parties are forever improvising their relationship, forever coordinating the multiple centripetal and centrifugal voices of contradiction. Instead of envisioning relationship development as a linear musical scale that progresses from lower to higher notes of intimacy, relationship change is more like a jazz improvisation of competing, yet coordinated, musical sounds.

Rethinking Praxis

The indeterminacy that characterizes relationship change is a direct result of the many praxical possibilities that can be enacted by relationship parties at any given moment. Relationship change thus can be envisioned as a tree with many branches, each of which fans out in a dense array and which changes over time. The path of change for a given relationship can follow any of multiple branching possibilities. To date, dialectically-oriented research has largely been in the business of documenting that contradictions exist and cataloguing them (for a more detailed review, see Werner & Baxter, 1994). Study of praxis, that is, the joint actions of relationship parties in response to the dialectical exigencies of the moment, has received fairly limited attention by researchers.

We have recently modified the list of praxis possibilities originally articulated in the 1988 *Handbook* chapter. Instead of six basic praxical actions, we now envision at least eight and are confident that this expanded list is far from exhaustive (Baxter & Montgomery, 1996). The praxis patterns are not equally functional. A functional praxis response is one which celebrates the richness and diversity afforded by the oppositions of a contradiction. Pearce (1989, p. 199) captures this spirit of celebration in his call for the development of "substantive irony", that is, learning to live on "friendly terms" with paradox, contradiction, and multivocality.

Two patterns are characterized by limited functionality, although they might appear with some frequency in relational life. The praxis pattern of *denial* is characterized by discourse in which the parties basically seek to extinguish the contradictory nature of their relationship, e.g., the couple who say they want to be together 24 hours a day or the pair who say they are always totally open with each other. The second praxis pattern is *disorientation*. This praxis pattern involves a fatalistic attitude in which contradictions are recognized as inevitable but negative. The relationship parties view their relationship as disorienting, that is, plagued with nihilistic ambiguities and uncertainties.

The remaining six praxis patterns display greater functionality than either denial or disorientation. They all show recognition of contradiction and involve proactive response patterns of one kind or another:

1. *Spiraling alternation* is characterized by a back-and-forth quality in which the relationship parties privilege different oppositional polarities at different times.
2. *Segmentation* is a response in which the relationship parties develop dialogic specializations, with certain topics or activities privileging one oppositional

polarity and other topics or activities privileging other oppositional polarities. As relationship parties shift from one topic or activity to another, different opposing themes are privileged.

3. *Balance* involves an effort to respond to all oppositions at one point in time through compromise. Each oppositional exigence is responded to only partially, given the nature of compromise.

4. *Integration* is a response in which the relationship parties manage to celebrate simultaneously and fully all polarities of a contradiction. Several scholars have suggested that rituals illustrate integration because they can hold all sides to a contradiction at once (see Werner & Baxter, 1994, for a more extensive discussion of rituals as dialectical).

5. *Recalibration* is characterized by a transformation in the form of the opposition, such that the initially experienced polarities are no longer oppositional to one another. Different from the teleologically-oriented dialectical concept of transcendence as a permanent resolution of a contradiction through synthesis, recalibration is a practice that only transcends the form in which a given opposition is expressed but without resolving the underlying contradiction.

6. *Reaffirmation*. This praxis pattern, like disorientation, involves an acceptance by the parties that contradictory polarities cannot be reconciled. However, unlike disorientation, reaffirmation celebrates the richness afforded by each polarity and tolerates the tension posed by their unity.

Some scholarly work has been done on dialectical praxis (e.g., Altman et al., 1992; Baxter, 1988, 1990; Baxter & Simon, 1993; Baxter & Widenmann, 1993; Braithwaite & Baxter, 1995; Conville, 1991; Rawlins, 1992; Sabourin & Stamp, 1997; Van Lear, 1991; Werner et al., 1993). Relationship parties appear to respond most typically to dialectical exigencies by invoking a spiraling pattern, in which one oppositional polarity is privileged and then another oppositional polarity is privileged in a waxing-and-waning pattern across time and across various topic or activity domains. Additionally, various communication rituals provide occasions where multiple oppositions can be symbolically voiced simultaneously. In short, existing dialectical work suggests that spiraling alternation, segmentation, and integration dominate the praxis of relating.

Although this research is insightful, it focuses on the molar level of analysis, failing to inform us about situated praxis, that is, meaning that is constructed in the moment-to-moment discourse between interlocutors (for a notable exception, see Van Lear, 1991). A finer-grained dialogic perspective would complement this molar-level work with information about the subtle nuances of contradiction in enacted talk. As Bakhtin (1981, p. 272) observed:

> Every concrete utterance of a speaking subject serves as a point where centrifugal as well as centripetal forces are brought to bear. The processes of centralization and decentralization, of unification and disunification, intersect in the utterance.

Bakhtin was critical of the dialectical tradition of Hegel and Marx because it was insufficiently grounded in the concrete practices of everyday sociality. As he argued, "Take a dialogue and remove the voices, remove the intonations, carve out abstract concepts and judgments from living words and responses, cram everything into one abstract consciousness—and that's how you get dialectics" (Bakhtin, 1986, p. 147). Sensitive to Bakhtin's critique, we call here for a dialectical approach that takes seriously and elevates centrally the details of enacted dialogue in relationships.

Rethinking Dyadic Boundaries

With some exceptions (e.g., Baxter, 1993; Brown, Altman, & Werner, 1992; Hinde, 1979, 1987; Montgomery, 1992; Rawlins, 1989, 1992; Werner et al., 1993), dialectical theorists have tended to view the personal relationship in a sociocultural vacuum. Thus, internal contradictions (i.e., those located within the boundary of the dyad) have received disproportionate attention in comparison to external contradictions (i.e., those located between the dyad and the larger social system). However, if one takes the dialectical principle of totality seriously, as Bakhtin urges with his emphasis on the chronotopic nature of social life, then our ability to understand even internal contradictions is limited until we incorporate information about the social context in which parties live their relationship. Relationship parties are always positioned concretely; they are embodied in real persons who are feminine or not, Euro-American or not, economically privileged or not, socialized in a dysfunctional family or not, and so forth. The relationship created between people exists in a socio-cultural milieu that is characterized by its own "interpersonal ideology", that is, widely recognized, legitimated, and prescribed beliefs about what a relationship is and how people ought to conduct their interpersonal lives (Fitch, 1994). There are no "clean slates" in relationships; no relationship "fresh starts". Instead, all relationships, as a social birthright, are heirs to the living history of social existence; at the same time, they are the guardians, the words, and the executors of that dynamic social estate. Partners relate or act into a relational context that is partly created in their acting and is partly the product of all other relationships in history. Any particular partners—by the way they interact with each other, their family, friends, neighbors, acquaintances, and even strangers—add to that history by reinforcing or modifying its patterns.

How relationship parties are chronotopically positioned affects the exigencies of contradictions in a number of ways. First, the very construction of "opposition" is accomplished socially and culturally. For example, the interplay between autonomy and connection among Euro-Americans who are socialized to believe in individualism no doubt differs from the autonomy–connection interplay among Japanese socialized to a sociocentric conception of personhood (e.g., Rosenberger, 1989). A similar, though not quite so pronounced, difference emerges when comparing Anglos to Hispanics and African–Americans (see Wood, 1995). These examples argue for a mindful consideration of cultural and social context in identifying contradiction. Second, relationship parties who are socially and culturally positioned with vested interests in different polarities of a given contradiction are likely to enact antagonistic struggles in the dialogue of their relationship. For example, to the extent that feminine socialization and masculine socialization are implicated in connection and autonomy, respectively, opposite-sex relations in American society are chronotopically predisposed to experience an antagonistic enactment of the autonomy–connection contradiction. Finally, chronotopic positioning undoubtedly affects praxis, as well. The range of praxical options that a couple perceives as viable, for example, is greatly affected by the ideology of relating that pervades the culture and the particular position of their relationship in the social matrix. To date, dialectically-oriented scholars have not taken as seriously as they must the sociocultural chronotopes in which relationships are embedded.

Rethinking Scholarly Inquiry

A dialogic view of dialectics extends to the process of inquiry with the warrants that theory and method are inextricably linked (Duck & Montgomery, 1991) and that inquiry is a kind of social interaction just as much as is relational communication. To the extent that we recognize and encourage a dialogic view of communication in personal relationships, we must also do so with regard to inquiry about communication in personal relationships.

Unlike some dialectical scholars, we do not limit dialectical inquiry to interpretive approaches. Neither are we advocates of exclusive reliance on traditional, quantitatively-oriented approaches. Rather, a dialogic view of inquiry is necessarily multi-vocal, respecting the internal integrity of all approaches to research. Dialogic inquiry is not merely a plurality of voices engaged in parallel scholarship. Dialogic inquiry assumes that understanding emerges from the active interchange among incommensurate views. We disagree with those who have offered critiques of pluralistic approaches based on the expectation that all participants in the dialogue will adopt the same evaluative criteria (e.g., Bostrom & Donohew, 1992; Burleson, 1991; Fitzpatrick, 1993; Miller, 1989). Instead, we agree with Pearce (1989) that the value of engaging incommensurate approaches depends partly on a kind of social eloquence rather than rhetorical eloquence. That is, the point of the dialogue is not to persuade, and it is not to produce coherence or convergence into a single point of view. Rather, the point is to elaborate the potential for coordination, a process Pearce describes as a kind of interaction that brings about an event that participants interpret as meaningful from their own, particular perspectives. Such coordination in the inquiry process does not require consensus. Approached eloquently, however, it does require recognition and appreciation of different viewpoints. Dialogic inquiry will be most fruitful when scholars collaborate to produce research in much the same way that people who mean different things can collaborate to produce a conversation. Collaborators do not necessarily have to agree; they do have to forge a relationship to produce something that works. Contradictory tensions between rigor and imagination, precision and richness, prediction and contingency, and creativity and verification push researchers to try different methods and to see different things in their data (see Guba, 1990). These tensions will not be escaped or transcended, neither are they necessarily negative outcomes or restraints on the productivity of ideas and understanding.

Beyond these meta-methodological issues, the study of relational interaction from the dialogic perspective must be attentive to its basic assumptions. The particular methods of choice are not as important as that the methods acknowledge that the "text" of any communication event emerges from the interaction of multiple voices, and that these voices are not uniquely identified with individuals but with the relationship between individuals (McNamee, 1988). Dialectics does not pit self-contained individual against self-contained individual. Certainly, antagonistic contradictions do occur from time to time in the form of interpersonal conflict, but users of methods of study must distinguish many more than two voices expressing the tensions of relating. Researchers must listen for those voices as they emanate between relational partners and also from the cracking, disjointed articulations of a single partner describing his/her contradictory experiences of the relationship. Such contradictory experiences are multivocal, not binary, involving complex webs of oppositions, all of which are unified and negated through time and space.

In arguing for multivocality in a number of ways—multiple perspectives in dialogue, multiple voices relating, multiple times and sociocultural locations of relating, multiple voices in research—dialogic inquiry challenges the "sacred cows" of agreement and consistency that have long driven the research enterprise. If one accepts a view of the world as dialogic, then such an outcome is inevitable. Problematic, for example, are the efforts in which researchers simply average the disparate scores of relationship parties in an effort to derive a single, unitary index of the phenomenon under investigation. Problematic as well are the efforts in which researchers privilege the outsider perspective as closer to objective truth instead of recognizing it as merely an alternative voice to those of the insiders. And the efforts in which researchers sustain universalizing generalizations are challenged, as well. The shift to multivocal inquiry is admittedly disconcerting. However, as Bakhtin (1986, p. 7) stated, "[M]eaning only reveals its depth once it has encountered and come into contact with another, foreign meaning".

CONCLUSION

Our purpose in this chapter has been to describe key concepts in, and approaches to, a dialectical perspective on social interaction in relationships. Taking a traditional scholarly approach to this explicative task, we have enumerated key assumptions like contradiction, change, praxis, and totality. We also have described the conceptual and methodological implications for understanding and studying such notions as the social self, relationship change, and dyadic interaction, and for viewing them as relationally situated. Finally, we have given examples of inquiry conducted form a dialectical perspective to illustrate the perspective's range of application. It would be inaccurate for us to claim that all of these concepts are unique to a dialectical perspective. Although an emphasis on contradiction as the key unit of analysis uniquely characterizes a dialectical approach, some aspects of other concepts we have examined (e.g., the social self, indeterminacy of change, totality) can be identified as well in other scholarship on personal relationships (e.g., Bateson, 1972, 1979; Duck, 1994a; Pearce, 1989; Gergen, 1994). In short, a dialectical perspective is both similar to and different from these other perspectives. A dialectical perspective thus joins the scholarly dialogue on personal relationships in its simultaneous unity with, and differentiation from, other scholarly voices.

Slighted in this scholarly rendering, however, is the spirit of a dialectical perspective. Partly because of the norms of scholarship and partly because of our own styles, we have found it far easier to present the digitized version of dialectics on these printed pages than the analogic version. But that version is every bit as important to grasp, for it extends understanding of a dialectical perspective beyond *what* assumptions and questions are central to *how* those are integrated into a dialectical view of relationships.

The spirit of dialectics is marked by a healthy dose of *irony*, a sense that things are both what they seem to be and something else as well. Irony entertains both belief and doubt, both hope and despair, both seriousness and play, and in these kinds of complexities it hints at the very nature of social dialectics. *Creativity* is another hallmark. As Bakhtin (1986, p. 120) observed, "it is much easier to study the given in what is created . . . than to study what is created". Dialectics demands that we reach beyond our "ready-made" vocabularies of generalized central tendencies to appreciate the uniqueness of each communicative moment. *Inclusiveness* is key as well. Dialectical approaches respect different meaning systems, are attuned to their distinct voices, and so represent a multivocal social reality. Lastly, we wish to stress the *fluidity* and *unfinalizability* that characterizes dialectical approaches. All is becoming, but never becomes.

We like the metaphor of the jazz ensemble to convey the dialectical spirit. Jazz is musically identified by its inclusiveness and its improvisation; collaboration of unique, sometimes discordant, instrumental voices happens in the service of spontaneous creativity. The musical score and deep structures of jazz provide just enough guidance to allow for that collaboration, but an accompanying irreverence for the music as written allows for the synergy of collaborative improvisation. These same themes of multivocal collaboration, respect for difference, and creativity of the interactive moment characterize our notion of relational dialectics.

Chapter 4

COMMUNICATION NETWORKS AND RELATIONSHIP LIFE CYCLES

Malcolm R. Parks

University of Washington, Seattle, WA, USA

Cynthia and John have just met at a social event sponsored by John's employer. Both are unattached and enjoying the unfolding conversation. We wonder, as perhaps they do, whether this conversation will mark the beginning of a romantic relationship. As scholars, of course, we also wonder how best to understand why John and Cynthia may have one relational future rather than another. Surely their individual needs and desires will matter. So, too, will the fact that they come from the same ethnic group and social class. But individual characteristics and societal categories are not suffi-cient. We must look at the interaction itself. But even that is not enough. We must look as well at the broader social context in which individual actions and relationships are woven together. It also may be important, for example, that Cynthia came to the party with Claire, who is John's co-worker and friend. It may be very important that Claire introduced them or that John is friendly with Claire's new husband. Whether Cynthia introduces John to her other friends or to her mother may make a difference later on.

These possibilities point to the fact that the way a given personal relationship changes over time will be intertwined with what happens in the participants' other relationships. To create a theory to account for these connections, we must first address two more basic questions. What is it that changes as a relationship develops or deteriorates? What are the features of communication networks that are most relevant for the particular dyads within them? After addressing these questions I will

Communication and Personal Relationships
Edited by Kathryn Dindia and Steve Duck. © 2000 John Wiley & Sons Ltd.

review previous research linking the developmental paths of personal relationships with the dynamics of the participants' surrounding social networks and then articulate a theoretic perspective for understanding these linkages.

CONCEPTUALIZING RELATIONSHIPS AND NETWORKS

The Relationship Life Cycle

Relationships exist in the structure and content of communication over time. While there are certainly cognitive, affective, and structural concomitances, relationships live in the communication between the participants. This is not to say that relationships are merely "undigested interactions" (Duck, 1988) or that what people think and feel does not matter. Rather, I emphasize the generative nature of communication. Interaction both stimulates changes in cognition and affect and is the medium through which those changes become real for the self and others.

The first task of a theory of relational life cycles is to identify the dimensions along which interaction changes as relationships develop and deteriorate. Many approaches commonly found in the literature on personal relationships fail to do this. Measuring the simple longevity of a relationship, for example, reveals nothing about the changes going on inside it. Categorizing relationships in terms of broad social labels (e.g., casual friend, friend, close friend) also does little to elucidate the underlying dimensions of the relational life cycle. Conceptualizing the relational life cycle in terms of single indicators such as satisfaction, attraction, or closeness suffers from the same problem. We must look more specifically at what changes when a relationship develops or deteriorates. I believe that a useful working definition of the relational life cycle would include at least six factors: (1) interdependence; (2) breadth or variety of interaction; (3) depth or intimacy of interaction; (4) commitment; (5) predictability and understanding; and (6) code change and coordination.

Interdependence

Interdependence has long been recognized as a defining feature of the developmental process (e.g., Kelley et al., 1983; Levinger & Snoek, 1972). I interpret interdependence generously to include three specific types of mutual influence. The first is true interdependence or mutual behavioral control. It represents the degree to which each person's outcomes are influenced by the way their overt actions and internal states fit with the other's (Kelley & Thibaut, 1978). For example, John and Cynthia would be interdependent in this way if each person's desire to see a particular movie varied with the other person's desire to see the same movie. Another kind of interdependence takes the form of simple mutual dependence. John's enjoyment of a movie may depend on how much Cynthia likes it, although Cynthia may find it possible to enjoy a movie regardless of how John reacts to it. On the other hand, Cynthia's tastes in music may be much more dependent on John's preferences than his are upon hers.

Although no one of these strands of dependency is binding, together they form a complex pattern of mutual dependencies that bind the couple together. A third form of interdependence is reflected in the degree to which each person's utterances in a sequence depend on the other's. The way relational partners introduce, develop, and retire topics, as well as the ways in which they negotiate identity claims, may involve considerable collaboration. Conversational interdependence is worth distinguishing because it focuses us on the give and take of ongoing conversation, on its true communicative character, in a way that outcome-based definitions do not. As the degree of mutual influence represented by these three types of interdependence increases, a relationship develops. As they decrease, the relationship deteriorates.

Variety or Breadth of Interaction

As relationships develop, the "breadth" or "richness" of interaction increases (Altman & Taylor, 1973). As they deteriorate, breadth decreases. Three aspects of variety or breadth warrant delineation. At the broadest level we may think of breadth as the variety of behaviors or resources exchanged. The exchange matrix expands with development and contracts with deterioration. In Hays's (1984) study of same-sex friendships, for example, friends who grew closer over a three month period displayed a greater variety of behaviors across a greater range of categories (i.e., task sharing, assistance, expressing emotion, mutual disclosure) than friends whose relationship stagnated or terminated. Breadth may also be conceptualized in terms of the variety of conversational topics. Taylor (1968), for example, tracked the number of different topics new college roommates discussed during their first three months and found increases in both non-intimate and intimate topics. Finally, breadth may be conceptualized in terms of the variety of communicative channels or contexts used. For instance, personal relationships started in computer-mediated channels, such as the Internet, often expand over time to incorporate other channels, including face-to-face contact (Parks & Floyd, 1995).

Depth or Intimacy of Interaction

The depth or intimacy dimension of the relational life cycle has most often been associated with self-disclosure and intimacy. While early approaches focused only on the simple revelation of personal information (e.g., Jourard, 1971), more recent approaches have emphasized the process-oriented, communicative aspects of this dimension. Intimacy is defined as a "process in which one person expresses important self-relevant feelings and information to another, and as a result of the other's response comes to feel known, validated, and cared for" (Clark & Reis, 1988, p. 628). Although the communicative turn represented by this definition is laudable, limiting the conceptualization of depth to this sort of positive affective intimacy makes it difficult to apply it to a wide range of relationships. I favor a more general approach, in which depth is conceptualized in terms of the subjective importance participants place on the topics they discuss and the behaviors they exchange. This definition would cover intimacy, but would also include depth in the sense of two business associates working on larger projects or taking greater risks together.

Commitment

Commitment is the expectation that a relationship will continue into the future. This expectation may be based on the feeling that one wants the relationship to continue, that it ought to continue, or that it has to continue. Johnson (1991a, 1991b) refers to these as personal commitment, moral commitment, and structural commitment. Johnson's tripartite model parallels two other approaches to commitment: Levinger's (1965, 1991) cohesiveness model and Rusbult's (1980, 1991) investment model. These models differ in how they categorize concepts, in the importance they place on moral factors, and in how explicitly they focus on the dyadic level. All three, however, share the view that commitment is a psychological state rooted in private judgments. They ignore the communicative nature of commitment. Yet what one's partner has said or not said about commitment is obviously important. Although some of the basic options for expressing commitment have been identified (Knapp & Taylor, 1994), we know little about how commitment is expressed or inferred in an ongoing way in different kinds of relationships. Put another way, the level of commitment people actually feel or think that their partners feel is highly contingent upon a whole set of factors having to do with the interactive dance of expression, with explicitness, with timing, and with mutual revelation.

Predictability and Understanding

Participants in a relationship must have some understanding and agreement about what behaviors are desirable, acceptable, what responses each is likely to have, and how each person's actions fit into larger relational sequences. They must become experts on one another (Planalp & Garvin-Doxas, 1994). Of course, uncertainty is never fully eliminated and our desire for novelty may sometimes cause us to increase rather than decrease relational uncertainty (Altman, Vinsel, & Brown, 1981; Baxter, 1993; Baxter & Montgomery, this volume). Nonetheless, the requirements for coordinated interaction will always impose the need to manage uncertainty and create understanding. The management of uncertainty therefore figures prominently in nearly every major theoretic perspective on the relational life cycle. It plays the title role in uncertainty reduction theory (Berger & Calabrese, 1975). It plays less explicit, but no less important, roles in social exchange models, such as social penetration theory and interdependence theory (Altman & Taylor, 1973; Kelley & Thibaut, 1978).

Communicative Code Change

Developing relationships create their own linguistic forms and cultural codes. I believe that three particular changes occur in communication codes as a relationship develops. The first of these is code specialization. Specialized language in the form of personal idioms, for example, both affirms the relational bond and increases the efficiency of communication. Research on personal idioms has consistently shown their use and variety to be related to perceptions of satisfaction and closeness (Bell, Buerkel-Rothfuss, & Gore, 1987; Bell & Healey, 1992; Bruess & Pearson, 1993). Less research has been conducted on the two other ways codes change as relationships develop. One of these is code abbreviation. As a relationship develops the participants may no longer need to elaborate as much (Bernstein, 1964). Their conversation is marked by rapid topic shifts, incomplete expressions, and frequent gaps in content (Hornstein, 1985). The other change is code substitution. Interaction that once required considerable verbal coordination now requires less and may often be managed with non-verbal communication. Non-verbal communication substitutes for verbal communication. Owing to a lack of research, we can only hypothesize what happens to these changes as relationships deteriorate. I believe that sharp reductions in the use of positive personal idioms are one of the harbingers of relational trouble. The ability to rely on less elaborated messages and on non-verbal messages should also be compromised as interactions become less coordinated and partners make contrasting assumptions.

The relational life cycle, then, may be defined in terms of changes along six dimensions: interdependence, breadth, depth, commitment, predictability, and communication code use. Three aspects of this conceptualization warrant further mention. First, while it is generally presumed that increases along these dimensions are associated with increases in affect, there is no assumption that the emotions associated with development must be positive or that deterioration necessarily weakens affect. We could, for example, use these dimensions to describe the development of a bitter rivalry. Second, this conceptualization encompasses the concept of relational maintenance which, after all, usually centers on sustaining a given level of development (Dindia & Canary, 1993). Finally, although the dimensions of change are continuous, change is rarely smooth or linear. There will be considerable, perhaps constant, fluctuation. Indeed, even the perception of stability may be a relational achievement (Duck, 1994). There may be sharp breaks in which major changes in several dimensions occur at the same time. People may experience these abrupt shifts as "turning points" and scholars may use them to mark the boundaries of different relational stages (e.g., Baxter & Bullis, 1986; Knapp & Vangelisti, 1992).

Communication Networks

No relationship exists in a vacuum. John and Cynthia, our couple from the introduction, for example, each have friends, co-workers, kin, and so on. Together these social contacts form a network. Although the idea of looking at sets of relationships as networks has a rich interdisciplinary history, the application of network concepts to the dyadic life cycle is a comparatively recent phenomenon. Understanding how this network becomes involved in the relational life cycle requires us first to specify who is counted as a network member and then to identify specific network dimensions for scrutiny.

Because people typically maintain networks containing several hundred contacts (Killworth, Bernard, & McCarty, 1984), researchers have always sampled members using one of two basic approaches. The first and most common approach is to sample people who are psychologically significant for the subject. Subjects may be asked to list people who are important to them or to whom they feel close (e.g., Johnson & Milardo, 1984; Parks, Stan, & Eggert, 1983). Sometimes researchers define particular social roles, such as friend or parent, as important on *a priori* grounds (e.g., Lewis, 1973). Another variation is to ask subjects to list confidants, sources of personal favors, or other people who serve particular functions (e.g., Fischer, 1982). The second approach is to sample members in terms of some prespecified rate or level of interaction they have with one another. When direct observation is not possible, subjects may be asked to create a record of their interactions with a log or diary or to respond to retrospective questions about their interactions within some specified period of time. In one study, for example, subjects were telephoned seven times during a three-week period and were asked on each occasion to list the people with whom they had interacted voluntarily for five minutes or more during the previous 24 hours (Milardo, 1989). The first approach yields what is referred to as the "psychological network", while the second approach yields an "interactive network" (Milardo, 1988, 1989).

These approaches yield quite different network rosters. When Milardo (1989) compared the psychological and interactive networks of spouses, for example, he found that only 25% of the people listed appeared in both networks. The relative merits of each approach have been the subject of considerable discussion elsewhere (Milardo, 1988, 1989; Surra & Milardo, 1991).

Four more general points, however, have been largely overlooked. First, neither approach yields the total network. Second, these are not mutually exclusive approaches. Fischer and his colleagues (1977, p. 45), for example, combined the two approaches by asking men to name "the three men who are your closest friends and whom you see the most often". Burt (1983) advocated identifying network members through a set of questions that captured both psychological importance and interactive frequency. Third, interactive and psychological networks are not so much different networks as different sectors within the same overall network. People will appear in one and not the other only when there is a large disparity between their stated importance to the focal person and their frequency of communication with the focal person. Finally, the choice of sampling procedure depends upon the research questions being asked. If one is interested in the effects of opposition or support from network members, for example, it may be more useful to look at the reactions of significant others, because their support or opposition may have a greater impact than that of less important network members. On the other hand, if one is interested in structural effects such as access to alternative partners, it may be more useful to look at a broader interactive network, because it better captures the everyday structure of the network.

Our present concern is with those aspects of network structure and content that are most intertwined with the dyadic life cycle. These include: (1) network distance; (2) network overlap; (3) cross-network contact; (4) cross-network density; (5) the partners' attraction to network members; and (6) support for the relationship from network members.

Network Distance

Everyone is linked directly to a set of people who are in turn linked to others, who are linked to still others, and so on. Everyone is thus connected indirectly to everyone else. As we know from the "small world" studies, five to ten links are usually all that are needed to connect any two randomly selected persons (e.g.,

Milgram, 1967). The distance between any two unacquainted persons is determined by the number of links separating them. This characteristic has been variously referred to as "reachability" (e.g., Mitchell, 1969), "network proximity" (Parks & Eggert, 1991), and "distance" (e.g., Surra & Milardo, 1991). Whatever term is used, the network distance between unacquainted persons should be closely related to their likelihood of initiating a relationship.

Network Overlap

Several important network characteristics are related to the more general concept of density—the extent to which network members are connected to each other. The overall density of the relational partners' network, however, will be less important than the density of specific local sectors or structures. If we think from the standpoint of a particular couple, say John and Cynthia, it quickly becomes apparent that we are most interested in the density of those sectors where Cynthia and John's individual networks come into contact with one another. One measure of this is network overlap—the number or proportion of people that are common members of the relational partners' individual networks. It is a measure of the extent to which partners have formed a joint network.

Cross-network Contact

Cross-network contact represents the degree to which each partner knows and communicates with members of the other's network. It is conceptually equivalent to network overlap when only the interactive network is considered. When the psychological network is considered, contact and overlap will differ. John and Cynthia, for instance, may both name Claire as a close friend (overlap) or perhaps only Cynthia will list her and John will be asked to report how often he communicates with her (contact). Sampling networks according to the type or importance of relationships preserves the subtle, but potentially important, distinction between "our friend" and "your friend with whom I have contact".

Cross-network Density

A broader measure of density is what I call a cross-network density—the extent to which members of each partner's network know and communicate with members of the other partner's network. In traditional network analytic terms, this measure would represent a special kind of "clustering" between members of the partners' separate networks (Barnes, 1969). This dimension has not been assessed in research on the relational life cycle, presumably because a rigorous measure of cross-network density would require contacting all network members.

The difficulties of contacting network members are illustrated in a study by Kim and Stiff (1991). First, they found that perhaps as many as 20% of the couples in their sample where lost because one or both members refused to give access to network members. Even with a reduced sample, however, data collection must have been a daunting task because nearly 1000 network members were named by approximately 75 couples. A more practical, but still useful, measure can be obtained by having the focal partners estimate the level of cross-contact between the members of their individual networks. In one prototype, for example, we asked dating partners to create a grid in which one person's contacts were listed along the rows and the other's were listed in the columns. They were then asked to determine jointly if each possible combination of people had ever met and, if they had, how often they communicated with each other.

Attraction to Partner's Network

People in relationships often come to see one another not simply as individuals, but as part of a social package. The course of any one relationship may thus be greatly influenced by each participant's attraction or repulsion for the partner's friends, family, work associates, and so on. Attraction may be based on the positive attributes of network members as individuals or on their value as a social links to other people and resources. Patterns of attraction have long been the subject of sociometric analysis (e.g., Cartwright & Harary, 1956; Davis, 1970), but less attention has been devoted to the role of attraction to network members in the development of dyadic relationships and still less has focused on the actual communication of attraction or repulsion. Yet the way in which partners talk about their feelings toward the members of one another's networks may well have an impact on the development of relationships that goes well beyond the feelings themselves.

Support from Network Members

Although there is a voluminous literature on social support, most of it has dealt with support for individuals rather than for relationships. The two types of support need not be the same. Supporting Cynthia as an individual does not necessarily mean that one is also supporting her relationship with John. Indeed, some network members may believe that the best way to support Cynthia as a person is to oppose her relationship with John. We know remarkably little about how people actually express support for relationships. Presumably networks act as "buffers" from stress and "channels" for resources at the relational level, just as they do at the individual level (Gottlieb, 1983). But relationships may be supported or opposed by network members in many other ways, including the symbolic reinforcement conveyed both explicitly through verbal comments and implicitly through devices such joint invitations (Lewis, 1973; Parks & Eggert, 1991).

Research to date has generally focused on the perceived supportiveness of network members. Concentration on global perceptions, however, may blind us to the more strategic process through which partners and network members negotiate what is known, presented, and expressed about the relationship.

CONNECTING RELATIONSHIPS AND NETWORKS

We are now in a position to explore how the private world of relationships becomes intertwined with the broader, more public world of the participants' social networks.

Relationships and networks are connected from start to finish, so I will look across three general phases of the relational life cycle: initiation, development and maintenance, deterioration, and termination.

Initiation and Before

If we want to understand how a relationship comes into being, we need to examine the conditions just prior to its formation. Some of these conditions exist in the inner qualities of the prospective partners. Others emanate from cultural and group norms. Still others reside in the physical context. The importance of physical proximity, for instance, is well recognized (e.g., Festinger, Schachter, & Back, 1950). Some physical settings are simply more conducive to relationships than others (e.g., Werner, Brown, Altman, & Staples, 1992).

When we think of relationship initiation from a network perspective, however, a new set of factors becomes apparent. As a case in point, consider the following account of how Julie met her future husband, Barry (*Seattle Times,* 1994):

> My husband and I met at my best friend's wedding. I was her maid of honor and he was her photographer. When I first saw him I thought he was the handsomest man I had ever seen. After that night I had to think of a way to see him again, so I took my nephew in for pictures. My future husband asked me out a few weeks later.

This account obviously notes psychological factors, such as Julie's strong physical attraction. Perhaps the physical and cultural context of the wedding itself also helped put romance in the air. But let's back up. Imagine that we could take a movie showing Julie and Barry's network in the months prior to the wedding. They already have an indirect relationship because each has a connection with the bride. Suppose we back up the movie still further and ask how Barry was selected as the photographer in the first place. We do not know, but it is probable that Barry had been recommended by someone who was close to the bride and perhaps knew Julie. As we move backward, then, we find a trail of indirect linkages between Julie and Barry long before they met. If we now move forward again, we would see Barry and Julie coming ever closer as their network distance shrinks. They are carried toward one another on the social plates of their networks by forces quite beyond their intention and control. This line of thinking points to social proximity effects in relationship formation.

Social Proximity Effects

As the number of links separating any two people decreases, their probability of meeting increases (Parks, 1995; Parks & Eggert, 1991). Social proximity is not the same thing as physical proximity. One is likely to encounter only a few of the many potential partners with whom one shares a given geographic space. Two people can be physically proximal, but socially distal (as in the case of neighbors who do not speak to one another). Conversely, people can be widely dispersed in a geographic sense, but relationally linked. Indeed, historical changes in organizational structure and technology have made it possible for many urbanites to create personal networks that are only vaguely tied to a particular geographic locale (Wellman, 1979; Wellman, Carrington, & Hall, 1988).

No-one has yet tested the social proximity hypothesis directly. Doing so would require measuring changes over time in the network structure for a large set of people. Nonetheless, the hypothesis is consistent with the structure of friendship choices in sociograms (e.g., Davis, 1970). A person who is a friend of one person is far more likely than not to be listed as a friend of that person's friends as well. Evidence from our studies of same-sex friendships and premarital romantic relationships is also consistent with the social proximity hypothesis (Parks, 1995; Parks & Eggert, 1991). In a series of large data sets collected in the mid-1980s, we asked respondents to obtain a list of their partner's 12 closest kin and non-kin contacts. Respondents were then asked to indicate how many of these people they had met prior to meeting their friend or romantic partner for the first time. If the social proximity hypothesis is correct, most of our respondents should have reported that they had such prior contacts. And indeed they did. Two-thirds (66.3%) of the nearly 900 respondents reported that they had met at least one member of their partner's network of close social network prior to first meeting their partner.

Although this result is consistent with the social proximity hypothesis, the precise extent of the effect remains unclear. Because it is based only on the partner's current network rather than the network the partner had at the time of the first meeting, our estimate of the social proximity effect may may be biased. If changes in the network between the first meeting and the time of data collection favored retaining people who knew the subject, as we would predict they would, reports of prior contact would be inflated. On the other hand, there are also good reasons to think that the 66% figure is probably an underestimate. Our method only counted the subject's contacts with members of the partner's network and not the partner's prior contacts with the subject's own network. Also, we only examined the closest 12 in a network of direct contacts that likely contains several hundred members (Killworth, Bernard, & McCarty, 1984).

Beyond the need for more direct, comprehensive data on the social proximity hypothesis itself, several related areas call for attention. In our samples there was substantial variation in the number of people with whom the subject had prior contact. While there were no significant sex differences, other individual differences may come into play and influence factors like network size or the willingness to reach out to new people and new situations. We found no age differences, but our samples were limited to high school and college students. Previous researchers have found age-related changes in the number and complexity of friendships across the adult lifespan (e.g., Blieszner & Adams, 1992) but have not examined differences in the sources of new friends or in patterns of initiation. Still, the school years are marked by easy access to a large number of potential friends and lovers within a relatively contained environment. Few environments in later life, save perhaps retirement communities, are likely to offer such easy access. Without such access, people may become even more dependent on common acquaintances and group ties. Finally, social proximity effects may vary according the type of relationship being examined. We found, for example, that prospective romantic partners had almost twice as much prior contact with members of each other's close networks as did prospective friends (Parks & Eggert, 1991).

Third Party Effects

While much of what leads up to the initiation of personal relationships is impersonal and structural, social networks also reflect the active choices and actions of individuals. Network members directly influence the initiation and early development of personal relationships in at least four ways.

Network members sometimes act as passive reference points for the judgments prospective partners make about one another. The process may be entirely visual, as in the case of one of our respondents, who saw her future boyfriend talking with some people with whom she had played volleyball. The fact that she liked them contributed to her positive appraisal of him. The use of network members as reference points also emerges in the talk between between prospective relational partners. Conversation analysts, for instance, suggest that interaction between previously unacquainted individuals is guided by "membership devices" that locate the participants in groups—such as place of residence, job, or academic major (Maynard & Zimmerman, 1984; Sacks, 1972). I would go one step further to suggest that these linguistic locators often include searches for common acquaintances. One is thus judged by whom one knows.

Network members may also an active role in the initiation and early development of others' relationships. Although the activities of "third-party helpers" beg for additional research, the broad outlines of their activities emerged in a study of third-party help in dating relationships by Parks and Barnes (1988). These researchers found that the friends of prospective romantic partners employed three general strategies on their behalf. One of these involved direct initiations, in which the third party introduced prospective partners, arranged for them to meet "by accident", or organized a blind or double date. A second general strategy involved a wide range of behaviors that functioned as attraction manipulations. Examples included telling one prospective partner positive things about the other and downplaying negative features, telling one of the other's interest in him/her, and emphasizing how much the prospective partners had in common or would like each other. In addition, network members did a variety of things that might be called direct assistance. These included relaying information back and forth between the prospective partners, providing one with information about how to contact the other, and coaching one person on what to say (and not say) to the other.

Third-party help is so common that it is almost normative. Nearly two-thirds (64%) of those who had started a romantic relationship in the previous year reported that they had received help from network members (Parks & Barnes, 1988). Moreover, they generally believed that this help had been important in the initiation of their relationship. This belief was supported by the finding that unattached people who did not receive third-party help dated less often during the previous year than those who did. Finally, it is worth noting that third-party helpers were most often acting in collusion with one or both recipients. In 80% of the cases at least one of the recipients was aware of the helpers' activity and in about 64% of the cases at least one of the recipients had asked or "hinted" for help.

Before turning to the development and maintenance of intepersonal relationships, it is worth pausing to appreciate just how different a social contextual view of relationship initiation really is. The vast bulk of previous research on personal relationships has either not addressed the process of initiation or has failed to recognize the crucial role of social context (Parks, 1995). The actual process of initiation can not be triggered merely by providing subjects with written descriptions or pictures of other people (e.g., Byrne, 1971, 1992; Snyder, Berscheid, & Glick, 1985). Neither can it be adequately modeled by procedures in which previously unacquainted individuals are paired by the researcher in the laboratory (e.g., Cappella & Palmer, 1990; Cramer, Weiss, Steigleder, & Balling, 1985; Sunnafrank, 1984; Van Lear, 1987). At best, such procedures create involuntary relationships that are disconnected from the subject's life world and that have no consequences for it (Parks, 1995). It is not surprising that psychological factors and processes are highlighted by such procedures. They may be so socially stripped that only these factors remain. To understand how actual relationships form, we must study the process *in situ*, in a context of existing relationships, commitments, network structures, and opportunities.

Development and Maintenance

More network factors come into play as personal relationships move beyond their early stages. Structural factors, like the degree of network overlap, cross-network contact, and density, become important. Support from and attraction to network members also influence and are influenced by development and maintenance. Indeed, the various life cycle factors and network factors outlined earlier define a complex matrix of possible links between networks and dyads. Not all of these have been examined, of course, and so the discussion below is meant not only to summarize existing research, but also to point to new areas for research.

Structural Factors in Development and Maintenance

Only two structural factors have been examined systematically. One of these is *network overlap*, the degree to which partners interact with the same people or name the same people as significant contacts. As romantic couples move toward marriage, they also develop a shared network (Krain, 1977). Milardo (1982), for example, found that about 30% of the network members of casually dating couples were shared, while almost 77% of the network members of engaged couples were shared. Both cross-sectional and longitudinal analyses revealed positive associations between network overlap and courtship stage, a global measure of relational development. Kim and Stiff (1991) measured relational development with an index composed of items tapping intimacy, predictability (uncertainty reduction), and commitment in heterosexual relationships. As predicted, this index of development correlated positively with the proportion of overlapping members in the partners' combined network. Studies of network overlap in marriage are not generally centered around developmental issues, but do generally show that network overlap and marital satisfaction are positively related (Julien & Markman, 1991).

Additional research is needed to evaluate the generality of the link between development and overlap. We do not know if overlap plays a greater role in some dimensions of development than others. Although we would expect network overlap to operate in similar ways across different types of relationships, the research to date has been limited to premarital romantic relationships.

More research has focused on the connection between relational development and *cross-network contact*. One measure of cross-network contact is the number or proportion of people one has met in the partner's network. This measure is positively related to a number of developmental indicators in romantic relationships, including measures of intimacy or love, closeness, predictability, and commitment (Eggert & Parks, 1987; Parks, Stan, & Eggert, 1983). It is also positively related to commitment in same-sex friendships among high school students, although it does not appear to be related to other developmental indicators, such as intimacy and predictability (Eggert & Parks, 1987). Another measure of cross-network contact is the frequency of communication with the known members of the partner's network. This, too, has been positively associated with a variety of developmental factors in romantic relationships. Increases in feelings of love, closeness, predictability, and commitment go hand in hand with increases in the frequency of communication with the partner's friends and family (Parks, Stan, & Eggert, 1983). Together, these results suggest that cross-network contact is indeed related to relationship development, although it appears to be more strongly related to commitment than to the other dimensions examined to date. It is not yet clear why this should be, or why cross-network contact appears to be more strongly related to development in dating relationships than in same-sex friendships.

Much less attention has been devoted to *cross-network density*, even though it is often implicated in theoretic discussions of development (e.g., Lewis, 1973; Milardo & Lewis, 1985; Parks, 1995; Surra & Milardo, 1991). The only data currently available on cross-network density come from Kim and Stiff's (1991) study of heterosexual relationships. These researchers found that couples who scored higher on a global measure of development also had a greater number of contacts between the members of their individual networks. Kim and Stiff's study is also notable because it is the only study to have gathered data directly from network members themselves.

Content Factors in Development and Maintenance

The information or content that flows through the network structure is, of course, at least as important as the structure itself. This content includes both discourse and perceptions among network members. Sometimes it is as generic as the extent to which members of a pair mention their activities with other network members or share news of other network members. Unfortunately, actual discourse about network members is rarely studied. Instead researchers have focused on perceptions of attraction and support.

To put it simply, attraction rubs off. That is, *attraction to members of the partner's network* and attraction to the partner should be related. Liking the partner's family and friends should lead to greater liking for the partner. By the same token, increases in attraction to the partner should render his/her family and friends more attractive. This connection is consistently supported in the research to date. Studies of hetero-sexual romantic relationships among both high school and college students report a strong positive relationship between how attracted partners are to the members of each other's networks and how intimate, close, and committed they feel toward each other (Eggert & Parks, 1987; Parks, Stan, & Eggert, 1983). Similar findings emerge from studies of same-sex friendship. Here, too, those who are more attracted to one another's network members also report greater intimacy, closeness, and commitment (Eggert & Parks, 1987).

One need not, of course, like all network members equally. In a study of young adult friendships, for example, we found that 82% of the subjects could think of at least one close friend who had a close friend who was disliked by the subject (Parks & Riveland, 1987). Although subjects typically reported having regular contact with the disliked person, most did little to resolve the imbalance. Instead, they avoided the topic when communicating with their friend or used cognitive coping strategies, such as trying to think about the disliked person's positive qualities or trying not to think about the disliked person at all. Much more remains to be learned about the choice of coping strategies, about the consequences of strategy choices, and about the factors that influence the level of imbalance that people are willing to tolerate. Many of the coping strategies reported in our exploratory study allow friends to think that network members like one another more than they actually do. Identifying the factors that influence how accurately people judge liking among network members is an obvious research priority.

The *perceived supportiveness of network members* also exerts a powerful role in the development of personal relationships. In two-earner families, for example, the best predictor of a father's involvement with childcare tasks is the extent to which his friends and other non-kin contacts support his father–child relationship (Cochran et al., 1990). As children form their own relationships, support from network members becomes important for them as well. Although there appears to be a gap in the research on network support in children's relationships, the importance of network support has been solidly established in research on adolescents. Among high school students, for instance, the perceived supportiveness of network members has been linked to the development of both same-sex friendships and opposite-sex dating rela-tionships. Subjects who perceive that the members of both their network and their partner's network support their relationship report higher levels of intimacy and commitment (Eggert & Parks, 1987; Parks & Eggert, 1991). Similar patterns hold for the development of romantic relationships and mate selection among young adults. The importance of parental support has long been recognized, not only in courtship but also in marital adjustment (e.g., Burgess & Cottrell, 1939; Locke, 1951). More recent research has systematically documented the positive link between support from the partners' networks and the development of intimacy and commitment in premarital romantic relationships (Krain, 1977; Leslie, 1983; Leslie, Johnson, & Houston, 1986; Lewis, 1973; Parks et al., 1983). In doing so, it has consistently rejected the notion that opposition from network members can intensify feelings of attachment. While this "Romeo and Juliet effect" (Driscoll et al., 1972) is deeply embedded in romantic mythology, it has little empirical basis.

Several distinct subprocesses are probably reflected in these findings. Some relationships may not be revealed to network members until the participants believe they will be supported (Baxter & Widenmann, 1993; Parks et al., 1983). Once the relationship is public, partners may lobby network members for support by providing reassurance, minimizing the partner's failings, highlighting the partner's good qualities, and strategically arranging social events to place the relationship in the best light. In one study approximately 85% of dating partners reported using such strategies with their parents (Leslie et al., 1986). As I noted in the previous section on initiation, network members also have their own strategies, should they wish to support the relationship. In addition, relational partners may simply withdraw from unsupportive network members. Knowing this, network members may express more support once it appears that the partners are committed to the relationship (Driscoll et al., 1972; Johnson & Milardo, 1984; Leslie et al., 1986).

Several other aspects of the role of network support remain unresolved. We have no data on either how accurately relational partners perceive the level of support from network members or how accurately network members judge the level of development in other members' dyadic relationships. Considerable inaccuracy should be expected, given the many strategic manipulations of information alluded to above. In addition, we know little about how the impact of support or opposition might vary across sources and relationships types. In adolescent romantic relationships, for example, support from the partner's network appears to be more strongly correlated with intimacy and commitment than support from the subject's own network. In adolescent friendships, however, the source of support does not seem to matter as much and, if anything, support from the subject's own network is a stronger correlate of development (Eggert & Parks, 1987; Parks & Eggert, 1991).

Deterioration and Beyond

As the social fabric weaving partners' networks together unravels, so does their personal relationship. The deterioration of personal relationships, like their initiation and development, is accompanied by changes in the structure and content of network relations. These changes flow both ways. Partners may seek to redefine their networks as their relationship deteriorates or changes in network structure and content may disrupt an otherwise viable relationship.

Structural Factors in Deterioration

Rifts in the shared network are particularly common as personal relationships deteriorate. *Network overlap* may fall as the partners shift their interaction from shared to unshared relationships. And once the problems in the dyad become apparent, network members may withdraw, either because of negative judgments or because they fear adverse impacts on their own relationships (Goode, 1956; Spanier & Casto, 1979). Alternatively, relationships may be stressed if social or environmental conditions isolate them or tear away their shared network. Whatever the direction of causal influence, reductions in network overlap should be associated with instability and deterioration. Milardo (1982), for example, found that both the size of the shared network and the amount of communication with it declined over time in deteriorating premarital romances. More generally, divorce rates tend to be higher in cultures where the spouses maintain comparatively separate networks (Ackerman, 1963; Zelditch, 1964).

Deterioration is also associated with reductions in both *cross-network contact* and *cross-network density*. That is, in deteriorating relationships there will be less contact with the members of the partner's network and the members of both partners' separate networks will have less contact with each other. Several different longitudinal studies support these predictions. Premarital romances, for example, are more likely to deteriorate over time when the partners have less contact with each other's friends and family (Parks & Adelman, 1983). Same-sex friendships are more likely to terminate if they are set in loosely knit networks rather than tightly knit networks (Salzinger, 1982). Cross-network density seems to be important in a variety of settings and relationships, as Hammer (1980) found in her study of relationships in a factory, a church group, and a doughnut shop. Relationships in each of these settings were more likely to be terminated when the partner's networks were comparatively unconnected.

Whether pulled or pushed, the parting of networks also marks a return to earlier network patterns. After marital separation, for instance, people typically focus more of their network activity with same-sex friends, drop contacts with the ex-spouse's friends and relatives, and generally develop a less densely interconnected network (Rands, 1988).

In many cases, however, images of relationships ending or networks fully separating are misleading. Most divorced parents who remain in the same geographic area, for example, continue to interact with each other directly (Ahrons & Rodgers, 1987). Their relationship is redefined rather than terminated. Even when former relational partners do not maintain direct contact, their *network distance* may not be very large. Ex-spouses who never speak may continue to be indirectly connected through children, friends, and relatives. Indeed, they may be quite strategic about maintaining such indirect linkages. We interviewed one recently divorced man, for example, who said he stayed in a car pool largely because one of the other riders could tell him what his ex-wife was up to. Systematic research on the use of networks to monitor former partners is essential not only for theoretic reasons, but also because ex-spouses so often react negatively, even violently, to what they learn about one another's activities.

Content Factors in Deterioration.

Just as attraction to the partner's network may bring relational partners closer, repulsion may drive them apart. This may happen gradually or quite suddenly, as in the case of romantic partners reacting negatively when they reveal a previously hidden relationship to disapproving family and friends. Unfortunately there is no systematic research backing the obvious prediction that reductions in *attraction to the partner's network* should be associated with the subsequent deterioration of the relationship. As this research is conducted, it may be important to examine changes in attraction to specific members of the partner's network as well as to the partner's network as a whole. We might also find wide differences in expectations regarding attraction, both at the individual level and across relationships types.

More research has been devoted to the *perceived supportiveness of network members*. Several studies, for example, have shown that dating relationships are more likely to dissolve when the participants believe that their friends and family are unsupportive (Johnson & Milardo, 1984; Lewis, 1973; Parks & Adelman, 1983). This effect also appears in marriage. Compared to those who remain married, those who divorce typically report far higher levels of family opposition before and during the marriage (Thornes & Collard, 1979).

These findings no doubt summarize a much more complex communication process that unfolds as relational partners and network members negotiate and renegotiate their stance on the relationship. Nearly everyone occasionally reveals relational complaints to network members. When people who are satisfied with their relationship discuss their complaints with confidants, they typically co-construct a conversation that supports both the expression of complaints and the maintenance of the relationship (Julien, Begin, & Chartrand, 1995; Oliker, 1989). The conversations of dissatisfied individuals with their confidants, however, do not show this delicate patterning of complaint and maintenance talk. Talk no longer contextualizes the expression of problems within general support for the relationship. Complaints are now treated as signs of deeper problems and the relationship is "spoiled" (McCall, 1982) in the eyes of network members. This in turn may trigger alliances which, while they may be supportive of the complaining partner as an individual, have the ultimate effect of undermining the relationship still further (Goldsmith & Parks, 1990).

THEORIZING ABOUT RELATIONSHIPS AND NETWORKS

The belief that personal relationships are purely private entities is a myth. As the research reviewed here demonstrates, personal relationships derive their life course not only from the character of their participants, but also from the larger social networks in which they are situated. From beginning to end, personal relationships are continuously embedded in the social context created by interactions with other network members and through which individual desires are enacted and cultural values are realized.

No one explanatory principle is sufficient to account for the linkages between personal relationships and their surrounding networks. Moreover, networks are not merely sources of influence, but are also resources that participants actively manipulate. Theory must therefore include processes that shape relationships in response to both structural imperatives and individual choices. Doing this brings us to several microprocesses that function to tie together the fates of relationships and networks. These may be grouped into two broader theoretic categories that I refer to as "uncertainty management" and "network structuring".

Uncertainty Management

Efforts to manage uncertainty are represented in several of the microprocesses that link the relational life cycle to networks. For example, people in close relationships generally expect to meet their partner's other close associates. Meeting the partner's friends, family, or close work associates satisfies a widely-held social expectation and thus contributes to the management of uncertainty. Failing to meet them may raise doubts about the partner's feelings or one's own desirability and thus retard or reverse the development of the relationship (Parks & Adelman, 1983). According to theories of cognitive balance in social relations (e.g., Cartwright & Harary, 1956; Newcomb, 1961), we also generally expect to like the people our partner likes. Attraction to the partner should create a cognitive strain toward liking the members of the partner's network. Similarly, attraction to members of the partner's network should create a cognitive strain toward liking the partner more. Imbalances in feelings for the partner and members of his/her network can create uncertainty, which may lead to either an attenuation of the relationship with the partner or coping strategies that have the effect of denying or concealing the imbalance (Parks, 1995; Parks & Riveland, 1987).

Linkages with network members open vast trade routes of information about the partner and the relationship. Even without explicit discussion, the relationships of network members create reference points against which partners evaluate their own relationship. Married couples, for instance, commonly compare their marriage to the marriages of their friends (Titus, 1980). Discussion with network members provides information about the past behaviors of the partner, ready-made explanations for his/her behavior as well as one's own, and opportunities to compare one's own judgments to those of others. Exchanges with network members yield information that goes beyond what can be learned from the partner directly. Perhaps this is why the frequency of communication with members of the partner's network is a better predictor of uncertainty in romantic couples than is the amount of communication directly with the partner (Parks & Adelman, 1983).

Some of the most important information exchanged with network members deals with whether network members support or oppose the participants' relationship. Almost without exception, research on friendship, premarital romantic relationships, and marriage reveals positive associations between relational development and support received from network members. Indeed, support is so important that it is the subject of considerable strategic activity by partners and network members alike. Participants and network members conspire to conceal, reveal, and distort information that may be challenging to their larger interests. Because their interests often do not coincide, the interactive dance between participants and network members typically unfolds as a series of signals, interpretive offers, and inferred responses.

Network Structuring

We may describe the social location of people relative to one another in terms of their structural positions in a larger network. Several measures of relative structural position are especially important for the life cycle of any given dyad within this larger network. These include distance, overlap, cross-network contact, cross-network density, and cross-network linkage. These factors are important not only because they contribute to the management of uncertainty, but also because they both represent and influence participants' broader relational behavior.

One reason for this is that the opportunity for any two individuals to interact is in large part a function of network structuring. Even before they meet for the first time, prospective partners may be carried toward one another by the physical and social structures they inhabit. The research on third parties demonstrates that people actively manipulate the network to create opportunities to interact with prospective partners. Once their relationship is established, relational participants realign the structure of their networks so that their opportunities to interact are maximized. They may, for instance, be drawn toward a shared network because a shared network gives them chances to be together that they would not otherwise have. If nothing else, the intertwining of network structure should be associated with development and stability because it reduces the number of conflicting demands on the dyadic partners' time and energy. On the other side of the relational life cycle, people may actively manipulate their network structures so as to minimize their time together when they feel their relationship is deteriorating. They develop independent relationships, spend less time with shared network members, and increase network distance by forcing the partner to gain information through intermediaries. These changes, of course, need not be deliberate. They could be unintended consequences of other actions, such as moving from one part of town to another, or they could result from larger social changes over which the individual has no control. Either way, changes in the network structure surrounding a relationship affect it because they alter the participants' opportunities to interact with each other.

Network structure also regulates both the desirability and availability of alternative partners. Although the notion of networks as barriers to dissolution has been around for some time (e.g., Levinger, 1979), there are probably more effects than have been previously recognized. For one thing, being embedded in a shared network or a heavily cross-linked network with a relational partner reinforces the desirability of the present relationship. This network may provide resources or other attractions that would not otherwise be available. Supportive network members are unlikely to introduce the participants to alternative partners. Simply being embedded in a shared, cross-linked network makes it more difficult to both meet and spend time with alternative partners of all kinds. Once a relationship has ended, the structure of the individual's network may make it easier or harder to find new partners. It has been hypothesized, for example, that divorced people's access to alternative partners is enhanced when their networks are predominantly composed of friends and reduced when kin make up the bulk of their networks (Milardo, 1987).

Looking Ahead

Some personal relationships never really get started. Some flower. Others wilt. Still others descend into hells of abuse. Whatever their path, all relationships change over time as the result of changes in individual abilities and wishes, changes in the external conditions impinging upon them, or both. There is no steady state. Understanding how relationships change over time is essential not only on general scientific grounds, but also because the social and individual consequences of disordered relationships are so high. To develop such an understanding, I believe we must ask at least four basic questions: What are the central dimensions of the relational life cycle? What aspects of social networks are most relevant for the relational life cycle? How are social networks linked to the relational life cycle? And, why?

The answers to these questions comprise a social contextual theory of the relational life cycle. Like all scientific theory, it is best viewed as work-in-progress. Indeed, one of the primary functions of theory is to point out how much you do not know. Although they have not been brought together as I have done here, there is considerable agreement about the salient dimensions of the relational life cycle. Theoretic statements typically incorporate all of most of the dimensions of interdependence, breadth, depth, commitment, predictability, and verbal and non-verbal code change (e.g., Altman & Taylor, 1973; Berger & Calabrese, 1975; Kelley et al., 1983). Yet our understanding of these dimensions is limited by our tendency to think of them in purely psychological terms. Thus, we know more about how psychological factors like satisfaction and perceived investment are related to psychological judgments of commitment than we do about how people actually express commitment to one another. We know more about uncertainty as a psychological state than we do about the actual communicative sequences people use to regulate their uncertainty.

Equally large gaps and opportunities exist in our knowledge of social networks. There is little question that both structural and content features are important. The findings to date justify attention to structural factors like overlap and content factors like support. Yet the importance of other factors, like network distance and attraction, is only beginning to be explored. Some, like cross-network density, have almost no research history. Although summary measures of content factors like attraction and support are useful, future theory may best be served by greater attention to the communicative dance through which relational partners and network members reveal, conceal, and distort their judgments. It is here that the real relationship between dyad and network is worked out.

The nascent status of social contextual theory is even more apparent when we bring the dimensions of the relational life cycle together with the salient network dimensions. Relatively few of the specific links between the six life cycle dimensions I have identified here have been investigated. Most investigators have relied on global indices or limited measures of relational stages, instead of specific measures of life cycle dimensions. In addition to studies investigating the links between specific dimensions of the life cycle and networks, future theory development would benefit from research on an expanded range of relationships. Most research to date has focused on romantic relationships and same-sex friendships among young adults. Yet the theoretic mechanisms that tie networks to the relational life cycle are in no way limited to these relationships. They should also emerge in work relationships, intercultural relationships, and relationships among older adults.

Even though much remains to be done, the social contextual perspective has already added already important new dimensions to our understanding of personal relationships. Models that incorporate network factors have been shown to do a better job of predicting relational events than models that are restricted to purely individual and dyadic factors (Parks & Eggert, 1991). While most theories of personal relationships are not triggered until prospective partners meet for the first time, the social contextual perspective offers an account of the forces that bring people into contact with each other. Perhaps most important, the social contextual perspective is unique in that it provides theoretic transport between the macro- and micro-levels of analysis. It is a vehicle for situating our understanding of individuals and relationships within larger structural and cultural processes.

Chapter 5

Face and Facework: Implications for the Study of Personal Relationships

Sandra Metts

Illinois State University, Normal IL, USA

Although there are many features of interactions that contribute to the quality and stability of personal relationships, one of the most pervasive, yet little studied, features is the degree to which partners enhance, preserve, or diminish each other's desired identity, or face. Indeed, even when relational deterioration appears to stem from such common issues as money management or sexual problems, closer analysis often reveals that the struggle occurs within a subtext of face concerns. That is, the conversations of troubled relationships tend to exhibit a prevailing lack of protection for, and validation of, one or both partners' desired identity. In the absence of such confirmation, one or both partners may avoid the aversive state of disconfirmation by withdrawing from problem-solving interactions or may engage in such interactions from a defensive posture. Ultimately, attempts to solve problems are cosmetic and unsatisfying. Conversely, the conversations of healthy relationships are marked by the ability and willingness to protect and validate the assertion of both partners' desired identities. In the presence of such confirmation, problems are resolved at the level of issues, leaving intact the integrity of each partner's desired identity.

The purpose of this chapter is to demonstrate the utility of a face perspective for the study of personal relationships. Because the terms "face" and "facework" have entered the common vernacular and scholarly writing with varying degrees of precision, this chapter begins with a discussion of face and facework based on the original writings of Goffman (1959, 1967). The contribution of this approach to personal relationships is illustrated with several common relationship stressors, with particular emphasis on complaints and conflict. The chapter then moves to a discussion of face and facework as elaborated by Brown and Levinson (1987) in politeness theory. The contributions of this tradition to the study of close relationships is illustrated with two problematic episodes, provision of social support and relationship disengagement. The chapter concludes with a brief discussion of possible avenues for future research.

FACE AND FACEWORK

Goffman's Model

Goffman (1967) employed the term "face" to refer to the situated public identities, or positive social values, that a person claims during an interaction. Ordinarily, face is granted and sustained as a routine and unnoticed consequence of interaction. However, in some instances, face concerns are the substance of the interaction. These occasions are personally relevant because people are emotionally invested in their face. When an interaction goes better than expected and face is enhanced, interactants feel positive emotions (e.g., pride); when an interaction goes worse than expected and face is diminished or lost, interactants feel negative emotions (e.g., embarrassment or shame). According to Goffman, "poise" is the ability to control emotional reactions and continue to interact even when one's face has been questioned by others as inappropriate or undeserved ("be in wrong face") or when one has no sense of the type of identity that should be projected in a situation ("out of face").

Facework refers to a variety of communicative devices available to interactants for preventing face loss (both their own and others), restoring face if lost, and facilitating the maintenance of poise in the advent of disrupted interactions (Goffman, 1967). "Avoidant facework" includes such practices as steering a conversation away from topics that would be embarrassing to self or other, pretending not to hear a belch or burp, or ignoring a rude comment. It also includes "disclaimers", statements used to preface remarks that could reflect negatively on a speaker (e.g., "I could be wrong, but …" or "Some of my best friends are Catholic, but …") (Hewitt & Stokes, 1975). Goffman also comments on more sophisticated strategies, or "tact", whereby people give options to the recipient of a message so that he/she is able to avoid face threats in giving a response. Goffman uses the example of social etiquette, which advises "against asking for New Year's Eve dates too early in the season, lest the girl find it difficult to provide a gentle excuse for refusing" (1967, p. 29). More recent illustrations might be found in the prevailing norm of indirectness in early stages of courtship. For example, scripted routines such as flirting afford both sender and receiver the opportunity to negotiate, with a minimum of face threat to both parties, whether affiliative communication actions will constitute signs of sexual intent or signs of conversational friendliness.

"Corrective facework" functions to restore face and re-engage routine interaction after a person's face has been lost or put in jeopardy. Typically, a ritualized sequence of four moves—challenge, offering, acceptance, and thanks—suffices to restore the social order. The remedial interchange begins when a challenge (sometimes called a "reproach") calls attention to some action that is inappropriate or inconsistent with a proffered identity. It may be verbalized (e.g., "You're late again"), or be non-verbally expressed (e.g., indications of surprise, an awkward silence, looking angry or hurt). An offering is the attempt to repair face damage by expressing regret or providing an explanation. The most deferential and self-deprecating offering is an apology; it not only acknowledges the severity of an offense, but also assumes responsibility for the act, disparages the "bad self" who did the act, offers atonement or restitution, and promises more appropriate behavior in the future (e.g., "I'm so sorry I'm late. I know how important it is to you that we get to the Jones' dinner party on time. I was terribly careless but I promise this won't happen again."). An excuse is a type of offering that provides an account for an offensive action by minimizing responsibility for the act (e.g., "I know I'm late and that getting to the Jones' on time is important, but I got caught in a meeting and it went on much later than I expected."). A justification is also an account, but focuses more on minimizing the severity of the offensive act than the person's responsibility (e.g., "I know I'm late but we still have plenty of time to get to the Jones' if we hurry; no harm done."). Offerings may also consist of the expression of appropriate emotions such as embarrassment, shame, or guilt without an accompanying account. Writings subsequent to Goffman (e.g., Cupach & Metts, 1994; McLaughlin, Cody, & O'Hair, 1983; Scott & Lyman, 1968; Semin & Manstead, 1983; Schonbach, 1980) provide more detailed typologies of offerings including, for example, humor, offers of restitution, expressions of empathy and support, denials, and refusals to provide an account.

Goffman (1967) contends that in most cases both avoidant and corrective facework are done in a cooperative manner. That is, people are reluctant to challenge another person's role performance and are willing to support a person's effort to maintain poise when their face has been threatened. If an offense has been committed, people readily offer an apology or account and expect that it will be accepted graciously. Such cooperation, according to Goffman, is the logical consequence of social and personal interests. As a general social maxim, it is rational for people to support the role performances of others because such support is likely to be reciprocated. If all interactants are willing and able to cooperate in the maintenance of face, interactions go smoothly. If persons are not willing or able to do so, then interaction breaks down and everyone feels awkward and unpoised. Even persons who have not themselves lost face will typically feel embarrassed for the person who has lost face (Cupach & Metts, 1990). In addition, individuals are motivated by more personal concerns, including, for example, the desire to present self as an honorable and compassionate person, out of a sense of moral obligation, and because he/she feels an emotional attachment to the face of the other person.

On occasion, however, facework is not done cooperatively, but aggressively. In such circumstances, a person attempts to protect, enhance, or restore his/her face at the expense of another's face. Success is determined not only by introducing favorable information about oneself and unfavorable information about the other person, but also by being better at the game of verbal dueling and "one-up-manship". Goffman does not elaborate on why supposedly rational people would be inclined to engage in aggressive facework, but several motivations can be inferred from his broader discussion. People might use aggressive facework when the speech event (e.g., bargaining) legitimizes it (see Wilson, 1992), when initial offerings for an offense (e.g., an apology) are rebuked, or when the role performance of another person is somehow counterfeit and must be stopped (see also Gross & Stone, 1964). In addition, Goffman notes that some individuals are simply less responsive to the affective consequences of face loss. He refers to persons who can witness another person's loss of face without emotional response as "heartless", and those who can experience their own face loss without emotional reaction as "shameless".

Perhaps because Goffman's notions of face and facework were conceived initially as a mechanism to explain the ritual order of social interaction, the applicability of his model to personal relationships has not been widely investigated. Its most systematic application to date lies in the research generated by politeness theory (Penman, 1994) and in integrative reviews of research from a face perspective (e.g., Cupach & Metts, 1994). Before moving to that literature, however, it is worth affirming that Goffman's original notions of face and facework have much to tell us about interaction patterns in personal relationships.

Goffman makes an observation about public interactions that is particularly relevant to interactions in personal relationships. He says that ordinarily the maintenance of face is a "condition" of interaction, not its "objective" (Goffman, 1967, p. 12). By this he means that the logical utility of reciprocal face support provides a structuring mechanism for interactions that allow people to meet their goals and accomplish their tasks in ways that are consistent with face. It is only when the mechanism breaks down by accident or by design that face maintenance becomes the explicit objective. This principle holds true in close relationships as well. Face maintenance is not typically the explicit objective of intimate interactions. Problems are negotiated and annoyances are voiced in ways that do not undermine the other's identity as a valued and competent relational partner. However, when this identity is seriously threatened by a person's own inappropriate behavior or by a challenge from his/her partner, then facework must be skillfully employed to repair the damage. Three examples of situations that hold the potential to seriously threaten face will be discussed briefly. These include the management of relational transgressions, the management of conflict, and the management of a couple's "joint identity" in public.

Relational transgressions are violations of cultural or idiosyncratic rules that a couple considers fundamental to the conduct of their relationship (Metts, 1994). When a violation is admitted or discovered, the couple is faced with the difficult task of managing not only the transgressor's loss of face but the collateral damage to the partner's face as well. Because the transgressor acted in a manner that undermined his/her own role performance as a trustworthy, honorable partner, he/she has impaired the partner's ability to act in a loving and trusting manner. Thus, facework is necessary at two levels, one to restore the interaction and a second to restore the legitimacy of role performance as a relational partner. In such cases, we would expect highly elaborated, cooperative, and partner-centered facework. The research on relationship repair episodes prompted by one partner's relational transgression (e.g., infidelity, deception, betrayal) supports this assumption. Regardless of the type of offense, an apology (i.e., admitting culpability, chastising self, and promising better performance in the future) is the type of facework most likely to appease partner and restore relational harmony (Hupka, Jung, & Silverthorn, 1987; Metts, 1994, Metts & Mongeau, 1994; Ohbuchi, Kameda & Agarie, 1989). In addition, when an apology is reinforced by non-verbal impression management tactics (e.g., "I acted guilty and ashamed") the combination is even more predictive of satisfaction with the confrontation episode and the likelihood that relationship stability will be restored (Aune, Metts, & Ebesu, 1991).

While an apology seems to be a necessary condition for successfully managing the initial trauma of a relational transgression, it is not a sufficient condition. The apology expresses the willingness to present self as a remorseful person, but it does not provide an explanation for the cause of the untoward behavior or its meaning to the relationship. Accounts serve this purpose. Excuses (acknowledging the seriousness of the offense but providing extenuating circumstances) are generally preferred over justifications (accepting responsibility but minimizing the seriousness of the event), perhaps because justifications tend to negate a partner's assessment of the act as important (Metts, 1994). However, when the transgression involves a real or potential infidelity, justifications are preferred over excuses and more strongly associated with commitment (Hupka et al. 1987; Metts, 1994). Apparently, when a transgression includes a third party who could threaten the viability of a relationship, assurances that the event did not entail emotional involvement are necessary in order to provide a sincerity condition for the apology (Metts, 1994).

This research suggests that, in general, the remedial interchange can be used successfully to manage potential relationship damage stemming from a partner's inappropriate behavior. However, the success of this process is influenced significantly by variations in the tone, directness, and degree of face threat implied in the initial reproach. As Schonbach and Kleibaumhuter (1990) have demonstrated, when a reproach entails a severe threat to a person's sense of personal control or self-esteem, it not only "strengthens an actor's tendency to refute the opponent's charge or justify his or her behavior during the failure event, but also markedly weakens the actor's readiness to offer some concessions" (p. 241). The research on complaints and conflict in personal relationships provides ample evidence of this pattern, particularly in unhappy couples. For example, complaint sequences of dissatisfied couples, compared to satisfied couples, are more likely to originate with complaints about a partner's personal characteristics rather than, for example, behavior (Alberts, 1988). These reproaches tend to be met with denials of the legitimacy of the complaint (Alberts & Driscoll, 1992), and/or countercomplaints (Alberts, 1988; Gottman, 1979).

It is no surprise that such complaint sequences routinely escalate into conflict that is characterized by aggressive facework. Indeed, the dysfunctional conflict patterns described by Gottman (1994) as the "Four Horsemen of the Apocalypse" might well be read as variations on the theme of aggressive facework. The first horseman, "criticism", is defined as "attacking someone's personality or character—rather than a specific behavior—usually with blame" (p. 73). The second, "contempt", is defined as the "intention to insult and psychologically abuse your partner ... lobbing insults right into the heart of your partner's sense of self" (p. 79). These strategies can be viewed as complaints and/or countercomplaints with increasingly strong attacks on partner's face. The third horseman is labeled "defensiveness" and defined as a response mode characterized by unwillingness "to take responsibility for setting things right" (p. 84) (e.g., denying responsibility, cross-complaining, yes-butting). This pattern reflects a heightened sensitivity to protect one's own face, to the point of refusing to offer even the semblance of an account. Finally, "stonewalling" is characterized by communicative withdrawal, lack of engagement, and passivity. According to Gottman, "it conveys disapproval, icy distance, and smugness" (p. 94). At one level, stonewalling represents an unwillingness to engage in the remedial interchange; apologies are no longer offered or accepted with sincerity, and accounts are perfunctory or not offered. At a deeper level, however, it may also indicate that remediation is not even necessary because partners no longer have an emotional attachment to aspects of face that are linked to the relationship.

Satisfied couples are able to keep these "horsemen" at bay by instituting regulatory rules that engage a more formal, public level of interaction during conflict. Jones and Gallois (1989) identified 45 rules that married couples believed to be important during conflict. Factor analysis using ratings of importance yielded five factors, three of which are remarkably similar to Goffman's notion of facework: consideration (e.g., not saying hurtful things), conflict resolution (e.g., being willing to say you are sorry), and positivity (e.g., being positive and supportive). In a study using the same items, Honeycutt, Woods, and Fontenot (1993) obtained a slightly different factor structure, but an underlying theme of regulating face threat still emerged. The primary factor, labeled "positive understanding", included such face-supportive rules as being able to say you are sorry, giving praise to the other, listening to the other, acknowledging the other, and seeing the other's point of view. Not only was the positive understanding rule cluster the dominant factor (accounting for 44% of the variance), it was also the only factor associated with relationship quality after controlling for multicollinearity among the rule dimensions. These findings seem to indicate that satisfied couples recognize the need to make one's own face vulnerable at the service of partner's face. This is evidenced in the high cost to speaker's face implicit in such rules as being willing to apologize, to listen, and to give praise, even during the emotionally charged exchanges characteristic of conflict. Less satisfied couples may not recognize the collateral damage that accrues to the relationship when protecting one's own face results in the destruction of partner's face. The problem, of course, is that interaction behaviors are strongly contingent; it is fairly easy to grant face to the partner when the partner is also granting face, but increasingly difficult to do so when the partner threatens face. Thus, regulative rules are only effective to the extent that both partners endorse and follow the rules.

In addition to providing insight into the way couples manage face in the private domains of relational transgressions and conflict, Goffman also provides insight into why face support from a partner is particularly salient in public forums. According to Goffman (1959), couples, families, and even co-workers form a "joint identity", or linking of individual identities. This connection implies that members will support each other's role performance because they are a "team" and the loss of face by any member discredits the role performance of the entire team. The greater the importance of the team to the individual, the greater the effort expended to maintain its public performance. When intimate couples constitute the team, the public performance of their relationship is generally characterized by mutual signs of respect, caring, and commitment, although, of course, these signs may be tacit or manifested in good-natured teasing and other rituals. Their joint identity implies an emotional attachment to the face of the partner similar to the emotional attachment felt to one's own face.

As a general rule, couples and families adhere to the norm of public face support: partners create idiomatic devices to communicate criticism while in public (Hopper, Knapp, & Scott, 1981), married couples confirm and support their partner's public recounting of their relationship stories (Dickson, 1995), and family secrets are kept at home (Vangelisti, 1994). Indeed, as with most ordinary interactions, face maintenance is automatic and non-remarkable. However, when violations do occur, they are likely to be relationally consequential. First, the information that intimates have about each other tends to be quite personal and perhaps inconsistent with more public images. Revealing such information can undermine role performance in uniquely devastating ways. Second, couples generally operate under the assumption that mutual face support is motivated by high regard for the public image of their relationship and by emotional investment in each other's face. Repeated and intentional violations of the norms of public face support may be interpreted by the couple (and even by observers in the social network) as lack of regard for the relationship and/or lack of emotional investment in the partner.

In a study of the nature and consequences of public embarrassment of romantic partners, Petronio, Olson, and Dollar (1988) found that public embarrassment was likely to take the form of revealing relational secrets (e.g., sexual behaviors, relational problems, intimate feelings) or acting in ways that discredited the joint identity of the couple (e.g., explicit sexual advances in public, openly flirting with other people, intentional inattentiveness). The frequency of these behaviors was negatively associated with length of relationship, quality of the relationship, and satisfaction with relational communication. Similarly, Argyle and Henderson (1984) found, among the rule violations most likely to lead to the end of a friendship, several that constitute public disregard for the other's face: not keeping confidences, criticizing you in public, not showing you positive regard, and not standing up for you in your absence.

Politeness Theory

Brown and Levinson (1987) were less interested in the corrective function of facework and more interested in the preventive function. In this regard, their conceptualization of facework is similar to Goffman's notion of avoidant facework. However, they extend Goffman's model by arguing that face concerns are motivated by two fundamental human needs, autonomy and validation. These motivate two types of face needs: negative face needs and positive face needs. Negative face needs refer to an individual's desire to be free of imposition and restraint, to have free access to his/her own territory and possessions, and to have control over the use of his/her time, space, and resources. To show regard for another person's negative face is to avoid imposing on their time or resources, to protect their privacy, to avoid intruding, and generally promote their autonomy and independence. Goffman's discussion of tact is implicitly a discussion of how people show regard for the negative face of others.

Positive face, on the other hand, is more akin to Goffman's notion that people value the attributes they claim during an interaction. Brown and Levinson (1987) define positive face needs as the desire to have the attributes or qualities that one values appreciated and approved of by people who are relevant to those attributes or qualities. To have regard for others' positive face is to show approval of their personality, attributes, accomplishments, appearance and so forth, as well as to show that they are considered likeable and worthy to be a friend and companion. Although Brown and Levinson do not distinguish between being valued and being liked, subsequent scholars have explored the possibility that these are distinguishable needs. Lim and Bowers (1991) and Lim (1990, 1994) argue that positive face should be divided into two types of face: (a) "fellowship face", defined as the desire to be included and to be viewed as a worthy companion; and (b) "competence face", defined as the desire to be respected for admirable traits (e.g., knowledgeable, intelligent, experienced, accomplished, and so forth).

Showing regard for the face needs of another person is often more complicated than it appears. First, although some messages threaten only one type of face need (e.g., a request threatens primarily negative face whereas a criticism threatens primarily positive face), other actions tend to threaten *both* negative and positive face (e.g., interruptions, threats, strong expressions of emotion, and requests for personal information). Interruptions, for example, might signal disregard or disagreement with a speaker's comments (threat to positive face), and signal that the speaker should stop talking and become a listener (threat to negative face). Requests for personal information not only constrain a person to answer when he/she may not otherwise have raised an issue (threat to negative face), but may also force revelation of information detrimental to his/her projected image (threat to positive face). This particular dilemma seems to be at the core of the prevailing preference among daters to assess the risk of HIV infection in a potential sexual partner through indirect and inferential strategies, rather than by direct, specific, and face-threatening questions about sexual history and drug use (Cline, Johnson, & Freeman, 1992).

A second, and in some ways more frustrating, complication for persons in close relationships is the fact that attempts to enhance one type of face can threaten the other. Because negative face is satisfied largely through deference and avoiding behaviors, whereas positive face is satisfied largely through connection and approaching behaviors, a tension exists between the two types of face needs (Brown and Levinson, 1987, p.74). Thus, a person who intends to show respect for another's privacy by leaving him/her alone may inadvertently send signs of disregard for his/her positive face. Likewise, a person who intends to show regard for another's positive face through frequent contact, signs of affection, and gifts may impose serious threat to the other person's negative face by making him/her feel obligated. In fact, a characteristic plateau in many developing relationships is reached when partners realize that the rewards for positive face gained from the partner's attention and solicitous behaviors are no longer significantly greater than the loss of autonomy necessitated by relationship obligations. The resolution of this tension determines whether the relationship continues to escalate or moves to termination (Eidelson, 1980).

A third complication identified by Brown and Levinson (1987) is that during the process of attending to the negative and/or positive face of a hearer, speakers can threaten their own negative and/or positive face. Brown and Levinson provide examples, such as giving thanks or accepting offers (which validate the other person's positive face but humble the speaker and incur a debt). Similarly, apologies, confessions, and emotional expressions (1987, p. 68) may address the positive face of an offended person, but potentially threaten the speaker's own positive face. An interesting illustration of this phenomenon is available in the analysis of the simple phrase "I love you" when uttered for the first time in dating relationships. Owen (1988) analyzed the naturally occurring conversations of couples where "I love you" was said for the first time. Often, the initial expression was met with "I love you too" and the positive face of the expresser was confirmed. Sometimes, however, the initial expression was met with "pseudo-reciprocation" in comments such as, "Well, I like you too", resulting in the positive face of the expresser being compromised. On occasion, the initial expression was met with "refutation" in comments such as, "You can't be in love; we've only known each other for three weeks". In these instances, the expresser's positive face is discredited, and perhaps even his/her negative face in the implicit injunction not to feel love, let alone proclaim it out loud.

Fortunately, languages provide members of a culture with mechanisms (verbal and non-verbal) for managing the threats to positive and negative face that are endemic to social interaction (Brown & Levinson, 1987). We routinely need to ask favors, borrow resources, express displeasure with someone's actions or personality, and so forth. Although speakers may sometimes choose not to do the face-threatening act (FTA), they sacrifice the chance to attain their goals in making that decision. Speakers may sometimes choose to do the FTA with no attention at all to face concerns, but in so doing, risk the consequences of having issued an unredressed face threat. More often, people will choose a middle ground between these extremes. They might do the FTA but do it "off record" through hinting and innuendo. This strategy will only work to the degree that the other person successfully infers the intention of the speaker. The most efficient and still face-saving strategy is to go on record with the FTA but employ politeness to minimize its severity. Positive politeness is manifested in such communicative acts as claiming common ground (e.g., similar attitudes, opinions, empathy, etc.), indicating that the listener is admirable, attending to the listener's needs, exaggerating approval, including listener in activities, seeking agreement and avoiding disagreement, joking, and giving gifts. Negative politeness is manifested in such communicative acts as providing a listener with options, hedging while making a request, avoiding the use of coercion, showing deference, apologizing, offering to be in debt in return, and being vague or ambiguous. The five suprastrategies for doing FTAs are presented in Figure 5.1.

According to Brown and Levinson, as the seriousness or "weightiness" of an FTA increases, a speaker will be more likely to use higher numbered strategies. That is, if the threat is not at all consequential, a person might well do it with little or no face redress (e.g., "Can I have a quarter?"), but do more elaborate facework if the threat is greater (e.g., "I hate to bother you, but I don't have time to get to the bank until after class; if you happen to have a little extra cash, could you possibly loan me $5.00 until tomorrow?"). What is important in determining the seriousness of an FTA, however, is not merely the nature of the act itself, but also the context in which the act occurs. For example, the request for $5.00 in the previous example might be made bald on

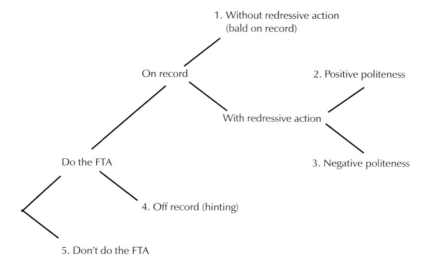

Figure 5.1   Strategies for doing FTAs

record ("Give me $5.00") if a husband were asking his wife for cash in order to tip a server in a restaurant after dinner. Brown and Levinson formalize these contextual features as a set of three sociological variables: (1) the *social distance* between the interactants (i.e., familiarity, closeness, interdependence); (2) the *power* of the hearer relative to the speaker (i.e., authorized or unauthorized ability to assert one's will over the other); and (3) the *ranking* of the face threat (i.e., the cultural and personal estimate of how much threat an act entails). The ranking of threats to negative face depends on the type of goods or services required (e.g., asking to borrow a quarter vs. five dollars), whether a legitimate obligation to comply exists (e.g., terms of employment), and whether possible enjoyment might be associated with performing the act. The ranking of threats to positive face depends on the discrepancy between a person's desired image in a given context (e.g., successful, beautiful, generous, intelligent, good parent, sensual, likeable, etc.) and the image conveyed in the FTA.

   One particular element in Brown and Levinson's model that has generated considerable discussion among scholars attempting to apply it to personal relationships is the position of privilege-afforded negative politeness. According to the model, negative politeness is more face-redressive (numbered higher on the hierarchy) than positive politeness. In fact, the only strategies more face-preserving than negative politeness are hinting or not doing the FTA. Brown and Levinson argue this position from a pancultural view of the importance of autonomy over validation. They claim that, in general, trying to minimize a face threat by telling someone we share common ground with them, or care about them, or admire them, is less redressive than being deferential, offering to incur a reciprocal obligation, and allowing the person maximum freedom in deciding how he/she will respond to the threat. According to Brown and Levinson, in most cultures, it is presumptuous to think our signs of inclusion and validation are as important to another person as his/her autonomy. Thus, threats to negative face are the more egregious offense and negative politeness is the more redressive action.

However, one of the defining characteristics of personal relationships is that partners expect increased interdependence to result in some loss of autonomy. Much as Brown and Levinson argue that "terms of employment" constitute a legitimate obligation that lessens the degree of threat to negative face, it might be argued that "terms of commitment" constitute a legitimate obligation in personal relationships— at least for relatively routine impositions ("Will you make dinner tonight?", "Can you get the kids after work?", etc.). Additionally, because "pleasure in performing an act" lessens the threat in being asked to perform it, we might assume that the negative face threat in many requests made of a partner is mitigated by the pleasure felt in making the partner happy or helping the partner in some way (e.g., "I know you're trying to finish that project, so I'll get dinner tonight."). Roloff (1987) suggests that intimates are not only expected to comply with requests from their partners, but to identify needs and fulfill them without being asked.

While partners may expect increased interdependence to result in some loss of autonomy, they do not expect it to result in loss of positive regard. Rather, they expect interdependence to afford increased opportunity for assurances of liking and inclusion from a valued significant other. Thus, threats to positive face in a personal relationship may be more highly ranked than in a social relationship because it is *not* presumptuous to think our expressions of regard matter, and because we have unique knowledge about traits, competencies, and qualities our partner would like to have valued. In general, then, threats to positive face should be the more egregious offense in personal relationships. In addition, when threats to negative face exceed some level of absolute magnitude, legitimate obligation, or vicarious pleasure, impositions on negative face eventually implicate positive face as well if the partner begins to feel exploited (i.e., under-valued). Thus, although the communication of intimates shows a general tendency to make direct (unredressed) impositions on negative face (Roloff et al., 1988), this does not mean that intimates are less polite to each other than to strangers. Studies that have manipulated levels of intimacy between a speaker and the target of a request find that intimates employ more overall politeness when making a request than do strangers (Baxter, 1984; Roloff & Janiszewski, 1989). Studies that have also manipulated the severity of face threat represented by a request find that intimates use more positive politeness in situations of greater negative face threat than do strangers (Leichty & Applegate, 1991; Lim & Bowers, 1991). Two situations are used here to illustrate the importance of positive politeness in attenuating potential damage to face in personal relationships: social support and relationship termination.

Providing social support to someone in need is both gratifying and problematic (Goldsmith, 1992, 1994). Each supportive interaction has the potential to restore an identity damaged by failure, loss, or rejection. However, it also has the potential to exacerbate a situation and do more harm than good (LaGaipa, 1990). Although a number of scholars have suggested that advice and problem-solving support is best tempered by messages that validate feelings (e.g., Burleson, 1994), the most systematic analysis of social support from a politeness perspective is offered by

Goldsmith (1992, 1994). Goldsmith notes that the support provider may feel constrained by having to give support (negative face), and may feel diminished if his/her efforts seem not to be effective or appreciated (positive face). Likewise, the support seeker may feel his/her positive face diminished by his/her own admissions of need, failure, or distress unless the support provider is able to confirm a more competent image.

As Barnes and Duck (1994) point out, most of these face dilemmas are regulated and diffused through the everyday communication of relationship partners. They argue that routine interactions allow partners to *detect* changes in mood or behavior that might warn them of possible problems before they become crises, to *ventilate* routine frustration and stress before it intensifies, and to *distract* partners, at least temporarily, from the strain of problems and other sources of stress. However, on any given occasion, when a particular event necessitates more focused supportive efforts, politeness, especially positive politeness, appears to be a key element in the success of the episode. In a study of comforting messages in close friendships, Goldsmith (1994) asked respondents to assess the degree of face threat in three types of social support messages given in response to a friend's experience of rejection (unwanted relationship termination) or failure (doing poorly on an exam). Each supportive message was accompanied by either positive politeness or negative politeness. She found, as expected, main effects for the type of supportive message. Advice posed the greatest threat to both positive face and negative face, whereas offers to help posed the least threat to positive face, and expressions of concern posed the least threat to negative face. However, when support messages were accompanied by positive politeness, the threat to face was moderated. In fact, ratings of how helpful a message was perceived to be revealed that advice with positive politeness was significantly more helpful than advice given bald-on-record and even advice given with negative politeness. Offers to help accompanied by positive politeness were also perceived to be more helpful than offers made bald-on-record or with negative politeness. Goldsmith speculates that positive politeness emerged as the more effective facework strategy because it not only mitigates the loss of autonomy and privacy implied by seeking support (i.e., negative face), but also "constructs an image of the friend as likeable and accepted following a breach in face created by the support seeker's disclosure of a failure or rejection" (pp. 41–42). Negative politeness may serve to mitigate the loss of autonomy and privacy, but does not additionally validate the positive face needs of the support seeker.

Although greatly simplified, an analogy can be drawn between Goldsmith's description of how face support operates in comforting situations and how it could, ideally, operate in disengagement episodes. The difference, of course, is that the person who terminates the relationship is the proximal, not distal, cause for the partner's loss of positive and negative face. As a consequence, the person who terminates a relationship, particularly when it is a unilateral decision, incurs an obligation to redress the positive face and negative face of partner, even though the attempt may place his/her own positive face and negative face in jeopardy.

The recognition that disengaging partners manage identities and provide accounts to the social network has been carefully explored (Harvey, Weber, & Orbuch 1990). Much less attention has been given to the fact that partners also manage identities in their interactions with one another during the disengaging episode(s). Implicit in the various typologies of disengagement strategies that have been offered, however, is the tension between asserting one's need to be independent of the partner (asserting own negative face needs) while not making the partner feel diminished (avoiding threat to the partner's positive face needs). For example, Cody and his colleagues (e.g., Cody, 1982; Banks, Altendorf, Greene, & Cody, 1987) have proposed five general categories of disengagement strategies: (1) avoidance ("I didn't say anything to the partner. I avoided contact with him/her as much as possible"); (2) negative identity management ("I told him/her that I was going to date other people and that I thought he/she should date others also"); (3) justification ("I fully explained why I felt dissatisfied with the relationship, that it hasn't been growing and that I believe we will both be happier if we don't date any more"); (4) de-escalation ("I told him/her that I need to be honest and suggested that we break it off for a while and see what happens"); and (5) positive tone ("I told him/her that I was very, very sorry about breaking off the relationship."). Each of these strategies communicates some element of concern for one's own or partner's face. Avoidance, for example, may entail threat to the disengager's negative face if he/she alters typical social habits, avoids certain places or people, and even hesitates to answer the telephone in order to avoid contact with the partner. However, by avoiding a disengagement episode, the disengager also protects his/her negative face (will not have to explain feelings or resist reconciliation attempts by partner) and his/her positive face (avoids possible accusations or recriminations from partner). Negative identity management illustrates a willingness to meet face-to-face, but is still an assertion of the disengager's own negative face needs and the imposition of this decision on the negative face needs of the partner. Justification illustrates the willingness to provide an account and to show concern for both one's own and the partner's positive face (i.e., we are both important enough to deserve happiness). De-escalation shows a more concerted effort to redress one's own positive face (as an honest or caring individual), the partner's positive face (this doesn't necessarily mean rejection), one's own negative face (temporary autonomy), and the partner's negative face (the option of re-engagement is possible). Finally, positive tone strategies are essentially apologies; they do little to redress the negative face needs of either person, but do a great deal to enhance the worthiness of the partner's positive face through the disengager's expression of remorse.

Baxter and her colleagues (e.g., Baxter, 1982; Wilmot, Carbaugh, & Baxter, 1985) created a similar list of strategies. These include: withdrawal; pseudo-de-escalation and mutual pseudo-de-escalation (false declaration of desire to retain some level of relationship); cost escalation (making the cost of staying in a relationship high by rude or hostile actions); fading away (partners share an implicit understanding that the relationship is over); *fait accompli* (simple and direct statement that the relationship is over); state-of-the-relationship talk (decision to leave is couched in the appearance of a discussion of the relationship's problems); attributional conflict (agreeing to break up but arguing over the reasons and placing blame); and negotiated farewell (sense-making session without blame). In a summary of this research program, Baxter (1985) organized these strategies along three dimensions: direct to indirect, unilateral to bilateral, and other-orientation to self-orientation. According to Baxter (1985), direct strategies are explicit statements of one's desire to exit the relationship, whereas indirect strategies attempt to achieve termination without an explicit statement of the goal. Unilateral strategies represent one party's intent to disengage, whereas bilateral strategies represent a fairly equal or mutual desire by both partners to disengage. Other-oriented strategies are those which avoid hurting, embarrassing, or manipulating the other person in the break-up, whereas self-oriented strategies "display primarily expedience for self at the other party's cost" (Baxter, 1985, p. 247). In general, greater face threat for the partner and less face threat for the disengager is associated with direct, unilateral, and self-oriented strategies. Less face threat for the partner and greater face threat for the disengager is associated with indirect, bilateral, and other-oriented strategies.

Although these typologies were not generated from a facework perspective, politeness theory provides a coherent framework for integrating a number of findings (for details, see Metts, 1992; Cupach & Metts, 1994). Politeness theory would predict that as the severity of a threat increases, the degree of politeness should increase. In the context of disengagement, this would mean that as the significance of the termination increased (e.g., breaking up a highly developed and committed relationship compared to a more casual involvement), the degree of elaborated and other-oriented politeness would also increase. To the extent that it does not, disengaged couples would report greater dissatisfaction with the process. This prediction is supported by the literature. In relatively low levels of threat (e.g., relationships of low interdependence and short duration), a minimal level of face redress is expected—minimal to the extent that the disengager is at least willing to provide a "face-to-face accounting" (Baxter, 1987), even if it is not marked by elaborated facework. When avoidance strategies such as withdrawal are used, the break-up is particularly unsatisfying for both the disengager and the partner, even in low-level relationships (e.g., Metts, Cupach, & Bejlovec, 1989; Wilmot et al., 1985). This lack of satisfaction can be traced, at least in part, to the ambiguity of not knowing whether the partner should continue to act as though he/she is still in a relationship (negative face is constrained for both), the unsettling sense of the disengager that he/she was not willing to "face the music" and state the desire to disengage (diminished positive face), and the perception of the partner that he/she was not significant enough to merit an accounting or an apology (diminished positive face). In relatively higher levels of threat (relationships of higher interdependence and longer duration), strategies that directly address both the positive and negative face of the partner should be even more important. De-escalation, pseudo-de-escalation, and mutual pseudo-de-escalation attempt to compensate for the loss of positive face implied in the disengager's decision to scale down the relationship by expressing continued desire to be in a relationship, to be friends, and to be affiliated. Positive tone strategies present the disengager as a person keenly aware of the seriousness of the act and remorseful over the role he/she is playing. Banks et al. (1987) found that disengagers were more likely to use positive tone, de-escalation, or justification when network overlap was high, the relationship was intimate, and post-disengagement friendship was desired. Metts et al. (1989) found that when an initiator used positive tone strategies, the couple was more likely to remain friends after the break-up, underscoring again the important role of positive politeness in the conduct of personal relationships.

FUTURE DIRECTIONS

Additional research is necessary before a full understanding of the role of facework in close relationships is realized. To date, the research tends to be of two kinds. One type is the "reading" of existing research from a facework perspective (e.g., Cupach & Metts, 1994). A second approach is to test the components of a facework theory, such as politeness, through a manipulation of relevant variables (e.g., distance and degree of imposition or severity of reproach) in a scenario or role play experiment. While both of these methods are useful, several additional research programs must be undertaken if we are to develop a comprehensive picture of the role of facework in close relationships.

First, it is essential to study facework processes as they are enacted in the everyday talk of ongoing personal relationships. Granted, close relationships emerge from the larger culture and thereby organize themselves within certain normative constraints. Thus, the basic principles of facework should be evident in couples' communication. However, intimacy, interdependence, and emotional investment reframe the notions of what counts as a face threat, what exacerbates severity, what constitutes legitimate explanations for face violations, and what counts as appropriate types and degrees of facework. The relative importance of positive face compared to negative face, for example, appears to be an important distinction between personal relationships and social relationships. Yet we know little about the mechanisms partners routinely use to avoid threats to positive face, to repair threats to positive face, and to enhance positive face. Idiomatic expressions, terms of endearment, and even unsolicited offers to help may function as positive politeness within the familiar context of personal relationships. It is doubtful that scenario studies will reveal these nuances. Patient analysis of couples interacting is likely to be the more informative approach.

This is not to suggest that linguistic features can or should be counted. Researchers who have attempted to use Brown and Levinson's exemplars as a classification system for coding politeness in discourse (e.g., Craig, Tracy, & Spisak, 1986; Tracy, 1990; Wood & Kroger, 1994), argue that the exemplars are difficult to use because they do not constitute equivalent or mutually exclusive categories. The exemplars include, for example, large units of speech and other actions (e.g., show interest in the speaker), sentences (e.g. an apology), and individual words (e.g. in-group markers such as "we" or hesitations such as "well ..."). In addition, some tactics are face-relevant because of their content, and others are face-relevant because of their form (e.g., indirectness). However, Brown and Levinson (1987) claim that politeness theory was never intended to be a mechanism for quantitative research and does not lend itself easily to that endeavor. They view facework as a kind of "speech act" that is performed in both the content and structure of messages, through a variety of techniques, with its ultimate effect residing in the interpretation of the interactants in a given context. Thus, messages that contain politeness features may be used to perform actions other than face redress, and messages that seem to contain no explicit politeness marker are nonetheless understood as polite by the people who share intimate knowledge of each other and their interaction practices. Therefore, the researcher interested in the role of politeness in personal relationships will need to enlist the help of the persons in those relationships, in order to isolate interaction patterns that represent both speakers' intentions to protect or repair face and listeners' interpretations of these patterns as polite in particular contexts.

A related area for future research is to find patterns of face threat and face support within personal relationships that distinguish satisfied couples from dissatisfied couples. The extant literature reviewed previously indicates a strong association between face issues and relational satisfaction. It is time to identify more precisely what those issues are. Several possibilities present themselves. Perhaps threats to negative face are non-problematic so long as they are "equitable" between partners. However, when one partner endures significantly more imposition relative to his/her partner, politeness, even in great measure, may no longer suffice. For positive face, however, more complicated patterns might be associated with satisfaction: e.g., (1) frequency of positive face threat; (2) the domain of positive face threat; (3) the proportion of positive face support relative to positive face threat; and/or (4) both partners' willingness to threaten their own positive face through concessions and apologies when appropriate. Of course, the challenge of this pursuit is to untangle the reciprocal influence of face-relevant actions on satisfaction from the influence of satisfaction on face-relevant actions (Fincham, 1992).

Finally, research would also profit from a more complete understanding of individual differences in face needs and facework competence. To date, efforts to create a measure of individual predispositions toward negative and positive face needs have met with only limited success (e.g., Cupach & Metts, 1993; Metts, Backaus, & Kazoleas, 1995). However, it seems self-evident that some people need a great deal of autonomy, whereas others need much less. Some people seem to have "thin skins" when it comes to criticism and others seem less sensitive to threats to positive face. The process of developing and maintaining a relationship is no doubt partly constituted in the communicative practices that reveal these individual differences and help partners to accommodate to them. To the degree that partners are willing and able to meet each other's particular face needs, even when they do not have similar face needs, we should expect that individual differences are not a problem. However, to the extent that differences in face needs cannot be accommodated, for example, when one spouse has a high need for positive face but the other is not willing or able to offer the desired level of positive face support, then individual differences may become important. This same argument is inherent in the theory of interpersonal needs proposed by Schutz (1958). Indeed, the similarity between the needs of inclusion and affection and positive face, and the similarity between the need for control and negative face suggest that the two lines of research could be mutually informative.

CONCLUSION

This chapter has attempted to illustrate the utility of facework for the study of personal relationships. For the most part, at least in satisfied couples, it recedes into the background of ordinary conversation. Care is taken, more or less consciously, to support the public identity of the relationship and the privately negotiated identities of the partners. Face threats are avoided through redressive actions and face damage is repaired through corrective sequences. However, when face issues become salient, even mundane relationship processes can become infused with escalating aggressive facework. Penman (1994) makes the observation that "the concepts of negotiating individual identity and relationship definition are remarkably similar to those of positive and negative face, respectively" (pp. 16–17). Although Brown and Levinson (1987) might not be entirely satisfied with this comparison, it does point out the inherently relational quality of facework. Although studying facework in personal relationships is admittedly a difficult undertaking, its contribution to the goal of understanding relationship processes make it an effort worth expending.

Chapter 6

Interpersonal Relationships and Mental Health Problems

Chris Segrin

University of Arizona

Every year, hundreds of thousands of people suffer from mental health problems. Mental health disorders such as depression, anxiety, and schizophrenia collectively afflict more individuals than certain health problems that have captured far more public attention, such as cancer and AIDS. For example, a prospective epidemiological investigation found that 9% of the male population and 25% of the female population had been treated for depression *by age 30* (Angst, 1992). It is likely that most people will experience a mental health problem or have a relationship with someone who does.

This chapter will show that many mental health problems are as much psycho*social* relationship and communication problems as they are psychological, and some can actually be precipitated by disrupted and distressed interpersonal relationships. In other cases, mental health problems have a direct corrosive effect on close relationships, or else mental health problems and distressed interpersonal relationships appear to be in a vicious cycle.

History of Interpersonal Approaches to Mental Health Problems

The connection between mental health problems and interpersonal relationships was hypothesized decades before an empirical verification of this association. Freud spoke of the causes and consequences of mental illness by referring to "the misfor-

---

Communication and Personal Relationships
Edited by Kathryn Dindia and Steve Duck. © 2000 John Wiley & Sons Ltd.

tunes of life from which arise deprivation of love, poverty, family quarrels, ill-judged choice of a partner in marriage, (and) unfavorable social circumstances" (Freud, 1917/1966 pp. 432). He stressed the importance of early interpersonal relationships, particularly with parents, in determining later mental health or illness, whereas neo-Freudians extended the thesis to other interpersonal relationships as causes of mental problems (e.g., Fromm-Reichmann, 1960). However, it was Sullivan (1953) who most strongly emphasized the role of interpersonal and social forces in the development of self and disruption of mental health, notably via his attention to same-sex adolescent peer relationships in the developmental process.

Later, Leary's (1957) *Interpersonal Diagnosis of Personality*, with an obvious lineage traceable to Sullivan, described the "interpersonal circle" as a method of defining a range of interpersonal behavior that included abnormal or disturbed extremes. Leary's interpersonal circumplex, defined by the dimensions of dominance–submissiveness and love–hate, has been revised and refined several times since its original appearance (e.g., Wiggins, 1982) as a tool for understanding interpersonal relations and mental health problems.

These early approaches have now developed into the "social-interactional viewpoint" (Carson, 1983) and the "interpersonal school" (Klerman, 1986), which Carson (1983) encapsulated in the view that "the underlying problems usually turn out to be interpersonal in nature—frequently having the form, 'I can't (do something interpersonal)'" (p. 147). Modern-day instantiations of this perspective stress the import of concurrent, as opposed to early childhood, interpersonal relationships and mental health problems and a wider variety of interpersonal relationships. Specific theories, models, and hypotheses derived from this perspective will be described in this chapter. Each shares the postulate that distressed and dysfunctional interpersonal relations are inextricably entwined with a range of psychological distress.

A review of depression, social anxiety, schizophrenia, eating disorders, personality disorders, and somatoform disorders will show that each of these distinct disorders has a common correlate: disturbed and dysfunctional relationships with other people. Although space limitations preclude an analysis of additional mental health problems, it should be noted that other disorders not reviewed here, such as alcoholism, substance dependence, loneliness, and psychogenic sexual dysfunction, are also marked by profound problems with interpersonal relationships, similar to those of the problems to be reviewed here. Notwithstanding the cognitive, neurochemical, life stress, genetic, and behavioral elements of these disorders, problematic interpersonal relationships also play a role in the development and/or course of these mental health problems. As such, they can be characterized rightfully as "psychosocial" disorders.

DEPRESSION

Major depressive disorder is a pervasive illness with a mortality rate of 15%, largely due to suicide (DSM-IV; American Psychiatric Association, 1994). Depressive episodes are marked by severely depressed mood, diminished interest in activities, significant weight loss or gain, sleep disturbance, psychomotor agitation or retardation, fatigue, feelings of worthlessness and guilt, difficulty concentrating, and recurrent thoughts of death or suicidal ideation (American Psychiatric Association, 1994).

Depression and Social Skills

Lewinsohn's (1974, 1975) behavioral theory of depression stressed that depressed people often exhibit *disrupted social skills*, making it difficult to obtain positive reinforcement from, or avoid negative outcomes in, relationships. This combination is thought to precipitate episodes of depression. Research is generally supportive of the notion that depressed people have social skills problems that can create relational difficulties (see Segrin, 1990, in press) and poor social skills have a strong association with interpersonal rejection (Segrin, 1992). Therefore, depressed people with poor social skills would be expected to experience difficulty in establishing and maintaining rewarding interpersonal relationships.

Depression and Interpersonal Rejection

An important interpersonal problem for people afflicted with depression is *rejection* by others. Much of the research on this phenomenon is guided by Coyne's interactional model of depression (Coyne, 1976a,b). According to this model, depressed people induce a negative mood in their interactional partners through a process of emotional contagion. This hypothesis is predicated on the assumption that it is an irritating, negative experience to interact with depressed people. As a consequence of this negative mood induction, others are expected to move from initially offering nongenuine reassurance and support to outright rejection and avoidance of the depressed individual. Depressed people appear to be quite aware of this rejection (Segrin, 1993), and such negative interpersonal feedback exaggerates their negative mood states (Segrin & Dillard, 1991).

A meta-analysis of the literature on interpersonal responses to depression indicates that the phenomenon of interpersonal rejection of depressed persons is very reliable and moderate in magnitude across studies (Segrin & Dillard, 1992). However, the extent to which depressed people create a negative affective state in others through social interaction is weaker and more sporadic. Interested readers may wish to consult Joiner and Coyne (1999) and Segrin and Dillard (1992) for fuller reviews of this literature.

Personal Relationships of Depressed Persons

The personal relationships of depressed people are characterized by dissatisfaction (Burns, Sayers, & Moras, 1994), diminished influence and intimacy (Nezlek, Imbrie, & Shean, 1994), and diminished activity and involvement (Gotlib & Lee, 1989). Some evidence indicates that the *quality* of social interaction with others is more strongly associated with depression than is the sheer *quantity* (e.g., Rotenberg & Hamel, 1988). As might be expected, the availability of a confidant with whom one can self-disclose and engage in rewarding conversation is negatively associated with depression. It is the case, however, that many depressed people lack a close relationship altogether, a lack that appears to create a heightened vulnerability to experiencing depression (Brown & Harris, 1978).

Research on the personal relationships of depressives leads to questions about the worth of their relational partners. For example, in Fiske and Peterson's (1991) investigation, depressed participants complained of dissatisfaction and anger with their romantic partners, as well as increased quarreling relative to non-depressed participants. These same respondents reported being hurt or upset by their romantic partners more frequently than did non-depressed controls, despite (or perhaps as a cause of) their greater desire for more love in the relationship. Depressed people also perceive their intimate partners as more hostile than do non-depressed persons (Thompson, Whiffen, & Blain, 1995). One group of depressed women reported that they received less social support from their confidants than did a non-depressed control group (Belsher & Costello, 1991). The confidants of these depressed women exhibited more depressogenic speech (e.g., "I can't do anything right anymore," "I'm never going to find a job") than confidants of either non-depressed or psychiatric controls. These friends may actually contribute to the depressed person's aversive psychological experience, and generally dysfunctional, hostile, and unsupportive relationships that are wanting in intimacy may precipitate depression and other undesirable affective states (Coyne et al., 1987).

Depression and Family Interaction

Depression is also associated with problems in marital interactions and family relationships (for reviews, see Beach, Sandeen, & O'Leary, 1990; Coyne, Kahn, & Gotlib, 1987). Research has shown that depression and marital distress go hand-in-hand (Beach et al., 1990). Estimates indicate that 50% of all women in distressed marriages are depressed (Beach, Jouriles, & O'Leary, 1985), and 50% of all depressed women are in distressed marriages (Rounsaville, Weissman, Prusoff, & Herceg-Baron, 1979).

The communication between depressed people and their spouses is often negative in tone and tends to generate more negative affect in each spouse than that of non-depressed couples (Gotlib & Whiffen, 1989; Ruscher & Gotlib, 1988). Biglan and his coworkers argued that depressed persons and their spouses find themselves in dysfunctional vicious cycles of interaction (e.g., Biglan et al., 1985). Depressed persons are "rewarded" by their spouses for emitting depressive behaviors in that the depressive behaviors tend to inhibit the hostile and irritable behaviors of the spouse. McCabe and Gotlib (1993) showed that over the course of a 10–15 minute marital interaction, the verbal behavior of depressed wives becomes increasingly negative, and that couples with a depressed spouse viewed their marital interactions as more hostile and less friendly than did non-depressed couples. Other studies find depression to be associated with poor communication during problem-solving interactions (Basco et al., 1992), verbal aggressiveness (Segrin & Fitzpatrick, 1992), and problems in establishing intimacy (Basco et al., 1992).

People with depression also experience problems as parents (e.g., Hammen et al., 1987). The parenting behavior of depressives is characterized by negativity, hostility, complaining, and poor interpersonal problem solving. Perhaps as a consequence, children of depressed parents are at elevated risk for behavioral, cognitive, and emotional dysfunction than are those of non-depressed parents (for reviews, see Downey & Coyne, 1990; Morrison, 1983).

SOCIAL ANXIETY

Definition and Symptoms

The term *social anxiety* refers to "anxiety resulting from the prospect or presence of personal evaluation in real or imagined social situations" (Schlenker & Leary, 1982, p. 642). Anxiety is experienced as an aversive cognitive and affective state that is accompanied by heightened autonomic arousal that can be extremely debilitating. In more extreme instances, this phenomenon may develop into clinical social phobia, a severe and debilitating disorder. People with social phobia have an intense and crippling fear of social or performance situations in which there will be exposure to unfamiliar others or scrutiny by others (American Psychiatric Association, 1994). To cope with this fear, many people will avoid any social situations in which this novelty or scrutiny may be present, sometimes culminating in a reclusive lifestyle. Less severe and/or more circumscribed forms of social anxiety include communication apprehension, public speaking anxiety, and shyness (Jones, Briggs, & Smith, 1986; Leary, 1983).

The Self-presentational Model of Social Anxiety

Leary built an approach around the concept of self-presentational concerns (Leary & Kowalski, 1995; Schlenker & Leary, 1982), arguing that social anxiety arises when people are motivated to make a desired impression on others but feel that they may not be successful in doing so. Social anxiety occurs when a person has some *motivation* to leave a desired impression on others, and their *subjective probability* for success in doing so is low.

Leary argues that some of the components of social anxiety may be functional when one considers the evolutionary basis for the need to belong. The emotional distress when people feel that they have made undesirable impressions on others can deter them from making such undesirable impressions in the first place, interrupt what they are doing to make the undesired impression, and/or motivate behaviors to repair the damage caused by their behavior (Leary & Kowalski, 1995). All of these are functional for social animals that depend on others for their livelihood and survival. Unfortunately, for some people this emotional distress becomes crippling and has the effect of drastically reducing their social contacts and/or producing exactly the kind of disastrous social behavior that they are worried they will create.

Social Anxiety and Social Behavior

People with social anxiety often exhibit a tendency toward emitting social behaviors that are associated with suboptimal interpersonal outcomes. For example, the social behavior of socially anxious people tends to be inhibited and withdrawn, especially when they anticipate evaluation from others (DePaulo, Epstein, & LeMay, 1990). When talking to others they make less eye contact than non-anxious people (Daly, 1978) and use gestures and pauses in such a way that may interfere with smooth turn-taking (Cappella, 1985), possibly as a result of greater cognitive load when in social situations. Indeed, socially anxious people tend to make more "safe" utterances, such as questions, acknowledgements, and confirmation, and avoid more "risky" utterances, such as those that express objective information (Leary, Knight, & Johnson, 1987).

Socially anxious people are sometimes rated as possessing or demonstrating lesser social skills than people who are socially secure (e.g., Beidel, Turner, & Dancu, 1985; Johnson & Glass, 1989). While socially anxious people also tend to evaluate their own social skills as poor, they tend to misperceive and underestimate their social skills (Segrin & Kinney, 1995), perhaps fueling expectations of rejection among people with social anxiety. This feeling is one of the more robust patterns of social cognition associated with social anxiety (Leary, Kowalski, & Campbell, 1988), and is consistent with the self-presentational model of social anxiety, particularly the doubt that one will be able to achieve a desired impression (Leary & Atherton, 1986). With that in mind, it should still be noted that poor social skills appear to contribute to development or worsening of social anxiety over time (Segrin, 1996).

Young adults with social anxiety report fewer interactions with members of the opposite sex, and greater dissatisfaction with their performance in those interactions than their non-anxious counterparts (Dodge, Heimberg, Nyman, & O'Brian, 1987). Similarly, adolescents who experience social anxiety have less frequent contact and intimacy with friends, compared to their less anxious peers (Vernberg, Abwender, Ewell, & Beery, 1992). Some evidence indicates that socially anxious high school students receive less desirable ratings as potential dates by conversational partners (Johnson & Glass, 1989).

SCHIZOPHRENIA

Definition and Symptoms

Schizophrenia is a formal thought disorder (actually a family of disorders) characterized by symptoms such as delusions, hallucinations, disorganized speech, grossly disorganized or catatonic behavior, inability to initiate and persist in goal-directed activity, affective flattening, and impoverished thinking evident in speech and language behavior (American Psychiatric Association, 1994). An additional diagnostic criterion is social/occupational dysfunction. Consequently, it is virtually true by definition that people afflicted with schizophrenia experience problems in their interpersonal relationships. Schizophrenia was one of the first psychological disorders to be associated with intensive theorizing, and research on its connection with interpersonal relationships and family interaction perspectives on schizophrenia remains prominent in the literature today.

Recent Family Approaches to Schizophrenia

Recent investigations of family relationships and schizophrenia center more on explaining the course than the cause of the disorder. Two family variables that have been, and continue to be, particularly influential in this area are *expressed emotion* and *communication deviance* (Wynne, 1981).

Early investigations of family expressed emotion (EE; Vaughn & Leff, 1976) identified a pattern of criticism, overinvolvement, overprotectiveness, excessive attention, and emotional reactivity that appeared to create a vulnerability to relapse and poor social adjustment among schizophrenic patients (for review, see Hooley, 1985). Patients who returned to a home with high EE relatives exhibited a 9-month relapse rate of 51%, whereas only 13% of those who returned to a low EE family relapsed (Vaughn & Leff, 1976).

Recently, Rosenfarb and his colleagues examined the functioning of a sample of young and recently discharged schizophrenia patients who returned to either high or low EE families (Rosenfarb, Goldstein, Mintz, & Nuechterlein, 1995). Patients from high EE families exhibited more odd and disruptive behavior during a family interaction approximately 6 weeks after hospital discharge than did patients from low EE households. Relatives in the high EE households were more critical of the patients when they verbalized unusual thoughts than low EE family members. Studies such as these clearly paint a picture of a vicious circle in high EE family relations: these parents respond to the patient with a lot of criticism because patients from these households appear to exhibit more bizarre and disruptive behavior than patients from low EE homes. It is likely that the negative reactions they receive from their families contribute further to the potential for relapse among the patients. Research on family EE continues to flourish (for review, see Hooley & Hiller, 1997). In addition to being a useful and reliable predictor of relapse, EE may also be understood as a familial risk indicator for schizophrenia (Miklowitz, 1994) as well as a family response to dealing with a schizophrenic member.

A considerable body of evidence indicates that families with a schizophrenic member will communicate in odd, idiosyncratic, illogical, and fragmented language, even when that member is not present. Topics of conversation will often drift or abruptly change direction with a lack of closure. This characteristic style of family communication has been labeled "communication deviance" (CD; Singer, Wynne, & Toohey, 1978). It is particularly intriguing that this distorted form of communication is highly reminiscent of the communication style that typifies the actual schizophrenic individual. Research by Goldstein and his colleagues indicates that parental CD precedes onset (Goldstein, 1987) and is therefore an excellent predictor of schizophrenia among premorbid adolescents (for reviews, see Goldstein & Strachan, 1987; Hooley & Hiller, 1997).

Miklowitz and his associates (e.g., Miklowitz et al., 1986; Miklowitz, Goldstein, & Neuchterlein, 1995) discovered that aspects of communication deviance, such as idea fragments (e.g., "But the thing is as I said, there's got ... you can't drive in the alley"), contradictions and retractions (e.g., "No, that's right, she does") and ambiguous references (e.g., "Kid stuff that's one thing but something else is different too") distinguish parents of schizophrenia patients from parents of healthy control subjects (for additional examples and CD constructs, see Miklowitz et al., 1991). As if to make a potentially disruptive family situation worse for the schizophrenia patient, it appears that families that are high in EE are also high in CD (Miklowitz et al., 1986). Consequently, patients may be dealt a double dose of problematic interactional exchanges with their family members. It is little wonder that patients discharged to parents high in EE, who are also likely to express unclear, odd, and fragmented ideas, are at such a high risk for relapse. In a longitudinal investigation, adolescents whose parents exhibited high CD and interpersonal aspects of EE, such as criticism, guilt induction, and intrusiveness, were more likely to develop schizophrenia-spectrum disorders compared to young adults from low CD & EE families (Doane et al., 1981).

The work on family expressed emotion and communication deviance is best summarized as follows: family EE is a good predictor of relapse among schizophrenia patients in remission; family CD is a good discriminator between families of schizophrenic persons and families of healthy controls (Miklowitz, 1994). While neither EE nor CD are specific to families with a schizophrenic member, each represents a potent risk factor for the course, and possibly onset, of the disorder.

Personal Relationships and Schizophrenia

Finally, it should be noted that problematic interpersonal relationships extend beyond the realm of family relations for the schizophrenia patient. Schizophrenia patients typically have smaller social networks, and report that they have fewer close friends than healthy controls or even other psychiatric patients (Erickson et al., 1989). Importantly, Erickson et al. observed a negative correlation between number of family members in the schizophrenia patients' social networks and their prognosis, whereas a greater number of friends and acquaintances was associated with better outcomes.

EATING DISORDERS

Definition and Symptoms

The American Psychiatric Association recognizes two distinct subtypes of eating disorders: anorexia nervosa and bulimia nervosa (American Psychiatric Association, 1994). The defining features of anorexia nervosa include a refusal to maintain a normal body weight, an intense fear of gaining weight, and a disturbance in body image perception. Bulimia nervosa is defined by recurrent episodes of uncontrolled binge eating, inappropriate compensatory behaviors to control weight gain (e.g., self-induced vomiting, misuse of laxatives or diuretics), and an undue influence of body shape and weight on self-evaluations. A chief difference between the two disorders is that individuals with bulimia nervosa are able to maintain their body weight at or above normally prescribed levels. Similar to depression and alcoholism, this is a disorder with a lethal component. The long-term mortality for those afflicted with eating disorders is estimated to be over 10% (American Psychiatric Association, 1994). Descriptions of these disorders in the *Diagnostic and Statistical Manual of Mental Disorders* (DSM-IV; American Psychiatric Association, 1994) contain references to interpersonal problems. Associated features of anorexia nervosa include "social withdrawal" and "diminished interest in sex". Episodes of binge eating associated with bulimia nervosa are often triggered by "interpersonal stressors". Family relationships in particular have been a focal point of this line of work in the last 25 years (for reviews, see Vandereycken, Kog, & Vanderlinden, 1989; Waller & Calam, 1994; Wonderlich, 1992).

Dysfunctional Family Relationships and Processes

Interest in the interpersonal relationships of people with eating disorders has focused largely, but not exclusively, on family relationships. These authors observed dysfunctional patterns of interaction among families with an anorexia nervosa patient. Their interactions, which often minimize conflict and adaptability, were argued to be entwined with the symptoms of the disorder.

Family relationships continue to receive a great deal of attention from those who seek to explain the origins and course of eating disorders (e.g., Wonderlich, 1992). Examples of this can be found in the investigations on family cohesion and adaptability. Systems-oriented researchers have emphasized family adaptability and cohesion as two dimensions of family relationships that are crucial to healthy family functioning, provided that neither is too extreme (Olson, 1993). A series of recent studies indicate that eating disorders are associated with perceptions of *low family cohesion* (Waller, Slade, & Calam, 1990). Although this finding has been relatively stable across child and parent reports of family cohesiveness (e.g., Waller et al. 1990), eating-disordered children give lower ratings to their family's cohesiveness than do their parents (Dare, le Grange, Eisler, & Rutherford, 1994). The fact that the parent and child with an eating disorder differ in their view of the family's cohesiveness is itself diagnostically significant.

Investigations of *family adaptability* have yielded less consistent results than those of cohesion. Some evidence indicates a negative association between family adaptability and symptoms of eating disorders (e.g., Dare et al., 1994; Waller et al., 1990). However, a study by Humphrey (1986) found more chaos, less organization, and more poorly defined boundaries in the family, all suggestive of greater adaptability, among patients with eating disorders. However, in most studies, the families appeared to be extreme in their adaptability (either too much or too little), indicating potentially detrimental family relations.

As in schizophrenia, *family expressed emotion* is beginning to emerge as an important family process variable in the eating disorders literature (e.g., van Furth et al., 1996). The van Furth et al. investigation indicated that aspects of maternal expressed emotion during family interactions with patients with eating disorders explained 28–34% of the variance in the patients' eventual outcome and response to therapy. The extent to which mothers made openly critical comments during the family interaction assessment was a stronger predictor of patients' outcomes than a host of other impressive predictors, such as premorbid body weight, duration of illness, body mass index, and age at onset.

Other family process variables that have been implicated in the eating disorders include disturbed affective expression (Garfinkel et al., 1983), parental overprotectivness (Calam, Waller, Slade, & Newton, 1990; Rhodes & Kroger, 1992) and excessive parental control (Wonderlich, Ukestad, & Perzacki, 1994). This latter variable has particular significance in that the symptoms of eating disorders may be an overt manifestation of a struggle for control.

Mother–Daughter Relationships

The ratio of females to males suffering from anorexia is approximately 10: 1 (Lucas, Beard, O'Fallon, & Kurland, 1988). Perhaps owing to the widely held importance of the relationship with the same-sex parent in a child's development, there has been a great deal of attention granted to mother–daughter relationships among anorexics. Girls with eating disorders tend to describe their mothers as overprotective (e.g., Rhodes & Kroger, 1992) and less caring (Palmer, Oppenheimer, & Marshall, 1988). In light of such findings, it is not surprising to discover that mothers of daughters with eating disorders have expressed a desire for greater family cohesion than they currently perceive (Pike & Rodin, 1991). A group of young women with eating disorders retrospectively reported maternal relations that involved more emotional coldness, indifference, and rejection, compared to a sample of controls (Rhodes & Kroger, 1992).

Investigations of mothers' attitudes towards their daughters' body image present an even more dim view of this relationship. Mothers of eating-disordered girls in one study thought that their daughters ought to lose significantly more weight than mothers of a group of non-eating-disordered girls (Pike & Rodin, 1991). Sadly, these same mothers rated their daughters as significantly less attractive than the daughters rated themselves! This is particularly amazing given that people with eating disorders typically have low self-esteem and a negative body image (Attie & Brooks-Gunn, 1989), and hence are unlikely to inflate ratings of their own attractiveness. Data provided by mothers in an interview study indicate that mothers of bulimics were more controlling and held higher expectations for their daughters than control mothers (Sights & Richards, 1984). The effects of being in a relationship with a mother prone to such negative and excessive evaluation could be extremely caustic for an adolescent girl.

Disturbances in Non-familial Relationships

The personal relationships of eating-disordered patients also appear to be problematic (e.g., Herzog, Pepose, Norman, & Rigotti, 1985). O'Mahony and Hollwey

(1995) recently conducted an intriguing study in which they compared interpersonal problems of anorexia nervosa patients to those of women who had an occupation or hobby that stressed physical conditioning and appearance (e.g., dance, athletics, professional models), as well women from the general public. The anorectic group in this study scored significantly higher on a measure of loneliness than either of the comparison groups. In addition, the correlation between loneliness and eating problems was higher in the anorexia group than either the weight-concerned group or the general public. A study of bulimic women indicates that such individuals perceive less social support from friends as well as family members (Grissett & Norvell, 1992). These women felt less socially competent than a group of controls in a variety of social situations, particularly those that involved seeking out social encounters and forming close relationships with others. Taken as a whole, currently available evidence paints a disturbed view of the personal relationships of people with eating disorders, indicating that their interpersonal problems extend beyond family relationships.

PERSONALITY DISORDERS

Definition and Symptoms

A personality disorder is an enduring and stable pattern of behavior and cognition that deviates from normative standards and expectations in one's culture (American Psychiatric Association, 1994). This pattern of behavior and experience is inflexible, pervasive, has its onset during adolescence or early adulthood, and leads to tangible distress and impairment. Most people who exhibit personality disorders by definition have interpersonal problems, such as affectivity, poor interpersonal functioning, and impulse control. The enduring pattern must be pervasive and inflexible across of variety of social situations, and it must lead to distress or impairment in social or occupational areas of functioning (American Psychiatric Association, 1994). The concept of "functional inflexibility" implies that the individual relates to others, expresses feelings, and resolves conflicts in a rigid fashion with tactics that are often ill-suited for the situation at hand (Millon, 1990).

Interpersonal Problems Associated with Various Personality Disorders

Currently, there are 11 different personality disorders recognized in DSM-IV. As a thorough review of the interpersonal implications of all personality disorders is beyond the scope of this chapter, several exemplary disorders will be examined (for a more comprehensive review, see Millon, 1981, 1990).

People with a *narcissistic* personality have an exaggerated sense of self-importance and entitlement, coupled with a nearly insatiable thirst for attention and acclaim from others. The negative effects of this behavior on others, as well as the wrongfulness of exploiting others for personal gain, are obscured by the arrogance of the narcissistic individual. Millon (1981) argued from a social learning perspective that the disorder has its origins in excessive and unconditional parental valuation and attention. Years of living in such an environment result in an unjustified sense of self-worth that must constantly be reinforced and polished in the face of any potential failure.

Those with a narcissistic personality disorder rarely develop satisfying, close personal relationships, often because of hostility and devaluation of others, known as the "narcissist's dilemma"—holding others in contempt while simultaneously relying on them for positive regard and affirmation (Rhodewalt & Morf, 1995). The other part of their interpersonal troubles lies in the rejection from others that is prompted by the narcissist's behavior (Carroll, Corning, Morgan, & Stevens, 1991).

Borderline personality disorder is one of the most commonly diagnosed personality disorders. Its most prominent feature is intense and variable mood, ranging from irritability to euphoria to impulsive anger and even self-destructive behavior. This moodiness is combined with more generally aberrant and aloof behavior, excessive daydreaming, and a dissociated self-image. It should be obvious that such individuals often have a long history of interpersonal problems, both professionally and socially, and close relationships that may best be characterized as stormy (Trull, Useda, Conforti, & Doan, 1997). Sadly, people with borderline personality disorder rarely learn from their interpersonal experiences and often recreate problems as they move from one relationship to another.

Poor maternal and paternal caring, to the point of neglect, are common themes among those with borderline personality disorder (Nordahl & Stiles, 1997), coupled with a greater overprotectiveness. Borderline patients also reveal that their mothers were autonomous and hostile toward them (Benjamin & Wonderlich, 1994). This perceived hostility also spills over to perceptions of current relationships with, for example, other patients and hospital staff. A similar theme is evident in the findings of Stern, Herron, Primavera, and Kakuma (1997), whose borderline patients also rated their fathers and mothers as attacking and rejecting. However, these patients also indicated that they too were attacking and rejecting toward their parents. This illustrates how the antecedents to the conflictual adult personal relationship clearly have their origins in adolescent, if not pre-adolescent relationships. These findings suggest that those with borderline personality disorder internalize abandoning, neglectful, and abusive childhood relationships in such a way as to promote self-abandonment and attack in adulthood (Benjamin, 1993).

Finally, people with borderline personality disorder elicit interpersonal rejection from others (Carroll et al., 1998). Given the preponderance of interpersonal conflict and emotional lability, the lack of acceptance from others is easily understood.

Perhaps the chief feature of *dependent* personality disorder is a strong sense of interpersonal submission. Such individuals are ill-equipped to handle mature and independent roles in life, while displaying a naive and gullible cognitive style (Millon, 1990). Because of their weak and fragile self-image they entrust others with the responsibility for addressing major tasks and fulfilling their needs. This excessive reliance on others appears to pay few, if any, dividends when it comes to establishing satisfactory personal relationships. People with dependent personalities report low frequencies of positive social behaviors, reduced directness of communication with others, less positive interactions with close friends, and less helpfulness from friends than those with less dependent personalities (Overholser, 1996). Despite their suggestible and compliant tendencies, people with dependent personalities report high degrees of loneliness (Overholser, 1996), which questions the value of the interpersonal connections that they may establish. It has been suggested that parental overprotectiveness, combined with authoritarianism, may serve to simultaneously reinforce dependent behaviors in the child while also preventing the child from developing a sense of independence and autonomy (Bornstein, 1992).

SOMATOFORM DISORDERS

Definition and Symptoms

Somatoform disorders entail the expression of some symptom or symptoms that suggest a medical problem, but are not fully explicable by a medical condition (American Psychiatric Association, 1994). These symptoms, such as severe back pain or chronic digestive problems, tend to cause significant distress or impairment for the individual expressing them. The experience of these physical symptoms is very real for the afflicted individual, and they are not intentional. Two of the more common types of somatoform disorders are pain disorder, the experience of pain that is severe enough to warrant clinical attention, while also interfering with social and occupational functioning, in the absence of any obvious medical cause, and hypochondriasis, preoccupation with fears of having a serious disease based on misinterpretation of one or more bodily signs or symptoms (for a description of these and other somatoform disorders, see Ford, 1995).

Potential Causes and Functions

Why would an individual experience and express "medical" symptoms in the absence of any precipitating medical or biological cause? Many have argued that there is a social function and perhaps even a social cause underlying this phenomenon. In a comprehensive review of the relationship between social psychological factors and somatic symptoms, Davidson and Pennebaker (1996) argued that "perceptions and reports of physical health may function as non-verbal indices of social health" (p. 114). Ford (1986) offered a list of possible etiologic explanations for somatization. Many, if not most, of these explanations entail some significant issue(s) in the area of personal relationships, such as primary or secondary gains, a solution to a systems problem in a family, or a means of communicating when other more direct forms of expression are blocked. Ford argues that many people with somatization disorders turn to health care professionals for social support that is otherwise lacking in their lives.

The concept of secondary gain has figured prominently in the somatization literature. When one is "sick", one is freed from normal and typical obligations and is generally absolved from any responsibility for being in the sick condition (Barsky & Klerman, 1983; Ford, 1986). The expression of physical symptoms also brings attention, sympathy, and support from others, not to mention more instrumental types of assistance, such as disability payments. For the individual who is unable or unwilling to solicit or secure social support from others through more standard means of social interaction, assuming the sick role may be a covert means of very effectively achieving this interpersonal goal.

Empirical Evidence of Social Dysfunction

Numerous studies suggest that people with somatoform disorders and otherwise inexplicable somatic symptoms concurrently suffer from some form of social dysfunction. For example, recent work in this area shows that people with hypochon-driasis often exhibit symptoms of social phobia and fear of criticism from others (Schwenzner, 1996), as well as elevated loneliness (Brink & Neimeyer, 1993). Patients with somatic symptoms that are not attributable to organic causes often report greater interpersonal and social problems than those with organically caused pain (e.g., Adler et al., 1997).

Studies of specific types of somatic symptoms present an equally compelling case for distressed interpersonal relationships at their core. Faucett and Levine (1991) compared a sample of people with myofascial disorders (muscular aching and tenderness in localized sites in the absence of organic pathology) to those with medically documented arthritis. Arthritis patients indicated that they had more available family and network support than those with myofascial disorders, who also appeared to experience significantly more conflict with members of their social networks. It should noted that the extent to which patients' close relationships were supportive rather than conflictual was significantly, and negatively, correlated with their reports of pain. A similar pattern of findings is evident in a study of elderly people (Hays et al., 1998), in which rated satisfaction with social interaction protected against the experience of somatic symptoms that are commonly associated with depression (e.g., trouble falling asleep, diminished appetite).

Given the preponderance of family relationship issues in the mental health liter-ature, it is understandable that family relationships that are conflictual or abusive have been linked to somatization. Patients at a university hospital who perceived high levels of family criticism made more office visits and reported poorer physical health than those who did not report as much criticism in their families (Fiscella, Franks, & Shields, 1997). On the other hand, reports of parental caring are negatively associated with the expression of somatic symptoms (Russek, Schwartz, Bell, & Baldwin, 1998). Patients with psychogenic pain problems indicated that their parents were physically or verbally abusive, that they tried to deflect the aggression of one parent away from the other and onto themselves, and that they had more concurrent problems with interpersonal relationships than patients with organically identifiable pain or disease (Adler et al., 1997). The findings on deflection of aggression nicely illustrate the family system problem hypothesis: as a child the patient was unable or unwilling to confront the aggressive parent, or intervene, so he/she exhibited somatic symptoms that at least temporarily preoccupied the conflictual parents, and calmed the family household.

Studies of patients with myofascial disorders have identified family relationships that are conflictual (Faucett & Levine, 1991) and overly involved and focused on success and achievement (Malow & Olson, 1984) as factors that discriminated such patients from those in other medical control groups. Findings such as these illustrate some of the ingredients in the secondary gain hypothesis. When the family places an excessive emphasis on success and achievement, the somatic symptoms relieve the patient from living up to these strict standards, with minimal loss of face. Even in marital contexts, one can see the functional value of somatization. The documentation of greater sexual problems and impairment in social roles among married pain disorder patients led Hughes to conclude that "the chronic illness or pain becomes a 'scapegoat' towards which the couple can direct their energies rather than to the underlying marital dysfunction, so affording the marriage a degree of stability" (Hughes, Medley, Turner, & Bond, 1987, p. 169).

CONCLUSION

An examination of the scientific literature on interpersonal processes and mental health problems shows that "mental illness" and "interpersonal illness" are often inseparable. There are clearly cases of mental illness whose origins lie in problematic interpersonal relationships. At the same time, it is clear that many, and perhaps most, forms of mental illness have serious negative interpersonal ramifications. People with mental health problems, regardless of the specific type of problem, will often find that their personal relationships are not what they were during their premorbid state. This deterioration of interpersonal well-being undoubtedly complicates the course of the mental illness, and thus the afflicted individual often winds up in a vicious cycle of interpersonal and psychological problems that perpetuate each other.

In stark contrast to the diverse range of mental problems and associated symptoms covered in this analysis (e.g., schizophrenia, depression, somatoform disorders) are the significant consistency and similarity of interpersonal problems that appear to cut across many mental health problems. I have argued elsewhere that at least some of these problems, such as poor social skills, create a *vulnerability* to the development of psychosocial problems such as those addressed in this chapter (Segrin, 1999; Segrin & Flora, in press). Why it is that the same vulnerability, such as parental neglect, may lead to one type of mental illness in one individual, a different illness in another, and no illness at all in yet another is not yet well-understood. The current search for moderating and mediating variables in this context holds great promise for answers to such questions.

Turning to some of the interpersonal problems that are common to multiple mental disorders, issues in the family of origin must be given serious consideration. It is widely understood and accepted that *parental neglect and abuse* are precursors to numerous mental health problems that include depression, personality disorders, eating disorders, and somatoform disorders, to name but a few. One might speculate that children, even those at a very young age, understand and desire the caregiving role and behavior of their parents. When that provider of care and support turns on the child through either neglect or more overt abuse, a corrupted interpersonal architecture is produced that in many cases will never support the construction of functional and satisfying personal relationships in the future.

It is a lesser known fact that *excessive parental attention and care-giving* may have equally devastating consequences for later personal relationships. When parents fail to maintain the delicate balance between a secure, nurturant environment, and a healthy dose of reality and responsibility, the child may develop a self-image that simply cannot be sustained by future relational partners. Once again, the blueprints for disaster, ultimately manifested in problems like personality disorder, may well be drawn before the child even leaves the home.

It would be premature to leave the topic of family issues without recognizing the widespread presence of an absolutely noxious combination of parenting behaviors: *parental overprotectiveness coupled with lack of parental warmth*. When parents are overly intrusive in the lives of their children, but at the same time emotionally distant, there is a high potential for serious psychosocial consequences that include eating disorders and schizophrenia, among others not reviewed in this chapter. The ubiquity of this parenting pattern in the mental health literature is as remarkable as the range of problems with which it appears to be associated.

The ill-effects of *conflict* on personal relationships are well established. The experience of excessive and hostile conflict can have equally severe intrapersonal consequences. Themes of destructive conflict are evident in the findings on eating disorders, personality disorders, schizophrenia, and somatoform disorders. In a very fundamental way, most people appear to seek and desire some form of harmony with at least a few other people with whom they share their lives. When this harmony is corroded by conflict, mental health problems often emerge. At the same time, the experience of a mental health problem, such as alcoholism or personality disorder, can also disrupt the harmony inherent in close personal relationships. This itself has the potential to propagate intense interpersonal conflict.

The importance of effective communication skills is underscored by the pervasiveness of *social skills deficits* in the interpersonal mental health literature. Some very well developed interpersonal theories of mental health stress the role of poor social skills in contributing to the development and course of problems such as depression, social anxiety, and schizophrenia. At the same time, effective social skills may play a prophylactic role by reducing the likelihood of mental health problems when faced with other stressors in life. Poor social skills are another interpersonal problem that may be a consequent or correlate of some forms of mental illness.

Interpersonal rejection is a social phenomenon that pursues most mental health problems. Although depression is one of the problems that has focused most attention on interpersonal rejection, per Coyne's interactional theory, this phenomenon is evident among people with many different psychological disorders. Human beings can be remarkably intolerant of those who present a less than "normal", competent, or personable image. The social interaction goals of most people leave little room for significant communication with others who have obvious symptoms of mental illness. Consequently, the mentally ill are often shunned and rejected by others—even those with whom they have shared a close personal relationship. Again, the potential for a vicious cycle between psychological and interpersonal problems is clearly evident.

Finally, one of the most fundamental and basic interpersonal problems associated with mental illness is a *lack of personal relationships*. The social networks of people with schizophrenia, depression, and social anxiety are notoriously impoverished. Here again, there is reason to suspect that this interpersonal problem is both a cause and a consequent of mental illness. By their social nature, most humans have a very basic need to seek out and form relationships with others. Mental health appears to deteriorate in parallel with the disappearance of opportunities for experiencing the pleasures of personal relationships.

Historically, scientific inquiry into mental health problems has emanated from a variety of perspectives. Psychodynamic approaches stress unconscious drives and early relationships with parents. Biological approaches emphasize the role of genes, and neuroendocrine and neurotransmitter malfunction. Cognitive theories illustrate how dysfunctional schemas and attributional styles can precipitate different types of mental illness, whereas behavioral theories explain how patterns of reinforcement and punishment can affect mental health. Although not as immediately recognizable and coherently organized, interpersonal approaches to mental illness highlight the role of interpersonal communication processes and close relationships as they may cause or be caused by mental health problems. The interpersonal approaches provide another useful and powerful tool for understanding mental illness. Their position alongside other orientations is as well-deserved as it is well-established by hundreds of research studies that indicate that problematic interpersonal relationships and mental health problems are inextricably entwined.

Chapter 7

Cross-sex Friendship Research as Ideological Practice

Kathy J. Werking

> ... in describing a given system, the scientist makes many choices. He chooses his words, and he decides which parts of the system he will describe first; he even decides into what parts he will divide the system to describe it. These decisions will affect the description as a whole in the sense that they will affect the map upon which the typological relationships between the elementary messages of description are represented (Bateson, 1991, p. 62; gendered language in original).

Scholars make choices as they reconcile various quandaries posed throughout the research process. These choices, as described by Bateson, profoundly influence the resulting descriptions of the chosen phenomena. However, by and large, the discussion in scholarly circles regarding our research decisions centers on issues of epistemology rather than ideology. Specifically, we enter lively and useful debates about theory, methodologies, and data analysis. Yet, our research decisions are permeated with ideological assumptions. In other words, these decisions are not neutral; rather, they reflect assumptions about what constitutes knowledge and what form of knowing will be privileged at particular historical moments.

Lannamann (1991) acknowledges the link between epistemology and ideology when he contends:

> To develop or maintain an epistemological stance is a social act like any other. It is subject to the same constraints, limitations, and contradictions as other social actions. An epistemology, then, is never neutral in terms of power or privilege. The choice of whose punctuation of power will become the influential myth in a dyad or society is

Communication and Personal Relationships
Edited by Kathryn Dindia and Steve Duck. © 2000 John Wiley & Sons Ltd.

never arbitrary. The choice follows from particular historical developments and social contingencies. Thus, to reduce power to an epistemological stance is to define away the importance of ideology in the study of interpersonal communication (p. 186).

As scholars interested in increasing our understanding of relationships, we must move beyond discussions about research findings and appropriate methodologies and begin a self-conscious examination of the latent ideological content of our work. The risk of neglecting the ideological underpinnings of research in the field of personal relationships is that scholars may perpetuate and reify particular ways of knowing, elevating them to the status of natural fact rather than acknowledging them as culturally constructed patterns of thought (Lannamann, 1991).

A critical examination of the existing cross-sex friendship literature is necessary and timely, because the study of friendship between women and men is attracting research interest and scholars of cross-sex friendships are debating epistemological issues. I have donned the role of "devil's advocate" in the spirit of invoking conversation of an ideological nature among such scholars. It is through this form of conversation and reflection that we gain new understandings regarding how we conduct research and what we do with the products of our research.

My overarching goal in this chapter is to address the ideological assumptions underlying research conducted in the area of cross-sex friendship, my chosen area of research. First, I argue that the selection of research topics reflects an ideological stance. I do this by tracing the history of cross-sex friendship research. Next, I contend that existing studies privilege an individualistic, heterosexist view of cross-sex friendship. In supporting this rather thick contention, I address each adjective in the above statement individually and provide illustrations of each adjective's presence in the existing cross-sex friendship literature. Throughout my discussion, I propose alternative ways of knowing that might be employed in the study of cross-sex friendship, sketching possible research projects for the future.

My observations and recommendations in this chapter are directed toward the cross-sex friendship literature specifically; however, I believe my comments will be useful to a larger audience of relational researchers, for many of the issues I raise in this chapter are found in other areas of research on personal relationships as well. For example, Rawlins (1992) critiques the social scientific literature on friendship in general for its lack of dyadic analysis and neglect of larger cultural contexts. Similarly, Duck (1993) argues that relationship researchers need to expand their focus to sustained consideration of the social context in which relationships are developed, sustained, and dissolved. Finally, several contributors to a special section on the study of personal relationships, published in the *Journal of Social and Personal Relationships* (1995), advanced suggestions similar to those included in this chapter, such as an increased emphasis on talk, context, and diversity in the types of relationships studied.

A HISTORY OF CROSS-SEX FRIENDSHIP RESEARCH

The story of research into cross-sex friendship is brief because this form of man–woman relationship has been largely ignored by scholars. The first empirical study was conducted by Booth and Hess (1974). This study emphasized the structural opportunities and normative constraints affecting the formation of cross-sex friendships of middle-aged and elderly persons.

The next study to include cross-sex friendship in its analysis was published six years later (Block, 1980). Several empirical studies on cross-sex friendship were published during the early 1980s. These inquiries focused on the affective qualities of cross-sex friendship, examining the relationship along a variety of dimensions, such as intimacy (Rose, 1985; Sapadin, 1988), stability (Davis & Todd, 1985), satisfaction (Argyle & Furnham, 1983), and self-disclosure (Hacker, 1981).

In general, one goal of these studies was the comparison of the above qualities with those found in same-sex friendship. A second goal was the comparison of men and women's perceptions of their cross-sex and same-sex friendships. The studies published during the 1980s are closely modeled by research conducted in the 1990s because, in general, researchers continue to focus on affective qualities, comparing these qualities across friendship type, and assessing women and men's perceptions of these qualities in their cross-sex and same-sex friendships (e.g., Monsour, 1992). The following review of the cross-sex friendship literature reflects these research foci.

Structural Opportunities for the Development of Cross-sex Friendship

Booth & Hess (1974) investigated the opportunities for cross-sex friendship development using a sample of middle-aged and elderly persons. First, their findings suggest that education and social class influence the experience of cross-sex friendship. Specifically, white-collar workers were more likely to have cross-sex friends than were blue-collar workers. In addition, married persons in their sample reported less frequent interaction with cross-sex friends than with their same-sex friends and a reduction in the amount of affect in their cross-sex friendships. Age was also a factor in the development of cross-sex friendship for, with increasing age, persons experienced a decline in the number of cross-sex friendships. In this study, sex appeared to interact with age because older females reported fewer cross-sex friendships than did their male counterparts. Sex appears to be a prime determinant of the number of cross-sex friends, because Booth & Hess found the number of cross-sex friendships reported by men in their sample was significantly higher than the number reported by the participating women.

The influence of age, sex, and marital status has also been documented in more recent studies. There appears to be a curvilinear relationship between age and the occurrence of cross-sex friendship. Cross-sex friendship in childhood and pre-adolescence is rare (Gottman, 1986; Maccoby, 1988). The number of cross-sex friendships rises during adolescence, but does not match the number of reported same-sex friendships (Kon & Losenkov, 1978). It appears that late adolescence and early adulthood are prime developmental periods for cross-sex friendship occurrence. For example, Rose (1985) found that all of her undergraduate participants experienced cross-sex friendship. Werking (1994a) reported that the number of reported friendships was highest during the high school and college years.

The number of cross-sex friends, however, decreases after early adulthood. Utilizing samples of persons in their mid-20s to mid-40s, Werking (1992; 1995) reported a decline in cross-sex friendship opportunities as persons married and raised families. The studies of Chown (1981) and Adams (1985) revealed that older participants report lower numbers of cross-sex friends and that age affects the number of cross-sex friends for women more than for men. The interaction of age and gender is also supported in other studies (Bell, 1981; Block, 1980; Rubin, 1985; Rose, 1985) which consistently found that men report a higher occurrence of cross-sex friends than do women.

The influence of marital status on the development of cross-sex friendship has also been evident in several studies. Specifically, Rose (1985) reported that 47% of the married women and 33% of the married men in her sample said they had no cross-sex friendships. This contrasts with the numbers reported by the single participants. All of the single undergraduates and male graduate students and 73% of the single female graduate students said they were involved in at least one cross-sex friendship. Likewise, Block (1980) reported that only 6% of his married participants named a cross-sex friend in his survey, and 78% of the men and 84% of the women in Rubin's (1985) sample of married or cohabitating persons said that they did not have a cross-sex friend. Finally, Werking (1994a) found that persons not involved in a cross-sex friendship cited marriage as a significant obstacle to the development of such a friendship.

In sum, the influence of age, sex, and marital status on the formation of cross-sex friendship is consistently documented in the existing literature. First, older adults are less likely to have a cross-sex friend than are young adults. Second, men are more likely to experience cross-sex friendship than are women. Lastly, unmarried persons are more apt to develop cross-sex friendships than married persons.

The Affective Qualities of Cross-sex Friendship

The findings of studies investigating the affective dimensions of cross-sex friendships have centered on comparing same-sex and cross-sex friendship along these dimensions and comparing women and men's perceptions of the levels of affect achieved in their cross-sex friendships. I will first review the studies comparing cross-sex and same-sex friendship.

Researchers have measured a variety of affective qualities by surveying participants about their cross-sex and same-sex friendships. The measured qualities include goodness and enjoyableness (Bukowski et al., 1987), intimacy (Aukett et al., 1988; Davis & Todd, 1985; Monsour, 1992; Rose, 1985; Sapadin, 1988), stability and supportiveness (Davis & Todd, 1985), loyalty (Rose, 1985), satisfaction (Argyle & Furnham, 1983), and self-disclosure (Hacker, 1981). Taken together, the above studies reveal several significant differences between the participants' perceptions of their same-sex and cross-sex friendships. For example, cross-sex friendships were less intimate and stable (Davis & Todd, 1985), less supportive (Rose, 1985), and less satisfying (Argyle & Furnham, 1983) than same-sex friendships. Hacker (1981) found that levels of self-disclosure were reduced in cross-sex friendship. Rose (1985) stated that cross-sex friends experienced less common interests, affection, acceptance, and communication while developing and sustaining their friendship than did same-sex friends.

Despite the many differences between the two friendship types, similarities are also found in existing studies. Specifically, Davis & Todd (1985) found no differences between cross-sex and same-sex friendship in the reported levels of trust, respect, acceptance, spontaneity, and enjoyment. Similarly, cross-sex and same-sex friends were nearly identical in the meanings they assigned to intimacy in their friendships (Monsour, 1992). Finally, Werking (1992) obtained similar descriptions of persons' ideal same-sex and cross-sex friendships.

Researchers have also been interested in assessing the mediating influence of biological sex on the reported affective character of cross-sex and same-sex friendships. Similar to the above comparative studies, significant differences between men and women's perceptions were discovered by several researchers. Men and women, however, also shared similar perceptions in a number of studies.

Overall, women tend to assign less intimacy to their cross-sex friendships than do men (Rose, 1985; Rubin, 1985). For example, Rubin (1985) reported that approximately two-thirds of the women named by a man as a close friend did not agree with the man that they had a friendship. Women are also more apt to discuss their personal problems with their female friends than with their male friends (Aukett et al., 1988). In comparison, men typically state that their friendships with their woman friends exhibit more caring and acceptance (Sapadin, 1988), security (Furman, 1986), and emotional support (Aukett et al., 1988) than their friendships with men.

Despite these differences, women and men also share many similarities in their descriptions of their friendships with one another. For both sexes, cross-sex friendship provides new understandings and perspectives of the other sex (Sapadin, 1988; Werking, 1992). Existing studies also found correspondence between men and women's reported amounts of intimacy and enjoyment (Monsour, 1992; Sapadin, 1988; Werking, 1995) and in the functions of help, availability, and recognition in cross-sex friendship (Rose, 1985). Gaines (1994) reported that men and women give as well as receive ample amounts of affection and respect in their cross-sex friendships and do not engage in respect-denying behaviors with their cross-sex friend frequently. Finally, both men and women tend to keep their friendships and sexual relationships as separate relationships (Sapadin, 1988; Werking, 1995).

Recent research has begun to expand its scope from the traditional focus on the affective qualities of cross-sex friendship to the study of other aspects of cross-sex friendship. Monsour, Betty & Kurzweil (1993) examined interpersonal perception in the context of cross-sex friendships and found that cross-sex friends tend to agree with one another regarding the intimacy in their friendship and the importance of the friendship. Werking (1994b) examined the talk and activities of close adult cross-sex friends. From this study, it appears that close cross-sex friends spend most of their time together talking with one another about personal issues. The majority of these conversations tended to take place face-to-face between the friends, rather than in a group setting. The participants also reported eating meals together, watching television, visiting friends, and shopping.

While researchers have been interested in why or how cross-sex friendships begin (e.g. Rose, 1985), Werking (1994c) researched the reasons why cross-sex friendships terminate and the strategies by which persons dissolve such friendships. Physical separation as a result of attending different colleges, moving to other geographical locations, and changing jobs or class schedules was by far the most frequently mentioned reason for cross-sex friendship termination. This reason is not unique to cross-sex friendship; however, it is interesting to note that the next two most frequently mentioned reasons centered around the management of romance and sexuality; issues that tend to be particular to cross-sex friendship. Taken together, 48% of the sample stated that their close cross-sex friendships ended because a romantic relationship between the two friends was not successful, one or both of the friends became romantically involved with another person, or one of the friends wanted a romantic relationship with their friend but the desire was not reciprocated. This study also explored the ways persons end their close cross-sex friendships and found that 38% of the sample said their friendships simply faded away. Other people stated that they simply cut off contact with their friend (23%) or intentionally avoided their friend (17%).

Theorizing about Cross-sex Friendship

Just as empirical research on cross-sex friendship has been limited in scope, theoretical work on the topic has been sparse. Rawlins (1982) published the first theoretical essay on cross-sex friendship, outlining a typology of man–woman relationship definitions. This typology consisted of five categories: (1) friendship, an affectionate and personal relationship lacking expressed sexuality; (2) platonic love, a relationship of deep intimacy and high emotional commitment without sexual activity; (3) friendship-love, an ambiguous relationship involving degrees of friendship as well as a potential for transition to a romantic relationship; (4) physical love, a relationship based primarily on sexual relations rather than emotional involvement; and (5) romantic love, an exclusive emotional and physical relationship.

In this article, Rawlins (1982) described the challenges facing cross-sex friends as they manage the internal dynamics of romance, sexuality, and sex role socialization. Rawlins also addressed the external dynamics of creating a viable public image of cross-sex friendship so that outsiders to the relationship perceive the relationship as a "friendship" rather than as a "romantic relationship".

The notion of "challenge" was further elaborated by O'Meara (1989). O'Meara identified four challenges, or potential difficulties, facing women and men as they forge friendships with one another. These challenges were: (1) reconciling ways of practicing friendship, because women and men typically enact same-sex friendship differently; (2) overcoming culturally-embedded power differentials between men and women; (3) negotiating the issue of romance and sexuality within the context of friendship; and (4) creating an image of cross-sex friendship that is considered legitimate by friends, family, romantic partners, and co-workers. In a response to data suggesting that structural and normative barriers exist which prevent opportunities for men and women to interact in environments conducive to the development of friendships, O'Meara (1994) added another challenge, the cross-sex friendship opportunity challenge.

Lastly, my own work (Werking, 1992, 1995) has extended the work of Rawlins and O'Meara as I have proposed a theoretical model of cross-sex friendship which weaves together the cultural and relational contexts in which cross-sex friendship is enacted. Specifically, my work has focused on the inherent tensions created between widely accepted cultural models of man–woman romantic relationships and the everyday practice of friendship between men and women. These tensions are a result of a "clash of relational ideologies". Primarily, current cultural models of woman–man relationships adhere to an ideology of heterosexual romance which may or may not include equality, is passionate in nature, and has a goal of marriage. In contrast, the ideology of friendship is based on equality, affection, communion, and is an end unto itself (Badhwar, 1987). Men and women engaged in friendship must, therefore, manage the disparities between these ideologies as they co-create their friendships. The model proposes that this management takes place simultaneously inside the friendship, as friends create relational definitions, and outside the friendship, as the friends address the perceptions of friends, family, co-workers, and romantic partners.

Although the number of published articles on cross-sex friendship has risen substantially in recent years, we still cannot claim that interest in cross-sex friendship is high. Further, few empirical studies have tested the theoretical propositions described above (see Monsour, 1994). Why have there been so few studies of cross-sex friendship? In response to this question, one could argue that friendship between women and men does not occur frequently enough to warrant research attention. This argument pales, however, on close scrutiny of the numbers of cross-sex friendships reported in existing studies.

Indeed, Wright (1989) averaged across the non-college samples of four studies conducted in the past 20 years (Bell, 1981; Block, 1980; Booth & Hess, 1974; Rubin, 1985), and found that 40% of the men and 30% of the women reported close cross-sex friendship. Further, Sapadin (1988) found that 89% of her sample of professional men and women reported engaging in cross-sex friendship. In college, the frequency of cross-sex friendship appears to be even higher, as all of the undergraduate and male graduate students and 73% of the female graduate students participating in Rose's (1985) study claimed at least one close cross-sex friendship outside of their romantic relationships. It appears, then, that women and men have been developing friendships with one another on a fairly frequent basis for quite some time. To understand the lack of research in this area, I contend that we need to investigate the deeply embedded cultural beliefs about woman–man relationships. Our choices of research topics arise within specific historical and cultural circumstances which legitimate certain areas of inquiry and overshadow other areas.

CULTURAL BELIEFS ABOUT HETEROSEXUAL RELATIONSHIPS

Heterosexism is an organizing principle in American society. This ideology assumes that heterosexuality is the norm and, as such, idealizes heterosexual romantic relationships. This type of relationship is widely recognized as the primary basis for marriage; therefore, women and men are encouraged to establish romantic relationships with one another. Messages regarding the importance, establishment, and sustenance of these relationships are provided to members of the culture by important social institutions, such as the media, family, friends, and the legal and educational system. In essence, heterosexual romanticism is the reigning ideology for woman–man relationships (Brain, 1976). Consequently, this ideology provides an interpretive framework for our thoughts, feelings, and behaviors in regards to personal bonds between men and women. Romantic relationships between women and men appear to be the "natural" form of male–female bond.

Because it seems natural, the ideology of heterosexual romanticism structures the possibilities for non-romantic forms of cross-sex bonds, as the legitimacy of alternative forms may be denied or questioned (Laws & Schwartz, 1981). One such alternative form of man–woman relationship is platonic friendship. Cross-sex friendship shares many similarities with romantic heterosexual relationships. For example, both relationships are voluntary in nature, involve feelings of affection and love, and require a substantial amount of emotional commitment if either type of relationship is to survive (Rawlins, 1993).

There are, however, important differences between ideal cross-sex friendships and ideal romantic heterosexual relationships. First, cross-sex friendship does not usually entail a strong sexual dimension (Rawlins, 1982; Werking, 1992). Second, the goal of cross-sex friendship is not marriage. In this regard cross-sex friendship stands in opposition to the dominant romantic ideology. Finally, cross-sex friendship is a relationship among equals. It is a relationship in which men and women hold equivalent rights and responsibilities as they relate to one another as persons *qua* persons rather than role occupants (Paine, 1974).

In contrast, researchers have constructed paradigm cases of romantic heterosexual love relationships and identified asymmetrical eligibilities as a characteristic of romantic relationships (Davis & Todd, 1985; Roberts, 1982). "Asymmetrical eligibilities" means that both relational partners do not have equivalent rights and responsibilities in romantic relationships. The presence of asymmetrical eligibilities, therefore, implies the possibility of an imbalance of power within romantic relationships. Several scholars of heterosexual romantic relationships (e.g., Argyle & Furnham, 1983; Cate & Lloyd, 1992) note that this imbalance of power underlies struggles with issues of dependency, control, and the management of relational resources in heterosexual romantic relationships.

Due to American society's preoccupation with heterosexual dating and marital relationships, we lack a cultural conversation about friendship between women and men. The media remain silent regarding cross-sex friendship, as portrayals of authentic cross-sex friendships are rarely seen in television sitcoms, films, and the popular literature (Werking, 1995). Typically, when cross-sex friendship, does appear in the media, it is sexualized because the plot often centers around what I call the "will they or won't they?" dilemma.

Further, in our everyday lives, the viability of cross-sex friendship is questioned, as cross-sex friends report receiving numerous and persistent questions regarding the nature of their relationship from friends, co-workers, family, and romantic partners (Swain, 1992; Werking, 1992). Cross-sex friends themselves recognize the deviant nature of their relationship when they label their relationship as "weird", "abnormal", or "unusual" (Werking, 1992).

Finally, researchers have not contributed to a conversation about cross-sex friendship. Instead, studies of heterosexual dating and marital relationships have dominated the personal relationship literature since the inception of the field (Blieszner & Adams, 1992; Hendrick & Hendrick, 1992). These types of studies are useful and needed, as they provide insight into a form of heterosexual relationship that is important in people's lives. However, by maintaining an almost exclusive focus on this form of heterosexual bond, researchers have mirrored cultural beliefs about woman–man relationships, rather than exposing these beliefs and presenting alternative forms of relating. We have to ponder, therefore, the degree to which we have reproduced the romantic heterosexual ideology in our work.

IDEOLOGICAL ASSUMPTIONS UNDERPINNING THE STUDY OF CROSS-SEX FRIENDSHIP

In addition to reflecting on our selection of research topics, we must also explore how we investigate our chosen topics. I now turn to two ideological stances enacted in existing cross-sex friendship studies. First, I discuss the ideology of individualism in cross-sex friendship studies. Second, I discuss the heterosexist nature of existing cross-sex friendship studies.

In many ways it is paradoxical that cross-sex friendship researchers tend to focus on the individual, because friendships are developed and maintained by the continual shared negotiation of a relational definition by *both* partners (see Duck, West, & Acitelli, 1997). Nevertheless, individualism, the notion that persons are self-contained beings acting in the world, is deeply ingrained in American society (Bellah et al., 1985) and in research on relationships (Duck, 1994; Gottman, 1982). From this perspective, individuals are "lifted" out of their social, historical, and cultural contexts and the locus of personhood is placed squarely with the individual rather than located in interactions with other humans.

The ideology of individualism is clearly evidenced in the cross-sex friendship literature in four ways: (1) the variables of interest are viewed as properties of individuals and not of relationships, because the unit of analysis is typically the individual rather than the dyad or social group; (2) studies center on persons' subjective appraisals of the cross-sex friendships, rather than their concrete friendship practices; (3) research is not embedded in the history of the studied relationships; and (4) research is acultural in nature. I will discuss each of these issues below.

The Individual as the Unit of Analysis

One consequence of employing individualism in our research is that the popular research concepts of gender, role, attitude, trait, and cognitions are conceptualized as possessions of individuals (Haley, 1963; Lannamann, 1992), rather than the creation of ongoing social processes.

For example, research assessing the role of gender (I use this example because of the large proportion of cross-sex friendship research concerned with this issue) in the development and maintenance of cross-sex friendship has conceptualized gender as a static individual characteristic brought to cross-sex friendships. Wright (1989) described this particular conceptualization of gender as the "dispositional approach" and, on reviewing the extant literature, asserted that "the friendship research exploring gender differences in general has overwhelmingly favored the dispositional approach" (p. 198).

One outcome of employing an individualistic perspective when studying gender and cross-sex friendship is the perpetuation of the belief that, through the socialization process, men and women have internalized culturally determined, and qualitatively different, "core" gender identities, which remain intact over time and across a variety of interpersonal situations (West & Zimmerman, 1987). Thus, the distinction between biological sex and gender has been demolished, as researchers assume that biological sex and its attendant cultural norms determine gender orientation. This assumption is clearly evident, as writers often interchange the biologically-based terms "males and females" (or "men and women") with "gender" (for a clear distinction between biological sex and gender, see Wood, 1993).

Relational scholars (e.g., Deaux & Major, 1987) are questioning the individualistic approach to gender and are advancing alternative constructions. Specifically, these scholars conceptualize gender as an emergent property of social relationships and their structural contexts (West & Fenstermaker, 1995). From this perspective, relationships are the *producers* of gendered identities as well as the *products* of gender-linked behaviors.

Although scholars are taking note of the work cited above, alternative forms of constructing gender have not appeared in the cross-sex friendship literature. Instead, cross-sex friendship researchers continue to equate biological sex with gender (but see Lin & Rusbult, 1995). Scholars simply ask respondents to check whether they are male or female on their surveys and then treat "gender" as an independent variable in their analyses. Further, in scholars' articulation of research goals and discussion of findings, claims are advanced regarding the influence of *gender*, rather than biological sex, on cross-sex friendship (e.g., Monsour, 1992; Rose, 1985; Sapadin, 1988; Werking, 1994).

An alternative to this approach, one that relates to the propositions advanced by West and others, is to view gender not exclusively as an independent variable in our studies, but as a dependent variable as well. In this way, researchers could assess how particular gender orientations are produced, maintained, and altered during the course of relationships. Specifically, cross-sex friendship scholars could examine how gender fluctuates as a function of relationship context and begin to answer the questions: does the gender orientation of a person depend on the gender orientation of the person with whom they are interacting?; how does gender orientation change over time in response to relationship experiences?; and is gender-linked behavior dependent on the type of relationship in which interaction takes place? My work suggests that the gender-linked practices of men and women are connected to whether or not the relationship is defined as romantic or platonic in nature (Werking, 1992, 1995). Specifically, behaviors which defy gender role stereotypes are possible and even facilitated in relationships where sex-typed gender identity is heightened, such as in same-sex friendship and romantic heterosexual relationships, or diminished, such as in cross-sex friendships. For example, men participating in my studies reported enacting a feminine type of friendship with their woman friends, while simultaneously exhibiting normative male friendship behaviors in their same-sex friendships and in their romantic relationships with women.

Individuals as Subjective Entities

In addition to conceptualizing social properties as the possessions of individuals, cross-sex friendship researchers have pictured individuals as subjective entities, because cross-sex friendship researchers have based their studies solely on persons' perceptions of interaction rather than investigating the interaction itself. These studies, therefore, underscore only one aspect of the complex processes surrounding interaction: the ability of humans to interpret the world around them. What is left out of this subjectivist stance is consideration of the concrete practices of cross-sex friends and the material conditions (the ideologically created context involving systems of language, meaning, and power relations) within which interaction takes place (Lannamann, 1991). For example, how do cross-sex friends talk about their friendship with outsiders when the friends are questioned about the nature of their relationship? Why do these inquiries arise? What language resources do the friends and the outsiders employ in these instances? What do cross-sex friends say to one another about such inquiries?

Furthermore, even though researchers are interested in investigating the friendship relationship, they have relied on the reports of only one party in deriving their conclusions. The use of the perceptions of one relational partner has been lamented in the larger literature on personal relationships as well (Duck, 1990, 1994). With few exceptions, the studies of cross-sex friendship generalize from one partner's perspective to the other partner's perspective and to the relationship they negotiate together. The possibilities of discrepancies in reports is rarely addressed (for exceptions, see Monsour, Betty, & Kurzweil, 1993; Werking, 1992), although extensive evidence for differential perceptions of shared relationships has been presented (Thompson & Walker, 1982). In neglecting both insiders' views of a relationship, researchers transform what originally was a single respondent's "perceptions of the relationship" to a summary description of "what is the relationship". In other words, one person's construction of the relationship becomes the objective report of the "reality" of the relationship. By neglecting the other's perceptions of the relationship, researchers risk limited and one-sided views of complex relational phenomena (Larson, 1974).

In short, cross-sex friendship scholars have not examined at first hand the *interaction* of cross-sex friends and the conditions under which these interactions take place. Instead, we have limited our analyses to our participants' *perceptions* of their relationships because we have confined our data collection methods to surveys and interviews. Typically, surveys gather cross-sex friends' perceptions of predetermined global relationship qualities, such as the amount of intimacy, loyalty, or companionship found in their friendships, through the use of Likert-type items. Interview studies are not as common as surveys in the cross-sex friendship literature. Interview studies encompass a wide range, varying from interviews consisting of two open-ended questions (Rose, 1985) to in-depth interviews with participants about their cross-sex friendships specifically (Werking, 1992, 1995) or about their friendships in general (Bell, 1981; Block, 1980; Rawlins, 1981, 1992; Rubin, 1985). Interviews may be designed to gather in-depth information about cross-sex friendship. Nevertheless, like surveys, data gleaned from interviews are participants' descriptions of their cross-sex friendship experiences, rather then segments of their actual friendship interactions.

Why might it be important for researchers to focus on the actual interaction of cross-sex friends? First, a focus on interaction necessitates a focus on the dyad rather than the individual, because, by definition, interaction takes place between two individuals. Second, researchers can examine specific cross-sex friendship interactions which may lead to the participants' assessments of relational qualities, such as affection, frustration, and companionship. If our participants say they are (dis)satisfied with their cross-sex friendship, how is this (dis)satisfaction conveyed in their talk with one another (Duck, 1994)? Third, through the analysis of interaction, researchers may investigate language-in-use and, therefore, analyze the ideological forces which shape the ways in which man–woman relationships are negotiated through talk.

Next, I present a segment of tape-recorded conversation between two cross-sex friends. I will use this excerpt to demonstrate the usefulness of examining the interaction of cross-sex friends in two ways: the window it affords into relationship negotiation and into the cultural/ideological context within which cross-sex friendship interactions take place.

I have been collecting the conversations of cross-sex friends by audiotape-recording 15–20 minute conversations. The following is an excerpt from a conversation between Mary, 25, and John, 24. Mary and John are Caucasian, heterosexual, college students. Both friends are involved in romantic relationships with other people. Mary and John have been close friends for three and a half years. In this excerpt, John and Mary are discussing how other people perceive their relationship:

M: can think of numerous specific examples of people comin' up to me and sayin', you know, "So what's up with you and John?" But ...

J: Well, even at the bar the other night, when that girl thought I was hittin' on you and I smiled and I told I wasn't, that you and I are ... it's the way that I say that, you know, people say I don't get defensive or anything, I just sort of smile ...

M: Yeah! (*laughing*)

J: ... because, I don't know. I don't deny it totally, it's not like I want to deny, 'cause then I would be like saying, "She's not my friend", you know ... 'Cause, you know, you're my best friend. In a way it's way beyond hittin' on you.

M: Right. Right!

J: So when people say that, I just sorta smile 'cause they are trivializing what it is. So, I guess that makes it harder for people to believe that there's not anything going on because I don't deny it.

M: Yeah. I follow that exactly because I suppose if both of us were like, "No way!", you know, then they'd believe us. I don't know, I guess, you know, I'm very fond of you and that's what people see when I say, "Oh, you know, we're just friends", or whatever. I guess they see that, you know, 'cause people read what you're, not only what the words are, but the message behind the words.

J: Yeah.

M: So, I guess if I didn't really care about you or whatever and I went like, "Naw", then it would be different.

J: I agree. When people ask me about you, I know I get that little, my eyes sort of (*pause*) they light up.

M: (*Laughs*)

J: You know, 'cause when I think about you, we really have fun, we laugh. You know, all we do is fun things and, you know, yeah, I can't anything hostile or ... I light up and people probably read that the wrong way.

M: Um hm. Then I guess it's actually *our* fault, you can't fault people for seeing that ...

In the above excerpt, we witness Mary and John conversationally struggle with the dilemma of being friends. On one hand, being friends necessitates feelings of caring and affection between John and Mary. Demonstrating these friendship qualities publicly, however, may be misinterpreted by others, since outsiders to the friendship may overlay a romantic template on affectionate behaviors. This interpretation of Mary and John's relationship is expressed in the phrases John and Mary use to describe the reactions of others, such as, "What's up?", "hittin' on you", "not anything going on", and "read that the wrong way". From their conversation, it is apparent that Mary and John do not want a romantic reading of their relationship because it is the "wrong" reading. Further, they feel this reading "trivializes" the relationship because their relationship is "way beyond hittin' on you".

In addition to functioning as a means to reveal their feelings about the misperceptions of others, this conversation is also a sense-making experience (Duck, 1994) for Mary and John because they attempt to explain to one another what their relationship means to them. In articulating their feelings toward one another, they use the words "fond", and "fun" and the phrase, "my eyes light up". They also cite the relational category of "best friends" to make sense of their experiences. Thus, this conversation provides information to researchers about feelings the friends have for one another and the specific ways these feelings are communicated to one another.

The ongoing negotiation of cross-sex friendship is a highly collaborative activity and is achieved through talk. In order to understand this activity, researchers should observe, tape-record, and transcribe the interaction of cross-sex friends. Through these activities, researchers may then witness for themselves cross-sex friends' affection for one another, their enjoyment of one another, and the enmeshment of their lives as they talk about themselves, friends, family, future plans, past events, and work with one another; not to a third party. As Duck (1994) notes:

… persons symbolize their relationship with others in many different ways through talking. That fact helps each person (and could help researchers) to discover something useful and important about the partner, the partner's vision, and the partners' attitudes toward one another. Talk provides them with evidence about the way in which another constructs the relationship and, more importantly, the frameworks of comprehension within which the other does so (p. 149).

Acultural

John and Mary's conversation may also be used as a way for researchers to examine the cultural context within which this interaction takes place. It is important for researchers to consider seriously the link between what occurs between cross-sex friends and their cultural and social contexts, yet, due to our focus on individuals, this type of analysis is rarely undertaken (e.g., Davis & Todd, 1985; Mahoney & Heretick, 1979; Sapadin, 1988). Several commentaries have been written about the potential influence of the cultural context on the nature of cross-sex friendship (e.g., O'Meara, 1989; Rawlins, 1982); however, extended analyses of cultural texts and the symbol systems available to participants for describing their experiences have not been undertaken.

Typically, when "cultural norms" or "sex roles" are offered as explanations of findings, researchers do not provide specifics on the nature of these norms and roles. For example, Hacker (1981) explains her finding of perceptions of lesser intimacy in cross-sex friendship for women than for men by simply pointing to "social norms" regulating the relationship between men and women friends (p.398). Hacker (1981) does not offer an explanation regarding the specific ways these norms regulate man–woman friendships. Similarly, the Bukowski, Nappi and Hoza (1987) finding, that men report greater intimacy in their cross-sex friendships than in their same-sex friendships, is explained by "cultural proscriptions" with regard to intimacy among males (p. 602).

Researchers need to consider seriously the connection between cross-sex friendship and the embracing culture, because the available tools for the conduct of relationships, language and metaphor, are informed by cultural ideologies (Duck, 1994). The prevailing heterosexual romantic ideology I described earlier in the chapter constrains the daily interactions of cross-sex friends, because it structures the possibilities for friendship (O'Meara, 1994) and brings to the fore specific issues in cross-sex friendship. These issues include the degree to which the friendship incorporates expressions of romance and sexuality if the man and woman are heterosexuals, or the extent to which outsiders to the friendship will accept the relationship as a "friendship" rather than a "romance".

Furthermore, the symbol systems utilized by cross-sex friends to address these and other issues are infused with a heterosexual romantic ideology, so that terms such as "just friends" are used to describe cross-sex friendship. Friends also struggle to create new ways of expressing their feelings for one another so that these expressions will not be misinterpreted as romantic in nature. Cross-sex friends particularly struggle to find substitutes for or clarify their use of "love" as an expression of feeling (Werking, 1995).

Clearly, in their conversation, Mary and John interactively reproduce the prevailing heterosexual romantic ideology. The ideology is reflected in their description of the misperceptions of others. Interestingly, Mary and John take responsibility for the misperceptions of outsiders by saying, "It's actually our fault, you can't fault people for seeing that". The ideology leaks into their own perceptions of their relationship as well, because they "trivialize" their relationship by using the phrase "just friends", implying that they too consider their friendship as "less than" a romantic relationship.

Studying the actual interactions of cross-sex friends is only one way researchers might tap into the cultural context in which cross-sex friendship is enacted. I focus on this method because it is underutilized by cross-sex friendship researchers. Interviews, surveys, and textual analysis of media images of cross-sex friendship would also reveal relevant information. Whatever the methodology of choice, our understanding of the challenges, tensions, and rewards associated with cross-sex friendship will be enriched by a description of the cultural contexts in which the studied friendships take place.

Acontextual

The social network of cross-sex friends also influences the character of cross-sex friendship (Parks, this volume). Nevertheless, cross-sex friendship researchers have just begun to chart the linkages between cross-sex friendship and other social relationships. For example, cross-sex friends' perceptions of the social network subsuming their dyad have been collected in only a handful of studies. In these studies, the marital relationship has been linked to participation in cross-sex friendship. Booth & Hess (1974) and Rose (1985) limited their documentation of this link to an analysis of the influence of marriage on the number of cross-sex friends. Other work has tapped into the connections between romantic relationships, same-sex friendships, family relations, and cross-sex friendship (Werking, 1992, 1995). For example, I (Werking, 1992) interviewed pairs of cross-sex friends about times when their romantic relationships with third parties influenced their friendships. This study revealed that the cross-sex friendships were often reconstructed during these times, either by not spending as much time with one another or by including the romantic partner in friendship activities, in order to reduce the romantic partner's insecurity about the cross-sex friendship. Ironically, the cross-sex friendship was viewed as more stable and beneficial than the romantic relationship by nearly all of the participants. This example also illustrates the overlap between cultural ideologies and the nature of social relationships at a personal level, because my participants reported privileging their romantic relationships over their cross-sex friendships while simultaneously describing their cross-sex friendships as more stable and beneficial. Work of this type is in its initial stages, and future research is needed prior to claiming understanding of the connections between cross-sex friendship and cross-sex friends' third-party involvements, such as same-sex friendships, work relationships, family relationships, and romantic relationships.

Ahistorical

I have argued that individualism is evidenced in the cross-sex friendship research in the conceptualization of research concepts, in the choice of the unit of analysis, and in the lack of focus on the cultural and social contexts of cross-sex friendship. A final consequence of individual-centered relationship research is that cross-sex friendship researchers rarely consider the studied relationships' histories.

The majority of existing cross-sex friendship researchers utilize the survey method. These surveys typically obtain minimal information about the friendships described by research participants. In general, the respondents' sex and age, the type of friendship (best, close, casual, etc.) and the length of friendship appear to be the only background information of interest. Because the type of information gathered through the use of surveys is abstract in nature, so too are the claims researchers may legitimately make regarding their results. In contrast to the survey method, interviews can provide detailed descriptions of the historical patterning of interactions within the studied friendships. Nevertheless, cross-sex friendship researchers do not necessarily choose to exercise this capacity (e.g., Hacker, 1981; Rose, 1985; Sapadin, 1988).

An alternative to ahistorical research is grounding research in the participants' relationships and examining their patterns of development and interaction. This perspective views relationships as co-constructed patterns of interaction which are built up over time (Bateson, 1978). These patterns compose a relational context which is in "continuous and reverberating motion" (Gergen, 1980, p. 243), unfolding as interactants choose and revise courses of action in tandem. Furthermore, the relationship and the acts of the partners are intertwined because the relationship is constituted by the partners' actions and, in turn, shapes their practices. A backwards look at these patterns thus reveals to the researcher the premises for interpreting the actions occurring within the relationship.

Only two interview studies (Rawlins, 1981; Werking, 1992), however, have grounded the analysis of the participants' descriptions of their close cross-sex friendships in the historical context of the studied relationship. Each of these researchers constructed "friendship histories" prior to interpreting their participants' descriptions of their friendships. A friendship history is in essence a story of the friendship as told to the researcher by *both* members of a friendship. This story consists of key relational events and themes, such as the friends' meeting, celebrations, special nicknames, and disagreements. Constructing such a history aids researchers' interpretations of the participants' responses to questions. For example, instances of physical contact between cross-sex friends may be interpreted by a researcher as being romantic and/or sexual in nature, unless the researcher has considered how touching has been interpreted by the friends in the past and how the relationship has been defined by the friends.

In sum, by lifting individuals' assessments of their cross-sex friendships out of the relational context, researchers have lost the ability to answer such questions as: how did these assessments arise in a particular form?; what led a participant to check off "very satisfied" rather than "somewhat satisfied" in response to the question, "How satisfied are you with your friendship with X?". Behind participants' responses are specific experiences and practices which remain unexamined by researchers.

Further, without historical information about the cross-sex friendships, to what do we anchor our participants' descriptions? How can we "interpret" their interpretations? Actions are accorded particular meanings because they are enacted in a particular context. By peeling the context from respondents' actions, cross-sex friendship researchers risk imposing researcher-owned categories of description on their participants' responses rather than participant-owned categories.

"Decentering" the individual in cross-sex friendship necessitates a profound shift in research practices (Lannamann, 1992) because it involves shifting our focus to interaction as it takes place within particular historical, relational, and cultural contexts. Such a shift reverberates through the questions we ask, to the methods we choose for data collection, to the ways in which we analyze our data.

THE IDEOLOGY OF HETEROSEXISM

The ideology of individualism has partly shaped what we know about cross-sex friendship. I now revisit a second organizing principle for cross-sex friendship research, the ideology of heterosexuality. I argued earlier in this chapter that heterosexism informs scholars' decisions about what constitutes viable research topics and is practiced in the everyday interactions of cross-sex friends. Unfortunately, heterosexism also undergirds many of the existing cross-sex friendship studies.

First, scholars often assume the participants in studies are heterosexual men and women, or specifically sample only heterosexual men and women (e.g., Swain, 1992; Werking, 1994) and thus neglect other forms of cross-sex friendship, such as friendships between gay men and lesbians. A recent literature review (Werking, 1995) uncovered no empirical studies of friendship between the gay and lesbian community and a limited number of studies investigating friendships between gay men and straight women (Malone, 1980; Nardi, 1992; Whitney, 1990).

Second, researchers exhibit a heterosexist ideology when we assume that issues of romance and sexuality constitute ongoing concerns only in cross-sex friendships between heterosexual persons, rather than acknowledging that these issues may be raised in varying degrees in same-sex friendships between homosexual and/or heterosexual persons (Nardi, 1992; Rawlins, 1994), or between cross-sex friends where one or both friends are homosexual. The danger in making this assumption is that researchers fall into dichotomous ways of thinking about sexual orientation. The scant research conducted into the friendships between gay men and heterosexual women questions this assumption. For example, the research of Malone (1980) and Whitney (1990) paradoxically reveals that, although many of their participants viewed their friendship as a safe haven from the perils of sexual and romantic relationships initially, sexual attraction and activity between the friends existed. The participants in both studies further reported that sexuality threatened their friendships and summoned feelings of frustration and anxiety.

Dichotomous thinking about sexual orientation may also be challenged by friendship between lesbians and gays. While studies have not yet been conducted in this area, an interesting collection of essays written by persons engaged in friendship highlights the close and complex relationships between gays and lesbians (Nestle &

Preston, 1994). These writings uncover the sensual nature of gay/lesbian friendship and, in this way, further undermine the heterosexist assumption that expressed or unexpressed sexual attraction occurs only between heterosexual men and women.

There is much to be learned about cross-sex friendship in the homosexual community, as well as cross-sex friendship between homosexual/heterosexual women and men. Such study is worthwhile because ignoring the various forms of cross-sex friendship limits our knowledge of the diversity of norms, rules, and societal contexts within which men and women forge friendships (Duck, 1994).

Lastly, romance and sexuality are important topics for study in the area of cross-sex friendship because these issues have been defined culturally as central to man–woman relations. Many participants in our studies reflect this centrality as they report that these issues are important to them in their everyday experiences in forging cross-sex friend-ships (e.g., Bell, 1981; Furman, 1986; Rubin, 1985). Cross-sex friendship scholars, however, should be cautious not to let investigation of sexual issues overshadow studies into other dimensions of the cross-sex friendship experience. Let us look beyond the issue of sex and pursue studies about other important cross-sex friendship dynamics, such as what cross-sex friends do and say with one another. And let us be cautious not to investigate these dynamics only as they occur between heterosexual persons, but as they are practiced between persons of differing sexual orientations.

CONCLUSION

The narratives told by research participants about cross-sex friendship are constructed within specific historical, cultural, and social configurations. So, too, are the texts produced by researchers. Both types of narratives are constrained by interre-lated complexes of ideological forces. Through our research practices ideologies gain their power, because these practices reaffirm and reify ideological assumptions. In this chapter, I have problematized what appear to be rarely questioned ways of thinking about and researching cross-sex friendship. Specifically, I have addressed the latent individualism and heterosexism evident in the cross-sex friendship liter-ature and charted the ways in which these ideological themes position our research. Such questioning is needed because the debate over the theoretical and method-ological approaches (in short, the stories we construct about cross-sex friendship) is constricted unless issues of ideology are addressed. As Shotter (1993) states:

> Stories may tell us what in certain particular circumstances we should do to fit our actions into a particular order, but their danger is, that by revealing in their telling only a selection of the possibilities open to us, they can so easily conceal from us what the range of possibilities is (p. 147).

Cross-sex friendship provides a unique opportunity to assess the interplay between cultural ideals and norms regarding woman–man relationships, unique relational patterns of interaction, and subjective individual experiences. Let us approach this opportunity thoughtfully and creatively so that our research is emancipatory rather than repressive in nature.

Chapter 8

Toward a Theory of Obsessive Relational Intrusion and Stalking

William R. Cupach

Illinois State University, Normal, IL, USA

Brian H. Spitzberg

San Diego State University, San Diego, CA, USA

Christine L. Carson

University of Wisconsin, Madison, WI, USA

The evolution of the field of personal relationships, with some notable exceptions, has focused on relationships that are largely mutual in nature. Research has extensively investigated conversation, acquaintanceship, workplace collaboration, friendship, sexual relations, love, marriage, and family relations (Duck, 1988b). To date, relatively few scholarly efforts have examined disjunctive relationships, such as enemyship (Wiseman, cited in Duck, 1994b) and unrequited love (e.g., Bratslavsky, Baumeister, & Sommer, 1998). Although processes that represent the dark side of close relationships (such as co-dependency and abuse) receive considerable attention, they typically occur in relationships that possess some level of

Communication and Personal Relationships
Edited by Kathryn Dindia and Steve Duck. © 2000 John Wiley & Sons Ltd.

reciprocity and mutual desire to sustain the relationship. However, not all relationships entail mutuality or overlap of intent to pursue the relationship. Some relationships are more disjunctive, whereby one party desires a type of relationship that the other party clearly does not want. A relational phenomenon that literally has only recently been named and investigated suggests a fundamentally disjunctive relationship.

Obsessive relational intrusion (ORI) is the "repeated and unwanted pursuit and invasion of one's sense of physical or symbolic privacy by another person, either stranger or acquaintance, who desires and/or presumes an intimate relationship" (Cupach & Spitzberg, 1998, pp. 234–235). ORI is an ongoing form of pursuit, harassment, and invasion of another person's life. Its objective, at least in part, is the escalation or redefinition of the relationship with an eye towards greater intimacy. The intimacy is desired by the pursuer, but the object of affection rejects and wishes to avoid this intimacy. In short, one person wants greater intimacy in the relationship, whereas the other person does not.

One characteristic of ORI is that it often involves activities that in another context could be viewed as appropriate forms of relationship pursuit. Leaving notes on a person's car windshield, showing up unannounced at the person's office, sending gifts and flowers, calling the person frequently, developing relationships with mutual acquaintances, and attempting to discover information about the person are all common courtship tactics. Pursuit becomes obsessive and intrusive when it "is persistent despite the absence of reciprocity by the obsessional object and despite resistance by the object" (Cupach & Spitzberg, 1998, p. 235). In other words, activities that constitute normal relationship pursuit are seen as excessive to the extent that the pursuer repeats them in the face of rejection.

ORI is closely related to the legal concept of stalking. Stalking is "the willful, malicious, and repeated following and harassing of another person that threatens his or her safety" (Meloy & Gothard, 1995, p. 258). Thus, activities such as following surreptitiously, breaking into a residence, sending thinly veiled threats, or engaging in coercion or violence designed to control another's movements and associations, are more clearly in the vein of stalking (Emerson, Ferris, & Gardner, 1998). ORI is a broader phenomenon than stalking, which represents an extreme and severe manifestation of ORI. Stalking involves a pattern of intrusion that a reasonable person would find threatening. Although ORI can be threatening, sometimes it is merely harassing or annoying.

Another distinction between ORI and stalking is that, whereas ORI seeks relational connection, stalking can occur due to other motivations, such as when an assassin pursues a political target (Holmes, 1993) or a sociopath seeks a victim. Nevertheless, research indicates that the vast majority of stalkers know their objects of pursuit (e.g., Burgess, Baker, Greening, Hartman, Burgess, Douglas, & Halloran, 1997), and that most stalking reflects the aftermath of relational decay (Tjaden & Thoennes, 1998). Indeed, one of the commonly recognized types of stalking is referred to as "domestic" stalking, in which a marriage or exclusive relationship dissolves and one of the parties refuses to let the relationship die and stalks the former partner (Holmes, 1993; Roberts & Dziegielewski, 1996; Wright et al., 1996). ORI and stalking, therefore, can be viewed as overlapping phenomena (see Cupach & Spitzberg, 1998).

The point at which relational pursuit becomes obsessive is not always clear and precise. Some perseverance in relational pursuit is expected and often desired by an object of pursuit. The processes of relational development (or reconciliation) are typically gradual and cumulative. Individuals certainly differ in their thresholds for tolerating unreciprocated overtures, and in some cases objects experience ambivalence about whether or not to reciprocate a relationship with a pursuer. Activities potentially defined as obsessive pursuit, "such as writing, calling, following, visiting, and gathering information about the other, also mark familiar, everyday courtship and uncoupling practices. Those who become the focus of such attention may initially frame these activities as romantic pursuit or friendship-building, only later reinterpreting them as stalking" (Emerson et al., 1998, p. 292). The obsessive nature of relational intrusion is therefore a matter of interpretation by the object rather than a pre-defined profile of behavior (Emerson et al., 1998).

Despite its disjunctive nature, ORI creates a form of relationship between pursuer and object. Some scholars have coined terms such as "obsessional following" (Meloy, 1996) and "relational stalking" (Emerson et al., 1998) to reflect this relational nature. The pursuer communicates with the object of affection in an effort to express relational interest and foster in the object favorable impressions of the pursuer. Despite the object's contrary goal, he/she is involuntarily drawn into recurring episodes of symbolic exchange with the pursuer. These exchanges collectively create a relational context that serves to frame each person's own intentions and interpretations regarding the other's behavior. Furthermore, each interaction serves as an enactment of a relationship between the pursuer and object, which further reifies the pursuer's sense that a relationship exists, even if it is not in the form that is desired. ORI thus involves what Emerson et al. (1998) refer to as *meta-relational troubles*. It is precisely "the nature of the purported relationship between the two parties—what it is, what it was, and what it will be—that is fundamentally at issue" (Emerson et al., 1998, p. 296).

ORI is a relatively common occurrence among college students (Cupach & Spitzberg, 1997; Spitzberg & Cupach, 1996). In addition, sizable percentages of college students and adults have been stalked (Fremouw, Westrup, & Pennypacker, 1997; Romans, Hays, & White, 1996). Indeed, according to the only nationally representative survey on the subject, 8% of women and 2% of men in the USA claim to have been victims of stalking (Tjaden & Thoennes, 1998). Research indicates that the average case of ORI and stalking lasts for many months to several years, and tends to produce a myriad of traumatic symptoms for the victim (Burgess et al., 1997; Hall, 1998; Pathé & Mullen, 1997). Victims of ORI and stalking are also more likely to be victims of sexual coercion (Spitzberg & Rhea, 1999) and physical violence (Tjaden & Thoennes, 1998).

A better understanding of the phenomena of stalking and ORI is clearly warranted. However, to date, there has been little conceptual grounding on which to cultivate a theory of ORI and stalking processes. This theoretical void seems to derive from at least two sources. First, as indicated previously, most theoretical work in the arena of personal relationships has emphasized reciprocal or mutual forms of relational development. There are few theoretical foundations for conceptualizing disjunctive relationships in which pursuit persists in the face of rejection.

Second, empirical inquiry regarding stalking and related phenomena has generally represented a strong clinical or forensic orientation. These orientations have presumably been grounded in the practical concerns of jurisprudence, clinical treatment, and prevention. Clinical and psychiatric approaches are brought to bear on such essential issues as competency to stand trial, assessment of violence-proneness, and nosological diagnosis. As useful as such perspectives are, they incur some limitations. First, clinical approaches for the most part are steeped in assumptions of childhood etiology, in which family of origin and childhood trauma are viewed as the distal causes of later complex patterns of adult behavior. Thus, the origin of current activity is rooted far in the past, rather than in relatively present mental and relational processes. Second, clinical approaches tend to be wedded to models of psychopathology, in which it is presumed that the pursuer's everyday fabric of "reality" has eroded, and he/she is enmeshed in a larger world of seriously distorted or delusional experience. Such approaches therefore locate stalking and ORI in the realm of "abnormality". This focus removes the study of stalking and ORI from the mundane processes of disjunctive relational development (Emerson et al., 1998), in which patterns of pursuit and escape originate in normal, common social behavior. Third, as has been found "with many forms of psychopathological behavior, there is no uniform or typical profile of an obsessional follower" (McCann, 1998, p. 668). Clinical approaches tend to yield classifications of pursuers that are predicated upon manifold etiologies and presenting symptoms. Such approaches locate relevant issues strictly within the individual, thereby ignoring the interactive and relational implications of pursuit.

There is a need, therefore, for a theory of stalking and obsessive relational intrusion located within the realm of ordinary individual experience and relationship processes. Before presenting such a theory, however, it is important to trace the outlines of regnant theoretical perspectives. We therefore begin by briefly summarizing some of the dominant theoretical work that addresses stalking and obsessive relationships from a clinical perspective. We then offer our own account of how common relational pursuit becomes obsessive and excessive.

PREDOMINANT CLINICAL PERSPECTIVES ON STALKING AND OBSESSIVE PURSUIT

Object Relations

Stalkers are often characterized as experiencing a fusion with their object of pursuit, being unable to distinguish between self and object. Object relations theory is directly pertinent to accounting for the ways in which people perceive self and other. The essence of object relations theory is that there is a developmental succession of phases in which infants increasingly differentiate their perception of objects in their environment from themselves, particularly their mother or primary caregiver (Mahler, 1986). This normal process of differentiation facilitates the development of a sense of self-efficacy, as the infant comes to realize that he/she is an autonomous entity interacting with other entities in a complex social environment.

The objects in this environment are not all equivalent. For example, the caregiver is more important for nurturance and security than most other objects. The affectionate bond between self and caregiver becomes more complex over time. The infant increasingly is cognizant of his/her dependence on and connection to the caregiver (i.e., object), and yet simultaneously is developing more exploratory independence from the caregiver. The infant develops a mental representation of the primary object, and his/her interaction with the object. Not only is the object viewed as a primary source of wish-fulfillment, but the object is visualized as behaving in certain desired ways with the infant. "If we see object relationships as being wish-fulfilments in a broad sense, then the fulfillment of the wished-for object relationship comes about through the finding of an object (in reality, in fantasy, or both) which will act and react in the appropriate way" (Sandler & Sandler, 1986, p. 283). People who experience disorders of their wish-fulfillments as infants may later pursue those objects in fantasy, and should they fixate upon an actual object who is viewed as potentially wish-fulfilling, stalking could be an obvious extension of this fantasy world.

Meloy (1992, 1998) and Kienlen (1998) have suggested the relevance of object relations theory to stalking. They identify the stages of object relations development, and propose that disruptions of these stages can presage abnormal idealizations and/or insecurities related to others. Some people never internalize appropriate distinctions between the object self and the objects of nurturing. Such a fusion could lead to the idealization of others, not only as the sole source of comfort and completion, but as essential extensions of oneself. Yet, the internalization, or intro-jection (Kernberg, 1986), of a model of one's primary caregivers may be essential as a basis of reference and comparison in the development of the self.

Alternatively, it has been suggested that disruption during a key separation–indi-viduation stage of development could lead to an aggressive orientation toward others. During such a stage, the infant is experiencing greater independence, but is simulta-neously anxious about the caregiver's availability. An emotionally unavailable mother, for example, could lead an infant to increase and exaggerate efforts to re-establish the mother's affection. Disruption could prefigure adult behavior that idealizes women as the source of caring, and yet produces anxiety and even rage at their unavailability (see Kienlen, 1998).

More specifically, Dutton (1998; see also Cogan & Porcerelli, 1996) argues that a particular process of object relations accounts for abusive personalities, especially in men. The developing infant is totally dependent on the caregiver, usually the mother. This dependency is generally comforting and fulfilling. But inevitably it fails in some ways. The mother is not always available, does not always do what the infant wants, and so forth. The infant, discovering that his/her primitive needs are rejected by the primary source of fulfillment, experiences rage. In order to reconcile this anger at the same object with which such strong positive attachment exists, a child sometimes fails to learn appropriate mechanisms, and instead learns to "split" his/her image of the mother; into the good mother (i.e., the Madonna) and the bad mother (i.e., the whore). This splitting, in turn, permits the infant to both love and hate the same object, albeit at separate times. Dutton (1998) interprets much of his empirical research on abusive relationships in terms of the husband abusing the wife when he is enraged by her, and subsequently is loving and supplicating when he sees her as a primary source of comfort and affection. This intermittent pattern of reinforcement, in turn, could be a powerful source of bonding for the wife, who consequently finds it difficult to leave the relationship. The analogue to stalking, in which the stalker vacillates between being passionately drawn to the object and subsequently enraged by the object, is suggestive of a key paradox of stalking.

Attachment Disorders

Attachment theory is an obvious source for theoretically grounding a model of stalking. Although the scope of attachment theory is intended to account for or apply to virtually all human relationships, disorders of attachment can lead to later processes that are uniquely relevant to stalking. Largely pioneered by the work of Ainsworth (1989) and colleagues (Ainsworth, Blehar, Waters, & Wall, 1978) and Bowlby (1969, 1973), attachment theory proposes that infants develop primary attachments early in life. The security and stability of these primary attachments, usually with the mother, come to represent core working models, schemata, or templates for later adult attachments and set up the conditions under which individual differences can emerge in attachment styles.

Bowlby summarized his theory in three core propositions. First, individuals confident that an attachment figure will be available when needed are less fearful of the social world than individuals who are not confident of the availability of an attachment figure. Second, expectations regarding attachment figures that develop during infancy and adolescence become relatively enduring and stable. Finally, these expectations become relatively accurate in depicting the individual's actual social experiences. Thus, if early primary attachments are disrupted, such as through abandonment, the individual develops a fearful or insecure set of expectations regarding attachment figures.

Particularly relevant to stalking is the further premise of an attachment system in which a person develops an attachment, that is, an affectional bond, with another. Two important extensions of this premise help elaborate the relevance. "First, relationships are dyadic, whereas affectional bonds are characteristics of the individual but not the dyad; they come to entail representation in the internal organization of the individual person" (Ainsworth, 1991, p. 37). Second, "[i]n an affectional bond there is a desire to maintain closeness to the partner" and "there is at least an intermittent desire to re-establish proximity and interaction ... Inexplicable separation tends to cause distress, and permanent loss would cause grief" (Ainsworth, 1991, p. 38).

Early theoretical work tended to focus on two to three attachment templates or styles (e.g., Hazan & Shaver, 1987). More recent formulations typically envision four or more styles (Bartholomew, 1993; Buelow, McClain, & McIntosh, 1996). Two positive–negative dimensions configure the four-style model: one's model of self and one's model of other. Thus, *secures* have a positive model of self and of other (i.e., attachment figure). *Preoccupieds* possess a positive view of others, but a negative view of self. Preoccupieds therefore fundamentally lack self-confidence, and are obsessed with achieving intimacy with desirable others. They are excessive in their demand for intimacy. *Dismissives*, in contrast, have a positive view of self but a negative view of others. Dismissives reveal a discomfort with intimacy, and instead emphasize self-reliance. *Fearful avoidants* possess negative models of both self and others. Lacking confidence in self, they need the reinforcement of another's love, and yet they simultaneously distrust and fear intimacy with others. This creates an ambivalent orientation toward intimacy.

Collectively, the preoccupieds, dismissives and fearful avoidants can be considered "insecure" attachment styles. Secures are least likely to have experienced unrequited love, and preoccupieds (also called anxious/ambivalents) are most likely to have experienced unrequited love (Aron, Aron, & Allen, 1998). Further, compared to secure attachment styles, insecures are more obsessive or desperate in their love styles (Sperling & Berman, 1991), more jealous and intrusive (Dutton, van Ginkel, & Landolt, 1996; Guerrero, 1998) and more abusive (Dutton, Saunders, Starzomski, & Bartholomew, 1994) in their relationships. Preoccupieds, in particular, appear more prone to aggressive behavior in relationships (Bookwala & Zdaniuk, 1998; Kalichman et al., 1993), although Kalichman et al. (1993) found fearful attachment style to be most correlated with anger and jealousy. Meloy (1996) specifically predicted that preoccupieds would be more likely to stalk others, given the importance of intimacy to their sense of self. The finding that stalkers have often experienced recent attachment losses is consistent with attachment theory (Kienlen et al., 1997).

Finally, it should be apparent that object relations theory and attachment theory are highly compatible. To formulate a working model of one's primary attachments, it is vital that perceptual processes permit proper differentiation of self from others. "Thus, attachment relations and object relations are inseparable for practical purposes, even though the constructs may be distinguished for theoretical purposes" (Buelow et al., 1996, p. 606).

In summary, object relations theory and attachment theory have been proposed to explain ORI and stalking. Although these approaches are informative, they focus more on psychopathology and peculiar cases; they focus less on processes that are manifested in more common instances of otherwise normal individuals engaged in relational pursuit that has run amok. In addition, these approaches, focusing on psychopathology, tend to be located in the individual. In other words, they do not allow for the communicative and relational factors that go hand-in-hand with ORI and stalking. We therefore propose a theoretical approach better suited to the everyday, garden-variety occurrence of obsessive disjunctive relationships.

TOWARD A THEORETICAL MODEL OF ORI AND STALKING

Overview

Obsessive pursuit is grounded in the pursuer's attraction to the object of pursuit and reflected in a desire for some form of relational connection to the object. There are two common pathways to this attraction. Most commonly, the attraction was developed and fostered in a personal relationship between pursuer and object. When the object attempts to redefine or terminate the relationship, the pursuer attempts to hold on to or re-establish the failed relationship. Alternatively, a pursuer may have initial contact with an object that stimulates attraction and thus creates the goal of developing a relationship with the object. This initial contact may be brief and fleeting, as in a chance meeting, or it can be based on the pursuer's observation of the object from a distance, perhaps through the media or across a company's conference table.

The attraction that a pursuer develops for an object leads to the formation of a relationship goal. In the case of a failed relationship, the goal is to restore or repair the previously experienced association with the former partner. In instances where the association between the pursuer and the object is nominal or hypothetical, the goal of the pursuer is to initiate and develop a close relationship with the object. In either case, the goal is pursued initially when the pursuer enacts common relational maintenance/repair strategies (Canary & Stafford, 1994) or affinity-seeking strategies (Bell & Daly, 1984). The pursuer sends messages conveying interest and affinity, sends gifts and other tokens, creates opportunities for interacting with the object of pursuit, attempts to ingratiate the object, and seeks reciprocation from the object. These efforts are interpreted in various ways by the object, ranging from benign, to annoying and pestering, to harassing, to menacing and threatening (Cupach & Spitzberg, 1997). The interpretation of the object then results in a response, which is sometimes avoidance and evasion, sometimes ambiguous rejection, sometimes overt rejection, and sometimes reliance on third-party intervention (e.g., Spitzberg & Cupach, 1996). The response may change over time, but at any given time, informs the subsequent perception of the pursuer. The pursuer interprets the object's behavior and responds accordingly, adjusting relational goal pursuit tactics to be commensurate with the level of ambiguity or resistance displayed by the object. Over time, to the extent that the relational goal is not achieved, pursuit activities persist, escalate, and gradually become more aggressive.

The potential for obsessive pursuit is rooted in the ordinary and often mundane experience of managing potential and actual personal relationships. "Unwanted relationship pursuit manifests itself in complex and subtle ways, owing to such commonplace experiences as jealousy, unrequited love, and divorce" (Cupach, & Spitzberg, 1998, p. 234). As Emerson et al. (1998) argue, "many forms of what comes to be identified as stalking grow out of glitches and discontinuities in two very common and normal relationship processes—coming together and forming new relationships on the one hand, and dissolving and getting out of existing relationships on the other" (p. 290). This partially explains why it can be difficult to specify a precise point at which pursuit "crosses the line" and becomes clearly excessive.

Although "abnormal" and borderline personality profiles can account for the propensity of certain individuals to develop obsessive attachments to others, relational pursuit can go awry even in the absence of dispositional psychosis. In the pages that follow, our aim is to elucidate the processes by which otherwise "normal" and acceptable (if annoying) pursuit becomes obsessive and inappropriate. Due to space limitations, we focus here specifically on the pursuer's interpretive processes that energize and catalyze the persistence of pursuit. We propose three fairly common and interrelated processes that transform normative affinity-seeking communication into obsessive intrusion and stalking: rumination, emotional flooding, and rationalization. Together, these three mutually reinforcing processes conspire to disinhibit a pursuer's conception of what is appropriate pursuit behavior. Consequently the pursuer's actions are interpreted by the object as excessive, inappropriate, and sometimes threatening. In the sections that follow, we discuss each of these processes.

Rumination

One of the important consequences of failing to make sufficient progress in the pursuit of an important goal is rumination (Millar, Tesser, & Millar, 1988; Martin & Tesser, 1989, 1996a). Rumination refers to the occurrence of repeated, intrusive, aversive thoughts. Virtually everyone has intrusive thoughts, but ruminative thoughts contain an obsessive quality, such that they "are more intense, longer lasting, more insistent, more distressing and more adhesive than the common variety of intrusive thoughts" (Rachman, 1997, p. 793). According to Martin and Tesser (1989; Martin, Tesser, & McIntosh, 1993), the realization that a goal is unmet motivates the individual to cognitively dwell on the goal and its pursuit (called a Zeigarnik effect). In addition, thoughts pertaining to an unattained goal become more easily accessed in memory.

> This accessibility makes it likely that people will detect goal-relevant information in the environment, interpret ambiguous information in terms related to the goal, and experience the motives and emotions associated with pursuit of that goal. The increased accessibility of goal-related concepts also makes it relatively easy for people to process information related to the goal. (Martin & Tesser, 1996a, p. 195)

As a consequence, rumination persists until either the goal is met, or pursuit of the goal is abandoned.

Because rumination stems from a desired state (i.e., goal) that is not achieved, the thoughts are distressing and unpleasant (Carver & Scheier, 1990). The more an individual ruminates about an unmet goal, the more unpleasant and aversive the rumination becomes. With the passage of time, rumination magnifies as repetition of the negative thoughts polarizes them, i.e., the thoughts become even more negative (Tesser, 1978).

Of course, not all unmet goals result in extended rumination. Goals are hierarchically organized, and goals lower on the hierarchy are easily abandoned when barriers thwart their achievement. For example, one could experience considerable sadness about an unrequited love, yet not engage in *obsessive* mulling about the unreciprocated relationship because it is not high in one's overall goal hierarchy. Only goals deemed important, particularly those higher in one's hierarchy of goals, merit rumination and persistent striving in the face of obstacles. *Linking* occurs when an individual believes that a lower-order goal is essential to achieving a higher-order goal. An obsessive pursuer, for example, links the lower-order goal of having a relationship with the object to a higher-order goal, such as life happiness (McIntosh & Martin, 1992) or self-worth (e.g., Pyszczynski & Greenberg, 1987).

Consequently, when the lower-order goal is blocked, the individual ruminates because failure to achieve the lower-order goal prevents achievement of the higher-order goal. Individuals are "very reluctant to give up a goal that promises long-term happiness. They may cling to such goals even in the face of much negative affect" (McIntosh & Martin, 1992, p. 243).

McIntosh and Martin (1992) suggest that "some people are likely to link more goals to happiness than others, and in that sense we can talk about people as linkers and nonlinkers" (p. 233). We propose that some relational pursuers who are rejected do not link the goal to happiness and therefore see the futility of persistence in striving for the relational goal, thus dropping the goal. Other pursuers are linkers, and consequently ruminate more about the desired (but unmet) goal. In other words, pursuers persist because they "link" the lower-order goal of possessing a relationship with the object to a higher-order goal, such as life happiness. Research by McIntosh and colleagues (McIntosh, Harlow, & Martin, 1995; McIntosh & Martin, 1992) demonstrates that linkers generally ruminate more than non-linkers. Moreover, McIntosh and Martin (1992) have shown the effect of linking on rumination specifically with respect to relational goals. They observed:

> Linkers who wanted a romantic relationship ruminated more than did linkers who currently had a romantic relationship. Non-linkers did not vary in how much they ruminated about romantic relationships, however, regardless of whether they currently had one or not. Looked at another way, among people who want but do not have a romantic relationship, linkers ruminated more than non-linkers. (p. 241)

Thus, the general tendency to associate lower-order goals with happiness fosters rumination about *specific* relationship goals that are unmet. Further, we suspect that the linking of a specific relationship goal to happiness (or another high-order goal) will be especially potent in stimulating rumination.

The rumination that occurs when an individual pursues an unreciprocated relationship represents a heightened form of *relationship awareness*, which Acitelli (1992) defines as "a person's thinking about interaction patterns, comparisons, or contrasts between himself or herself and the other partner in the relationship. Included are thoughts about the couple or relationship as an entity" (p. 102). Clearly, when relational pursuers ruminate about the object of pursuit, they focus to some degree on potential, desired, and actual relationship interaction patterns with the object.

In summary, it is proposed that linking leads to rumination, which tends to foster persistent pursuit. Certainly all individuals do not follow this pattern of interaction. However, individuals who tie the importance of a specific relationship to higher-order goals, such as happiness or self-definition, will tend to cognitively dwell on and persist in pursuing that relationship, even in the face of apparent obstacles to the relationship goal. Rumination is absorbing and pre-occupying, and drives the motivation to pursue the relational goal because goal achievement is the only pathway to relief from the distress of rumination. As long as the pursuer clings to the relational goal, rumination intensifies over time, as does the corresponding effort to accomplish the relationship goal. If rumination serves as the engine of pursuit, it is fueled by the concomitant experience of emotional flooding.

Emotional Flooding

Absorbing Negative Affect

We borrow the term "emotional flooding" from Gottman (1994) to describe the sense of feeling swamped by negative emotion. The arousal felt by obsessive pursuers is frequent—indeed ongoing—and absorbing. As we indicated previously, "rumination can lead to negative affect because (a) it is aversive in and of itself and (b) it may cause people to polarize the negative feelings they associate with their failure to attain their goals" (McIntosh & Martin, 1992, p. 228). Rumination is positively associated with depression (McIntosh et al., 1995; Millar et al., 1988; Pyszczynski & Greenberg, 1987), unhappiness (McIntosh & Martin, 1992), and the perpetuation of dysphoric moods (McIntosh, 1996). Furthermore, McIntosh and colleagues (McIntosh & Martin, 1992; McIntosh et al., 1995) found that rumination mediates the connection between linking and these negative states. Thus, rumination results from goal blockage, and in turn, rumination produces negative affect.

The emotional distress of rumination is self-perpetuating. The experience of negative affect leads to an appraisal of the circumstances producing the emotion (Lazarus, 1993). Such appraisals stimulate rumination insofar as they inform the appraiser that an important goal has not been achieved (Martin & Tesser, 1996a, b). In other words, for the relationship pursuer, ongoing negative affect serves as a constant reminder of goal discrepancy, thus further fueling rumination. The pursuer gets trapped in a vicious cycle of absorbing and aversive rumination and affect. Rumination leads to greater negative affect, which in turn increases rumination, and so on, thereby perpetuating persistence in the recovery or development of the desired relationship.

In addition to the general flooding of affect that co-occurs with rumination, we argue that specific emotions play a role in fostering obsessive pursuit. Here we focus on two emotion clusters that are particularly pertinent to obsessive relational pursuit: the cluster of jealousy and possessiveness, and the cluster of guilt, shame, and anger. Although many (if not most) people experience some degree of these emotions in relationships, especially relationships in which rejection has been communicated, the ruminative process may provide a state in which these affects are intensified through cognitive focus and reinforcement. Such intensification, in turn, should assist in both reducing cognitive control of these affective states, as well as providing a ready target for the expression of these emotions.

Jealousy and Possessiveness

Jealousy is a complex set of emotional, cognitive, and behavioral reactions to the apprehension that some rival, typically another person or persons, threatens one's relationship (Guerrero & Andersen, 1998). Jealousy is one of the most common experiences of relational partners, and it produces both positive and negative consequences (Guerrero & Andersen, 1998). Since obsessive pursuers perceive that they are losing a desired or imagined relationship, jealousy accounts for much of the emotional undercurrent of ORI and stalking.[1]

Jealousy is clearly tied to the concept of possessiveness, which "refers to a constellation of attitudes, feelings, and behaviors that seek to initiate and maintain control over the actions of another person in a relationship" (Pinto & Hollandsworth, 1984, p. 273). Posessiveness manifests itself in protective activity intended to encourage a partner's dependency in the relationship (Pinto & Hollandsworth, 1984). Jealousy could easily predispose a person to engage in tactics to take and maintain possession of an object of affection (Spitzberg & Cupach, 1999). This pattern of possessiveness is represented by such characteristics as believing that the partner's friends threaten one's relationship with the partner, discouraging the partner's individual or external interests, and restricting the partner's privacy (Pinto & Hollandsworth, 1984).

A jealous person who perceives, correctly or delusionally, that he/she is in a relationship with another person, is likely to engage in a wide variety of activities, to protect the relationship from actual or potential rivals, including surveillance and guarding, communication with the rival, and signaling possession (Bryson, 1991; Buss, 1988; Guerrero et al., 1995). Many of these activities are similar to stalking behaviors (Spitzberg & Cupach, 1999). When the need to protect the relationship is particularly intense, jealousy often is considered a proximal cause of relational coercion and violence (Barnett, Martinez & Bluestein, 1995; Sugarman & Hotalling, 1989).

Rumination influences the ways in which a jealous person communicatively manages romantic jealousy. Carson and Cupach (1999) found that jealous rumination was positively associated with communicative responses to jealousy, such as spying on the partner, controlling the partner's access to a potential rival, concocting tests of the partner's commitment to the relationship, showing signs of possession of the partner, and attempting to improve the relationship by doing nice things for the partner. In fact, an examination of reported and unreported data from the Carson and Cupach study reveals that rumination was associated with greater use of all types of responses to jealousy (including violent communication) *except* integrative communication. Thus, rumination appears to "motivate a jealous person to step up efforts to solidify and secure the relationship" (Carson & Cupach, 1999, p. 18). Since jealousy can also occur over a past relationship (Buunk & Bringle, 1987), we predict that rumination fosters persistent attempts to restore a terminated but highly desired relationship. In a similar way, rumination may fuel pursuit of an imagined relationship.

Guilt, Shame, and Anger

When the desire for a relationship is not reciprocated, guilt, shame, and anger are among the emotional responses that eventually can occur. These emotional responses may grow out of feelings of jealousy, feelings of abandonment, or the realization that previously enacted pursuit behaviors were inappropriate. Shame and guilt are similar constructs in that they both are moral emotions; however Lewis (1971) differentiates between the two as follows:

> The experience of shame is directly about the *self*, which is the focus of evaluation. In guilt, the self is not the central object of negative evaluation, but rather the *thing* done or undone is the focus. In guilt, the self is negatively evaluated in connection with something but is not itself the focus of the experience. (p. 30)

Guilt is not as strong an emotion as shame, but it may spur an individual to persistent pursuit behaviors. Pursuers who are rejected may feel that they have transgressed against the object, either by being too persistent, or by thinking that they did not work hard enough to earn the object's reciprocation. Those who experience guilt "often report a nagging focus or preoccupation with the transgression—thinking of it over and over, wishing they had behaved differently and could somehow undo the deed" (Tangney, 1995, p. 1135). Guilt, therefore, is yet another source of potentially debilitating rumination. Although guilt tends to be a healthier emotion than shame, focusing on the behavior instead of the self (Tangney, 1995), the preoccupation with the "transgression" and "a desire to ... repair the damage that was done" (Tangney, 1995, p. 1138) may lead the individual to become obsessed with reinstating/creating a relationship with the object of affection. Thus, obsession becomes manifested when rejection leads to guilt, which motivates attempts to repair or restore the relationship, which leads to more rejection, leading to more guilt, and so forth. The degree of persistence is a function of linking and rumination that co-occur with the guilt. The potential for aggressiveness in pursuit, however, is much greater when the rejected pursuer experiences shame rather than guilt.

Shame tends to be a more painful and severe emotion than guilt (Tangney, 1995). Retzinger (1995) proposes two types of shame: *overt shame,* which may cause people to "feel paralyzed, helpless, passive, childish, out of control of the situation" (p. 1106), and *covert shame*, which might cause individuals to "function poorly as agents or perceivers" and where "thoughts, speech, or perception may be obsessive or overly rigid" (p. 1106). Further, Retzinger (1991) proposes that shame is a direct product of rejection by a valued other. "Threat or damage to social bonds (e.g., unrequited love, loss of face, rebuke, unworthiness in the eyes of others) is the primary context for shame; shame follows directly from separation, which then often leads to angry conflict or silent impasse" (p. 55). By definition, such rejection is likely to be experienced by pursuers in all cases of stalking and ORI.

Corresponding to the two types of shame, there are two ways of managing shame: withdrawal (similar to overt shame), and anger at others (similar to covert shame) (Tangney et al., 1996). Those individuals who experience shame and withdraw are less likely to engage in ORI behaviors, while those who experience shame coupled with anger are more likely to engage in hostile or violent actions. Individuals who feel shame are less likely to be concerned about the other's pain or hurt (Tangney, 1995). Shame coupled with anger can lead to defensive retaliation against the object, who is blamed by the pursuer for causing the feeling of shame (Lewis, 1971). The hostility directed at self for failure is redirected toward the object in an effort to compensate for the damaged sense of self that the pursuer experiences. At this point, the initial goal of having a relationship with the object is displaced by the goal of revenge against the object. In a sense, the menacing behaviors of a shamed and angry pursuer maintain a type of relationship with the object by exerting some "control" over the object's life.

Individuals who possess the propensity to experience shame may be particularly susceptible to expressing anger when a relational goal cannot be met. Tangney et al. (1992) found that "Shame-proneness was consistently positively correlated with anger arousal, suspiciousness, resentment, irritability, a tendency to blame others for negative events, and indirect (but not direct) expressions of hostility" (p. 673). In keeping with these findings, another study showed that shame-proneness "was associated with maladaptive and unconstructive responses to anger" (Tangney et al., 1996, p. 806). Those who feel shame and anger about their inability to have a relationship with the person they desire are more likely to engage in hostile, even violent, communication with the desired partner.

Rationalization

Rationalizations made by individuals pursuing unreciprocated relationships co-occur with rumination and emotional flooding. These rationalizations pertain to perceptions regarding the object and the object's behavior, as well as the pursuer's own behavior. Rationalizations contribute to the overall development of the pursuer's disinhibition with regard to obsessive pursuit. As a counterbalance to the increasingly aggressive and inappropriate communication directed at the object, the pursuer rationalizes the "normalcy" of escalating pursuit.

To begin with, obsessive pursuers construct and preserve, at least for a time, a rose-colored view of the object of pursuit. The object is highly idealized by the pursuer, who distorts perceptions about the object in a positive direction. In this way, the obsessive pursuer acquires some of the qualities of a limerant lover. As Tennov (1979) explains, limerant lovers show "a remarkable ability to emphasize what is truly admirable in [the object of affection] and to avoid dwelling on the negative, even to respond with a compassion for the negative and render it, emotionally if not perceptually, into another positive attribute" (p. 24). Ironically, even when an object of pursuit withholds expression of positive sentiment towards the pursuer in an effort to discourage pursuit, the pursuer focuses on positive qualities of the object, thus reinforcing the relational goal and heightened efforts to communicate with the object.

Not only is the object seen in the most flattering light, but also the object's behavior is distorted to show signs of encouragement for the potential relationship. Similar to limerant lovers, pursuers possess an "acute sensitivity to any act or thought or condition that can be interpreted favorably, and an extraordinary ability to devise or invent 'reasonable' explanations for why the neutrality that the disinterested observer might see is in fact a sign of hidden passion" in the object of affection (Tennov, 1979, p. 24). Despite the object's desire to avoid a relationship with the pursuer, the object's behavior is seen by the pursuer as communicating reciprocal interest.

This cognitive tendency to observe reinforcement or encouragement by the object, even in its absence, extends to the pursuer's misconstrual of rejection by the object. Emerson et al. (1998) explain that: "... most relational rejections are delivered in ways that offer the proposer at least some opportunity to save face. Thus, it may well be that persistence trades on ignoring the rejecting message being conveyed, or submerging the negative content of the communication in favor of its civil, face-saving form" (p. 306). Indeed, the indirectness of rejection is often misinterpreted by the pursuer as a sign of affection and encouragement (Bratslavsky et al., 1998; de Becker, 1997).

Pursuers who are particularly persistent may be especially inclined to rationalize the appropriateness of their behavior by drawing on cultural scripts that seem to represent normative practices to the pursuer, but in actuality represent an exaggerated caricature of courtship communication. Feminist and cultural analyses of courtship (e.g., Holland & Eisenhart, 1990) suggest that persistence, especially male persistence, is strongly reinforced by media typifications and cultural rules of courtship. For example, Bratslavsky et al. (1998) contend that "Movies, books, and songs often portray the would-be lover's persistence as paying off when the rejector comes to his or her senses and recognizes the would-be lover for the wonderful person he or she is" (p. 251). If ambiguity is a key component of flirtation (Sabini & Silver, 1982), and initial resistance is a way of preserving an image of selectivity and desirability, then a pursuer's persistent communication with the desired relational partner is a rational strategy to overcome this initial resistance.

Furthermore, a double standard is considered still in force, in which males are expected to pursue sex *qua* sex, whereas females are expected to pursue sex *qua* relationship (Metts & Spitzberg, 1996). Consequently, females are cast in the role of "gatekeeper", in which they specialize in tactics of resisting male tactics of romantic (i.e., sexual) pursuit. This role reinforces the desire to appear selective, which is, in turn, read by males as token resistance to the presumed inevitable outcome of romantic congress. In such a cultural archetype, male persistence is viewed not only as normative, but also as one of the only available tactics for overcoming the expected resistance of women to men's romantic advances. In this light, stalking by men is merely a somewhat extreme extension of normative courtship practices, and the line between the two becomes significantly blurred in the minds of obsessive pursuers. This may explain why Tjaden and Thoennes (1998) found that approximately 87% of stalkers are men and about 80% of stalking victims are women.

As pursuit escalates to the point of menacing harassment, the overly zealous pursuer further rationalizes persistence by downplaying the negative consequences of pursuit behavior for the object. The pursuer exonerates him/herself from blameworthiness because pursuit is justified "in the name of love" (Bratslavsky et al., 1998). The pursuer's "honorable intentions" prevent the pursuer from realizing how aversive and potentially threatening the pursuit behaviors are to the object. Even when a pursuer is overtly accused of being excessive, systematic self-serving biases are reflected in accounts offered regarding the persistence of pursuit. Research by Stillwell and Baumeister (1997) indicates that individuals cast in the role of perpetrator (e.g., of a relational transgression) highlight the benevolence of their actions while downplaying the negative consequences for the victim and ignoring responsibility for the victim's woes.

SUMMARY AND IMPLICATIONS

The study of communication in relationships has traditionally focused primarily on people with the mutual intention of pursuing a relationship. However, there is a class of relationships in which one person persists in attempts at communication to establish a relationship that the object of this pursuit clearly wants to avoid altogether. This is the domain of stalking and obsessive relational intrusion. Thus far, theory and research relevant to these phenomena have derived almost entirely from the clinical literature, which tends to emphasize childhood etiology, taxonomic distinctions in types of underlying disorder, and a relative lack of attention to affective and interactional characteristics of the process of pursuit. In this chapter, we have attempted to develop the outline of a theory of stalking and obsessive relational intrusion. The resulting framework proposes that disjunctive relationships of this type are the product of the pursuer linking the goal of a relationship with the object to a higher-order goal, such as happiness. Ongoing ruminative and rationalizing processes that maintain the cognitive salience of the object of attraction mutually reinforce this linking. As the object inevitably rejects the increasingly obsessed pursuer, emotional flooding fuels the very nature of the obsession.

Obsessive thought and overwhelming affect typically translate into obsessive pursuit. Rumination and emotional agitation spur the relationship pursuer to interact with the object in order to bring relationship definitions into alignment. Initially, the communication between pursuer and object reflects the common and accepted everyday workings of relationship negotiation. The intensity of efforts by the pursuer escalates gradually over time. At some point, a point often difficult to specify, the pursuer's attempts to relate to the object persist, even in the face of clear and multiple rejections. Such persistence is preoccupying and obsessive for the pursuer, and distressing and creepy for the object. When patterns of repeated suveillance, threatening messages, and/or violence occur, ORI has escalated to stalking.

The primary advantage of this theoretical model is that it suggests cognitive and emotional processes underlying *all* cases of obsessive relational intrusion, regardless of original developmental pathways through which a person ultimately reaches the position of unwanted pursuit. A thorough understanding of these processes provides the possibility of insight that eventually may direct more productive avenues of intervention and prevention. In particular, if rumination, flooding, and rationalization have direct correlates in a person's discourse and behavior, a reliable profile may be refined, such that potential partners can ascertain their risk long before the obsession becomes fixed in the pursuer's mind. Finally, such a theory provides one of the few attempts at conceptualizing disjunctive relational processes. The understanding of such processes is essential if the "dark side" of relationships and communication is to be integrated into a comprehensive theory of human experience (Duck, 1994b; Spitzberg & Cupach, 1998).

ACKNOWLEDGMENTS

The authors gratefully acknowledge the constructive input on this chapter provided by Kathryn Dindia and Steve Duck.

---

[1] It could be argued that envy, which is closely connected to jealousy, is also relevant to some cases of ORI. Envy pertains to wanting something that one does not have. We have chosen to focus on jealousy, however, because: (1) jealousy is typically considered to be a broader concept than envy; (2) individuals usually experience jealousy as a stronger emotion than envy; and (3) envy focuses more on competition with (and resentment toward) a rival, rather than protection of a relationship (see Guerrero & Anderson, 1998).

as well as SD as relational communication, have been virtually ignored in the personal relationships literature.

Although others since Pearce and Sharp have argued that SD is a transactional process, theory and research on SD in personal relationships has been relatively unaffected by this view and predominantly reflects a static, linear, one-way, cause–effect view of SD. For example, three types of *effects* have been consistently studied in the literature on SD and relationships: reciprocity of SD, SD and liking, and SD and relationship development (Berg & Derlega, 1987). Research on reciprocity of SD typically examines the effect of one person's SD on another person's SD, rather than viewing SD as *mutually* interdependent (Dindia, 1994). Research on SD and liking has studied three effects: (1) do we like others who disclose to us?; (2) do we disclose more to people we like?; (3) and do we like people as a result of disclosing to them? (Collins and Miller, 1994). SD is the independent variable for the first and third effects; SD is the dependent variable for the second effect. Research on SD and relationship development examines the one-way effect of SD on relationship development. Longitudinal studies of SD and relationship development are rare (Taylor & Altman, 1987); typically, cross-sectional comparisons of SD are made between relationships at different stages of development, with SD treated as the independent variable and relationship development as the dependent variable (for a review of this research, see Taylor & Altman, 1987).

There is some research on SD in personal relationships that begins to examine the process of SD. Time-series analysis of conversational sequences (Dindia, 1982, 1984; Spencer, 1993c) and ethnography of natural conversation (Spencer, 1993b) have been used to examine short conversational sequences centering around SD. In particular, these studies focus on the comments occurring directly before and after SD. However, these studies implicitly assume that SD is a one-time event occurring within the confines of a single conversation, typically within a single utterance. Research by Van Lear (1987) examines the process of SD across six conversations between zero-history dyads. This study identifies patterns of SD across conversations, including changes in levels of SD and reciprocity of SD. However, all of these studies make the "act" the unit of analysis.

Self-disclosure as a Dialectical Process

Relational dialectics subsumes all the assumptions of a transactional perspective (i.e., process, interdependence, contextual embeddedness; see Baxter & Montgomery, this volume, for elaboration of these assumptions from a dialectical perspective) but adds the unique and fundamental assumption of a dialectical perspective, contradiction. According to a dialectical perspective, relationships are viewed as involving contradictory and opposing forces (Baxter, 1988; Baxter & Montgomery, this volume, 1996; Montgomery, 1993; Montgomery & Baxter, 1998).

Several theorists have posited openness–closedness as a dialectical tension in relationships (cf., Altman, Vinsel, & Brown, 1981; Baxter, 1988; Rawlins, 1983b). According to this perspective, individuals continually face the contradictory impulses to be open and expressive vs. protective of self and/or other. Self-disclosure is necessary to achieve intimacy, but SD opens areas of vulnerability. To avoid hurting each other, people must undertake protective measures (Rawlins, 1983b). Thus, the contradictory tension between information openness and information closedness requires decisions to reveal or conceal personal information (Rawlins, 1983b).

Although a number of theorists and researchers have recently argued that SD is a dialectical process, there is little research examining SD from a dialectical perspective; in addition, some of the research that does exist still studies SD as a static phenomenon (e.g., Baxter & Simon, 1993). However, some research on SD in personal relationships examines SD from a dialectical perspective. For instance, Rawlins's (1983b) research on the dialectics of SD in friendships elaborates and illustrates the contradictory impulses between expressiveness and protectiveness in conversations between friends. Rawlins's definition of SD included revealing personal aspects of oneself to another as well as commenting about another's individual qualities. Rawlins interviewed 10 pairs of close friends, eliciting their subjective interpretation of their ongoing interaction, and then conducted an interpretative analysis of the transcribed interviews. Rawlins found two conversational dilemmas resulting from the contradictory impulses to be open and expressive vs. protective of self and/or of other. In deciding whether to disclose information regarding self, an individual confronts the contradictory dilemma of protecting self by restricting personal disclosure and of striving to be open by confiding in the other. Disclosing personal information to another makes one susceptible to being hurt by the other. The decision to self-disclose will be a function of at least two things: an individual's need to be open about a given issue, and the individual's trust of the partner's discretion (his/her ability to keep a secret and exercise restraint regarding self's sensitivities). The decision to reveal or conceal involves assessing what will be gained or lost by either choice (Rawlins, 1983b).

In deciding whether to disclose information regarding the partner, an individual confronts the contradictory dilemma of protecting the partner by restricting negative feedback and of striving to be open and honest to build trust in the relationship. The decision to disclose information regarding the other will be a function of the self's need to be open and honest about a given issue and the amount of restraint appropriate to the topic. An individual develops an awareness of topics which make the other vulnerable to hurt or anger. In particular, *"self must determine whether telling the truth is worth causing the other pain and breaching the other's trust in self's protective inclinations"* [emphasis in original] (Rawlins, 1983b).

Privacy Regulation as a Dialectical Strategy

Several scholars (Altman, 1975; Derlega & Chaikin, 1977; Petronio, 1988, 1991) view SD as a privacy regulation mechanism. Altman (1975) defined privacy as:

> ...an interpersonal boundary process by which a person or group regulates interaction with others. By altering the degree of openness of the self to others, a hypothetical personal boundary is more or less receptive to social interaction with others. Privacy is, therefore, a dynamic process involving selective control over a self-boundary, either by an individual or by a group (p. 6).

Communication boundary management theory (CBMT) (Petronio, 1988, 1991) extends Altman's privacy regulation theory and more specifically relates it to SD. CBMT argues that individuals manage their communication boundaries in balancing the need for disclosure with the need for privacy. The basic thesis of CBMT is that revealing private information is risky because one is potentially vulnerable when revealing aspects of the self. Receiving private information from another may also result in the need to protect oneself. To manage both disclosing and receiving private information, individuals erect a metaphoric boundary as a means of protection and to reduce the possibility of being rejected or getting hurt (Petronio, 1991).

Three assumptions underlie CBMT. First, individuals erect boundaries to control autonomy and vulnerability when disclosing and receiving private information. Second, because disclosing and receiving private information is risky and may cause potential vulnerability, partners regulate their communication boundaries strategically to minimize risks. Third, decision-making rules are used to determine when, with whom, and how much private information is disclosed, as well as how to respond to the disclosure (Petronio, 1991).

Privacy regulation and communication boundary management have been proposed as theories of SD. However, I view privacy regulation/communication boundary management as strategic responses to the dialectical tension of the need to reveal and conceal. By regulating privacy (or managing communication boundaries), individuals employ a strategy designed to satisfy the oppositional forces of openness–closedness. By setting a hypothetical boundary, individuals designate some things as appropriate for disclosure and some things as inappropriate for disclosure. This strategy is similar to Baxter's (1988) "segmentation" strategy, which differentiates topic domains into those for which SD is regarded as appropriate and those for which SD is regarded as inappropriate (i.e., taboo topics). In studying the existence of, and response to, dialectical tensions in relationships, Baxter (1990) found that the most dominant strategy reported for the openness–closedness contradiction was segmentation. The difference between Baxter's segmentation strategy and privacy regulation, viewed as a dialectical strategy, is that segmentation is conceived of as a static strategy, whereas privacy regulation is conceived of as a fluid process.

Disclosure of Stigmatized Identities

Theory and research on disclosure of stigmatized identities, such as sexual abuse, homosexuality, HIV antibodies, and AIDS, illustrates the principles of SD from a dialectical perspective (for a more comprehensive review of this literature, see Dindia, 1998). Although this research lies outside the field of personal relationships, it provides examples for personal relationships researchers of how SD can be conceptualized and studied as a process.

The process perspective is not evident in all of the literature on disclosure of stigmatized identities. Some of the research on disclosure of stigmatized identities invokes the "SD as action or event" perspective. For example, several researchers have examined the strategies used to disclose stigmatized identities and the outcomes of such disclosure (cf., Edgar, 1994). Others have assessed how, when, where, why, and to whom gays and lesbians disclose their sexual orientation (Wells & Kline, 1987). The research I will review conceives of, and studies, disclosure of stigmatized identities as a dialectical process.

The term "stigma" refers to a stable characteristic of an individual that is perceived as damaging to the individual's image or reputation. Stigmas include, but are not limited to, physical disability, membership in some stigmatized group, character defects, which are manifested by some discrediting event in the person's past or present, and disease. Goffman (1974) differentiated those who are stigmatized into the "discredited" and the "discreditable". The discredited is one whose stigma is already known about or is immediately perceivable by others. The problem for the discredited is managing tension generated during mixed social contacts (i.e., contacts with "normals"). The discreditable is one whose stigma is not known about or immediately perceivable by others. Thus, the major problem for the discreditable is information control, or the management of undisclosed discrediting information about self:

> To display or not to display; to tell or not to tell; to let on or not to let on; to lie or not to lie; and in each case, to whom, how, when, and where (Goffman, 1974, p. 42).

Theory and research on the disclosure of stigmatized identities is not limited to disclosure of homosexuality, sexual abuse, AIDS, etc., but is generalizable to SD of intimate, negative, and risky information in general. As Goffman (1974) pointed out, the problem of stigma control is not a case of a few who are stigmatized and the majority who are not:

> Stigma management is a general feature of society, a process occurring wherever there are identity norms. The same features are involved whether a major differentness is at question, of the kind traditionally defined as stigmatic, or a picayune differentness, of which the ashamed person is ashamed to be ashamed (p. 130).

All people suffer some discrepancy between their virtual identity and their actual identity and thus are faced with the problem of identity management and must make decisions regarding SD (Goffman, 1974).

Research on the disclosure of stigmatized identities employs interview and observational methods to elicit conversational sequences of SD, which extend across a particular conversation, to multiple conversations, and sometimes to the life-long process of SD. Limandri (1989) studied the process of disclosure of stigmatizing identities from the perspective of the discloser. Limandri conducted a qualitative analysis of 29 interviews of disclosure of women's abuse, AIDS, or HIV antibodies, and herpes. Limandri found that SD is a process, not an event:

> On the surface, disclosure seemed to be a dichotomous variable composed of disclosure or concealment. However, with further examination of the interviews, there appeared to be smaller categories of disclosure ... there seemed to be an unlayering process to disclosure (Limandri, 1989, p. 73).

Similarly, Dindia and Tieu (1996) studied disclosure of homosexuality. Fifteen gays and lesbians were interviewed about their "coming out" story. A qualitative analysis of the results indicated that disclosure of homosexuality, or "coming out," is not a single, dichotomous event in which the person has disclosed or has not disclosed (i.e., is out of the closet or is not out of the closet). As stated by one of their study participants: "I ... am in the process of coming out ... When you say, 'heh, I'm gay', that's the beginning. Yeah, coming out to yourself and then slowly coming out to other people as well". Another participant said, "I think it [disclosure of homosexuality] occurs in increments". He reported disclosing to a male friend, a female friend, his sister, another female friend, and his mother, in an incremental process over a 20 year period. Another respondent spoke of going through stages of disclosure: (1) if asked would lie; (2) if asked would say nothing; (3) "if someone asked I wouldn't deny it but I don't wear a sign".

MacFarlane and Krebs (1986) described the process of children's disclosure of sexual abuse as the "no–maybe–sometimes–yes" syndrome. They frequently observed children who initially said "no" without any qualifications to an inquiry of abuse, who later acknowledged that "maybe it happened sometimes", and who finally fully revealed sexual abuse.

SD of stigmatized identities often involves a process of "testing the waters", in which the discloser tests the reaction of the recipient before self-disclosing in more detail (Miell, 1984). Limandri (1989) found that disclosure of stigmatizing conditions usually begins with a small revelation to test the environment. MacFarlane and Krebs (1986) state that children frequently tell what happened to them in small pieces, saving the worst part until they see how the recipient reacts to the things they disclose first. Spencer and Derlega (1995) report that because many people are afraid of those who are HIV-positive, disclosure of HIV antibodies requires the discloser to investigate the attitudes of a potential recipient before disclosing HIV status. Spencer and Derlega provide the following example from one of their study respondents:

> I was dating someone not too long ago, went out, was asked out. I didn't tell them right at that point. The way I handled it on the first date, I steered the conversation around to AIDS-related topics; because of my own volunteer work, I was able to do that—start talking about them and seeing what their reaction was. Were they going to try to change the subject, were they uncomfortable, or were they comfortable and compassionate with the whole thing? That was it for the first time, and the second time I brought it up again. I brought up that a former lover of mine had recently tested positive, which he had. Which sort of puts it into their mind that I probably would be, too, and if they were horrified, well that was it and I wouldn't see them again. If that went fine, then the next time it was, "Yes, I have tested positive myself" ... But that's the way I do it; just sort of a gradual thing, test the waters a bit, not just jump right in it, telling them and scaring them to death (p. 4).

However, SD doesn't necessarily move from non-disclosure to disclosure in a linear fashion. In studying the process of disclosure of stigmatized identities, Limandri (1989) found that some would conceal for a while, disclose, then retract back into concealment:

> This [deciding whether to tell or to conceal] is not a simple decision or a decision that is made only once, but rather the process simulated a swinging gate or valve that could be completely open, completely closed, or partially open ... disclosure occurs many more times than once ... people can retract their disclosure at times, and ... the process can expand and contract over time (Limandri, 1989, p. 76).

Similarly, several of the participants in Dindia and Tieu's (1996) study described a circular process of disclosure, in which they revealed, then concealed, then revealed homosexuality to others. One participant described the process this way: "Coming out for me has basically moved from wanting to tell everybody, to not wanting to tell anybody, to kind of going in between those two". Participants in Dindia and Tieu's (1996) study also reported the need to establish a balance between the two extremes of total concealment and total disclosure. As stated by one of the participants:

> I know that I've had to find a sense of equilibrium. I don't feel comfortable wearing a sign that says, "I'm gay"..... But I am becoming less tolerant, as time goes on, with the "game playing" that I did in my own head for a lot of years.

Summit (1983), in discussing child sexual abuse, states that whatever a child says about sexual abuse, he/she is likely to reverse it. Summit refers to disclosure—retraction as being the "normal" course of children's disclosure of sexual abuse.

Sorenson and Snow (1991) studied 630 cases of alleged child sexual abuse in which the authors had been involved as therapists and/or evaluators. Qualitative analysis of clinical notes, conversations, audio- and videotapes, and reports revealed four progressive phases to the process of children's disclosure of sexual abuse: denial, disclosure (which contains two sub-phases, tentative disclosure and active disclosure), recantation, and reaffirmation. *Denial* is defined as the child's initial statement to any individual that he/she had not been sexually abused. *Tentative disclosure* refers to the child's partial, vague, or vacillating acknowledgment of sexual abuse. *Active disclosure* refers to a personal admission by the child of having been sexually abused. *Recantation* refers to the child's retraction of a previous allegation of abuse. *Reaffirmation* is defined as the child's reassertion of the validity of a previous assertion of sexual abuse that had been recanted. According to this model, children typically begin by denying that they have been sexually abused and this is followed by tentative, then active, disclosure. Some children recant and later reaffirm sexual abuse.

Sorensen and Snow (1991) tested their model of the disclosure process in a qualitative analysis of 116 case studies involving sexually abused children from three to 17 years of age who were eventually confirmed as credible victims. The results were that 72% of the children initially denied having been sexually abused. Denial was most common when (a) children were initially questioned by a concerned parent or adult authority figure, and (b) when children were identified as potential victims and initially questioned in a formal investigative interview. Tentative disclosure was the common middle stage for the majority of these children (78%), with only 7% of the children who denied moving directly to active disclosure. Active disclosure, a detailed, coherent, first-person account of the abuse, was eventually made by 96% of the children (including children who originally did not deny having been sexually abused). In approximately 22% of these cases, children recanted their allegations; of those who recanted, 92% reaffirmed their allegations of abuse over time. The results of these studies provide evidence that SD does not necessarily move from non-disclosure to disclosure in a linear fashion, and instead indicates that individuals may reveal, then conceal, then reveal in a circular manner.

A central aspect of a dialectical process of SD is that it takes place over time. Sorenson and Snow (1991) found that the time frame involved in the progression through the stages of SD (denial, tentative disclosure, active disclosure, recantation, full disclosure) was unique to each case. Some children moved from denial to tentative disclosure to active disclosure in a single session; others took several months to reach the active phase.

The process of SD of stigmatized identities is ongoing and continues throughout the lifespan of individuals and relationships. You can never fully reveal yourself (e.g., you are never totally out of the closet). Research on disclosure of stigmatizing identities has found that disclosure of stigmatizing identities continued as long as the person had the stigmatized condition (Limandri, 1989). Similarly, "coming out" is a lifelong process for gays and lesbians (Herdt and Boxer, 1992; Mazanec, 1995). As stated by one of Dindia and Tieu's (1996) study participants:

> I'm not certain whether anybody really can ["come out"] …. You can "come out" to all your friends and family and such, but then you can do things like move to a more conservative area and that creates a whole new issue. You can acquire new friends and depending upon how they are it creates new issues …. When I moved to the Canyon … I ended up … back in the closet. The minute you step there … you're essentially "back in". You can think of yourself, as far as I'm concerned, back in the closet every time you enter a new room. Okay? … There's a whole new process of coming out again as you count the ranks (p. 18).

Although there is no research that examines SD over the lifespan, there is research which examines the role of SD in the development of a stigmatized identity. Goffman (1974) referred to the similar "moral career" of persons who have a particular stigma, arguing that these people tend to have similar learning experiences regarding their stigma and go through similar changes in self-concept; thus, they go through a similar sequence of personal adjustments. For Goffman, in the first phase of this process the stigmatized person learns and incorporates the standpoint of society regarding the particular stigma. In the second phase, the person learns that he/she possesses a particular stigma and the consequences of possessing it. Learning to "pass" or conceal the stigma constitutes the third phase in the socialization of the stigmatized person. In the fourth phase, the stigmatized individual "can come to feel that he should be above passing, that if he accepts himself and respects himself he will feel no need to conceal his failing" (Goffman, 1974, p. 101). It is here that SD fits into the moral career.

Similarly, SD is conceived as one of the phases in the "coming out" process. Coming out, in popular American culture, refers to public disclosure of a gay or bisexual identity. However, in the scholarly literature, "coming out" refers to the larger developmental process of acquiring a gay identity, of which disclosure of gay identity, is only a part (Paradis, 1991). A number of models of coming out have been advanced (cf. Berzon, 1992; Cass, 1979; Coleman, 1982; Mazanec, 1995; Plummer, 1975). In these various models, disclosure of gay identity is typically a stage of the coming-out process. For example, Coleman (1982) describes a five-stage model; "coming out" is the second stage, during which individuals begin the process of SD to others. Berzon (1992) describes a turning point process, in which disclosure to a non-gay person is the third turning point and disclosure to family, friends, and co-workers is the seventh and final turning point.

Disclosure of stigmatized identity is typically viewed as a developmental task in the process of gay identity development (Coleman, 1982). Wells and Kline (1987) state that "prerequisite to the emergence of a positive homosexual identity is the communication of one's sexual orientation to significant others". According to this perspective, SD to accepting individuals is paramount in affecting positive identity development (Wells and Kline, 1987). The function of SD is self-acceptance:

> Recognizing the need for external validation, individuals risk disclosure to others in hope that they will not be rejected. This is a very critical point, for the confidants' reaction can have a powerful impact. If negative, it can confirm all the old negative impressions and can put a seal on a previous low self-concept. If positive, the reactions can start to counteract some of the old perceived negative feelings, permitting individuals to begin to accept their sexual feelings and increase their self-esteem (Coleman, 1982, p. 34).

Although the term "dialectics" is not used in the literature on the disclosure of stigmatized identities, these researchers are positing disclosure of stigmatizing identities as a dialectical process. In particular, the circular nature of SD is hypothesized to be the result of the dialectical tension between the needs to reveal and to conceal. Limandri (1989), in the study of disclosure of women's abuse, AIDS/HIV and herpes, states that informants in her sample "were confronted with the need to tell or to conceal" (p. 76). Dindia and Tieu (1996) also reported that participants struggled with the dialectical tension of whether to reveal or conceal homosexuality. As stated by one of the study participants:

"I'm really struggling with this [who to tell] for about the past year .... I want to tell—hard to lie—hate to lie. Something pulls the other way [not telling], I don't know what."

Similarly, Gershman (1983) described the "Catch 22" of disclosure of homosexuality: one experiences anxiety in disclosing one's true feelings, yet failure to disclose engenders the anxiety of not being oneself. Gard (1990) argued that disclosure of HIV infection to parents may also involve a similar Catch 22.

According to Limandri (1989), the dialectical process of disclosure of stigmatized identities is due to the fact that stigmatizing conditions contribute to feelings of shame and the wish to conceal or hide; however, those who experience such conditions often need to confide in others and seek help from professionals. Marks et al. (1992) explain:

> One may feel the need to inform a significant other for purposes of support but may fear rejection from that person. Similarly, one may feel an ethical obligation to inform medical providers (e.g., dentists) but may simultaneously fear that disclosure will result in refusal of services (p. 300).

Research on the disclosure of stigmatized identities also provides evidence of privacy regulation/communication boundary management as strategic responses to the dialectical nature of SD. Because disclosing stigmatized identities is risky and may cause potential vulnerability, partners regulate their communication boundaries strategically to minimize risks. Decision rules are used to determine to whom, how much, when, where and why to disclose. For example, Limandri (1989) found that her subjects considered the costs and rewards of disclosing their stigma. Specifically, to decide whether to disclose, subjects tried to anticipate how the other person would respond. If the anticipated response was negative, the discloser might decide not to risk SD. Similarly, Marks et al. (1992) argued that disclosure of HIV infection is a reasoned action that follows from the perceived social, psychological, and material consequences of informing others. People with a stigma evaluate the consequences of informing a particular target person before a disclosure is made. Further, the factors considered in deciding whether to disclose to a particular person (e.g., a parent) differ from the factors considered in deciding whether to disclose to another target (e.g., a sexual partner). Siegel and Krauss (1991) found four considerations that influenced whom individuals told they were HIV-positive: (1) fear of rejection; (2) the wish to avoid the pity of others; (3) the wish to spare loved ones emotional pain; and (4) concerns about discrimination. Dindia (1998) describes a number of commonly used strategies to regulate disclosure of stigmatized identity.

CONCLUSION

SD is not a dichotomous event defined by whether the person has disclosed (e.g., is out of the closet) or has not disclosed (e.g., is not out of the closet). Instead, SD is an ongoing process that is extended in time and is open-ended, not only across the course of an interaction or series of interactions, but also across the lives of individuals as their identities develop/unfold, and across the life of a relationship as it evolves. The process of SD is circular; SD does not necessarily move from non-disclosure to disclosure in a linear fashion. The end state of this process is not full disclosure. Although some theorists argue that the ideal end state is full disclosure (e.g., it is often argued in the gay literature that you should come out of the closet; similarly, Jourard (1971) argued that to be healthy one must disclose oneself), this is not realistic, given the inherent risk involved in the disclosure of intimate information. Additionally, full disclosure (or total concealment) is impossible from a dialectical perspective (see Baxter & Montgomery, this volume). SD is contextual and is embedded in the larger processes of self-identity and relationship development. The process of SD is interdependent with processes of self-identity and relationship development. Who we are as individuals, as well as who we are in relationship to each other, affect and are affected by SD. Finally, the process of SD is inherently dialectical; disclosure is governed by the dialectical tension between the need to reveal and the need to conceal. Privacy regulation or communication boundary management is the fluid mechanism for responding to this dialectical tension.

The dialectical perspective on SD has important ramifications for theory and research on SD in personal relationships. SD can not be conceptualized as a one-time event. Personal relationships researchers need to examine the ongoing conversational patterns of SD over time within real-life relationships. Hopefully, by reviewing research on disclosure of stigmatized identities, personal relationships researchers will see how SD can be conceived of and studied as a process.

ACKNOWLEDGMENTS

The author would like to thank Steve Duck, Robert McPhee, and Jack Johnson for their feedback on earlier drafts of this chapter.

REFERENCES

Acitelli, L. K. (1988)   When spouses talk to each other about their relationship. *Journal of Social and Personal Relationships*, **5**, 185–199.

Acitelli, L. K. (1992)   Gender differences in relationship awareness and marital satisfaction among young married couples. *Personality and Social Psychology Bulletin*, **18**, 102–110.

Acitelli, L. K. (1993)   You, me, and us: Perspectives on relationship awareness. In S. W. Duck (Ed.) *Individuals in relationships* (Understanding relationship processes 1): (pp. 144–174). Newbury Park: Sage.

Acitelli, L. K. (1997)   Sampling couples to understand them: Mixing the theoretical with the practical. *Journal of Social and Personal Relationships*, **14**, 243–261.

Ackerman, C. (1963)   Affiliations: Structural determination of differential divorce rates, *American Sociological Review*, **69**, 13–20.

Adams, R. G.(1985)   People would talk: Normative barriers to cross-sex friendships for elderly women. *The Gerontologist*, **25**, 605–611.

Adler, M. J. (1927)   *Dialectic*. New York: Harcourt.

Adler, M. J. (1952)   (Ed.). *The great ideas: A synopticon of great books of the Western world*. Chicago: Encyclopaedia Britannica.

Adler, R. H., Zamboni, P., Hofer, T., Hemmeler, W., Hurny, C., Minder, C., Radvila, A., & Zlot, S.I. (1997)   How not to miss a somatic needle in a haystack of chronic pain. *Journal of Psychosomatic Research*, **42**, 499–506.

Ahrons, C. R., & Rodgers, R. H. (1987)   *Divorced families: A multidisciplinary developmental view*. New York: W. W. Norton.

Ainsworth, M. D. S. (1989)   Attachments beyond infancy. *American Psychologist*, **44**, 709–716.

Ainsworth, M. D. S. (1991)   Attachments and other affectional bonds across the life cycle. In C. M. Parkes, J. Stevenson-Hinde & P. Marris (Eds) *Attachment across the life cycle* (pp. 33–51). New York: Routledge.

Ainsworth, M. D. S., Blehar, M. C., Waters, E., & Wall, S. (1978)   *Patterns of attachment: A psychological study of the strange situation*. Hillsdale, NJ: Erlbaum.

Alberts, J. K. (1988)   An analysis of couples conversational complaints. *Communication Monographs*, **55**, 184–197.

Alberts, J. K., & Driscoll, G. (1992)   Containment versus escalation: The trajectory of couples' conversation complaints. *Western Journal of Communication*, **56**, 394–412.

Altman, I. (1975) *The environment and social behavior: Privacy, personal space, territory, and crowding.* Belmont, CA: Wadsworth.

Altman, I. (1977) Research on environment and behavior: A personal statement of strategy. In D. Stokols (Ed.) *Psychological perspectives on environment and behavior: Conceptual and empirical trends* (pp. 303–323). New York: Plenum.

Altman, I. (1990) Toward a transactional perspective: A personal journey. In I. Altman & K. Christensen (Eds) *Environment and behavior studies: Emergence of intellectual traditions* (pp. 225–256). New York: Plenum.

Altman, I. (1993) Dialectics, physical environments, and personal relationships. *Communication Monographs*, **60**, 26–34.

Altman, I., & Gauvain, M. (1981) A cross-cultural and dialectic analysis of homes. In L. Liben, A. Patterson, & N. Newcombe (Eds) *Spatial representation and behavior across the life-span* (pp. 283–320). New York: Academic Press.

Altman, I., & Taylor, D. (1973) *Social penetration: The development of interpersonal relationships.* New York: Holt, Rinehart & Winston.

Altman, I., Brown, B., Staples, B., & Werner, C. M. (1992) A transactional approach to close relationships: Courtship, weddings and placemaking. In B. Walsh, I. Craik, & R. Price (Eds) *Person–environment psychology* (pp. 193–241). Hillsdale, NJ: Erlbaum.

Altman, I., Vinsel, A., & Brown, B. B. (1981) Dialectic Conceptions in Social Psychology: An Application to Social Penetration and Privacy Regulation. In L. Berkowitz (Ed.) *Advances in Experimental Social Psychology*, Vol. 14 (pp. 107–160). New York: Academic Press.

American Psychiatric Association (1994) *Diagnostic and statistical manual of mental disorders*, 4th edn. Washington, DC: American Psychiatric Association.

Andersen, P. A. (1993) Cognitive schemata in personal relationships. In S. W. Duck (Ed.) *Individuals in relationships* (Understanding relationship processes 1) (pp. 1–29). Newbury Park: Sage.

Angst, J. (1992) Epidemiology of depression. *Psychopharmacology*, **106**, S71-S74.

Antaki, C. (1987) Performed and unperformable: A guide to accounts of relationships. In R. Burnett, P. McGee, & D. Clarke (Eds) *Accounting for Relationships* (pp. 97–113). London: Methuen.

Antaki, C., & Rapley, M. (1999) "Has anyone said you have a mental handicap?" Problems in inferring knowledge of category membership. Paper presented at the annual conference of the Social Psychology Section of the British Psychological Society, Lancaster, September.

Archer, R. L. (1979) Anatomical and psychological sex differences. In G. J. Chelune and Associates (Eds) *Self-disclosure: Origins, patterns, and implications of openness in interpersonal relationships* (pp. 80–109), Jossey-Bass, San Francisco, CA.

Archer, R. L. (1987) Commentary: Self-disclosure, a very useful behavior. In V.J. Derlega & J.H. Berg (eds) *Self-disclosure: Theory, research, and therapy*, (pp. 329–342). New York, Plenum.

Argyle, M., & Furnham, A. (1983) Sources of satisfaction, and conflict in long-term relationships. *Journal of Marriage and the Family*, **48**, 849–855.

Argyle, M., & Henderson, M. (1984)   The rules of friendship. *Journal of Social and Personal Relationships*, **1**, 211–237.

Aron, A., Aron, E. N., & Allen, J. (1998)   Motivations for unreciprocated love. *Personality and Social Psychology Bulletin*, **24**, 787–796.

Askham, J. (1976)   Identity and stability within the marriage relationship. *Journal of Marriage and the Family*, **38**, 535–47.

Attie, I., & Brooks-Dunn, J. (1989)   Development of eating problems in adolescent girls: A longitudinal study. *Developmental Psychology*, **25**, 70–79.

Aukett, R., Ritchie, J., & Mill, K. (1988)   Gender differences in friendship patterns. *Sex Roles*, **19**, 57–66.

Aune, R. K., Metts, S., & Ebesu, A. S. (1991, November)   Managing the outcomes of discovered deception. Paper presented at the Speech Communication Association Convention, Atlanta, GA.

Badhwar, N. K. (1987)   Friends as ends in themselves. *Philosophy and Phenomenological Research*, **XLVIII**, 1, 1–23.

Bakhtin, M. M. (1965/1984)   *Rabelais and his world* (H. Iswolsky, Trans.). Bloomington, IN: Indiana University Press.

Bakhtin, M. M. (1981)   *The dialogic imagination: Four essays by M. M. Bakhtin* (M. Holquist, Ed.; C. Emerson & M. Holquist, Trans.). Austin: University of Texas Press.

Bakhtin, M. M. (1984)   *Problems of Dostoevsky's poetics* (C. Emerson, Ed. and Trans.). Minneapolis MN: University of Minnesota Press (original work published 1929).

Bakhtin, M. M. (1986)   *Speech genres and other late essays* (E. Emerson & M. Holquist, Eds; V. McGee, Trans.). Austin: University of Texas Press.

Ball, R. (1979)   The dialectical method: Its application to social theory. *Social Forces*, **57**, 785–798.

Banks, S. P., Altendorf, D. M., Greene, J. O., & Cody, M. J. (1987)   An examination of relationship disengagement: Perceptions, breakup strategies and outcomes. *Western Journal of Speech Communication,* **51**, 19–41.

Barlund, D. C. (1970)   A transactional model of communication. In J. Akin, A. Goldberg, G. Myers, and J. Stewart (Eds) *Language behavior: A book of readings in communication* (pp. 43–61). The Hague: Mouton.

Barnes, J. A. (1969)   Graph theory and *Social Networks*: A technical comment on connectedness and connectivity. *Sociology*, **3**, 215–232.

Barnes, M. K., & Duck, S. W. (1994)   Everyday communicative contexts for social support. In B. R. Burleson, T. L. Albrecht, & I. G. Sarason (Eds) *Communication of social support: Messages, interactions, relationships, and community* (pp. 175–194). Thousand Oaks, CA: Sage.

Barnett, O. W., Martinez, T. E., & Bluestein, B. W. (1995)   Jealousy and romantic attachment in maritally violent and nonviolent men. *Journal of Interpersonal Violence*, **10**, 473–486.

Barsky, A. J., & Klerman, G.L. (1983)   Overview: Hypochondriasis, bodily complaints, and somatic styles. *American Journal of Psychiatry,* **140**, 273–283.

Barthes, R. (1983)   *A Lover's Discourse*, New York: Hill & Wang.

Bartholomew, K. (1993)   From childhood to adult relationships: Attachment theory and research. In S. W. Duck (Ed.) *Learning about relationships* (Understanding relationship processes. 2), (pp. 30–62). Newbury Park, CA: Sage.

Basco, M. R., Prager, K. J., Pite, J.M., Tamir, L.M., & Stephens, J.J. (1992) Communication and intimacy in the marriages of depressed patients. *Journal of Family Psychology*, **6**, 184–194.

Bateson, G. (1972)   *Steps to an ecology of mind*. New York: Ballantine.

Bateson, G. (1978)   The pattern which connects. *The Coevolutionary Quarterly,* Summer, 5–15.

Bateson, G. (1979)   *Mind and nature: A necessary unity*. New York: E. P. Dutton.

Bateson, G. (1991)   Naven: Epilogue 1958. In R.E. Donaldson (Ed.) *A sacred unity: Further steps to an ecology of mind* (pp. 49–69). New York: HarpersCollins.

Baumeister, R., & Newman, L. (1994)   How stories make sense of personal experiences: Motives that shape autobiographical narratives. *Personality and Social Psychology Bulletin*, **20**, 676–690.

Baxter, L. A. (1982)   Strategies for ending relationships: Two studies. *Western Journal of Speech Communication,* **46**, 223–241.

Baxter, L. A. (1984)   An investigation of compliance-gaining as politeness. *Human Communication Research*, **10**, 427–456.

Baxter, L. A. (1985)   Accomplishing relationship disengagement. In S. W. Duck & D. Perlman (Eds) *Understanding personal relationships* (pp. 243–265). London: Sage.

Baxter, L. A. (1987)   Cognition and communication in the relationship process. In R. Burnett, P. McGhee, & D. D. Clarke (Eds) *Accounting for relationships* (pp. 192–212). London: Methuen.

Baxter, L. A. (1988)   A dialectical perspective on communication strategies in relationship development. In S.W. Duck (Ed.) *A Handbook of personal relationships*. pp. 257–273. Chichester: Wiley.

Baxter, L. A. (1990)   Dialectical contradictions in relationship development, *Journal of Social and Personal Relationships*, **7**, 69–88.

Baxter, L. A. (1992)   Forms and functions of intimate play in personal relationships. *Human Communication Research*, **18**, 336–363.

Baxter, L. A. (1993)   The social side of personal relationships: A dialectical perspective. In S. W. Duck (Ed.) *Social Contexts of Relationships* (Understanding relationship processes 3) (pp. 139–165). Newbury Park, CA: Sage.

Baxter, L. A. (1994)   A dialogic approach to relationship maintenance. In D. J. Canary & L. Stafford (Eds) *Communication and relational maintenance* (pp. 233–254). New York: Academic Press.

Baxter, L. A., & Bullis, C. (1986)   Turning points in developing romantic relationships. *Human Communication Research*, **12**, 469–493.

Baxter, L. A., & Montgomery, B. M. (1996)   *Relating: Dialogs and dialectics*. New York: Guilford.

Baxter, L. A., & Simon, E. (1993)   Relationship maintenance strategies and dialectical contradiction in personal relationships. *Journal of Social and Personal Relationships*, **10**, 225–242.

Baxter, L. A., & Widenmann, S. (1993)   Revealing and not revealing the status of romantic relationships to *social networks*. *Journal of Social and Personal Relationships*, **10**, 321–338.

Bazerman, C. (1987)   Codifying the social scientific style: The APA publication manual as a behaviorist rhetoric. In J. S. Nelson, A. Megill, & D. N. McCloskey (Eds) *The Rhetoric of the Human Sciences: Language and Argument in Scholarship and Public Affairs* (pp. 125–144). Madison: UWisc Press.

Beach, S. R. H., Jouriles, E.N., & O'Leary, K.D. (1985)   Extramarital sex: Impact on depression and commitment in couples seeking marital therapy. *Journal of Sex and Marital Therapy*, **11**, 99–108.

Beach, S. R. H., Sandeen, E.E., & O'Leary, K.D. (1990)   *Depression and marriage*. New York: Guilford.

Beidel, D. C., Turner, S.M., Dancu, C.V. (1985)   Physiological, cognitive and behavioral aspects of social anxiety. *Behavior Research and Therapy,* **23**, 109–117.

Bell, R. A., & Daly, J. A. (1984)   The affinity-seeking function of communication. *Communication Monographs*, **51**, 91–115.

Bell, R. A., & Healey, J. G. (1992)   Idiomatic communication and interpersonal silidarity in Friends' relational cultures. *Human Communication Research*, **18**, 307–335.

Bell, R. A., Buerkel-Rothfuss, N. L., & Gore, K. E. (1987)   "Did you bring the yarmulke for the cabbage patch kid?" The idiomatic communication of young lovers. *Human Communication Research*, **14**, 47–67.

Bell, R. R. (1981)   Friendships of women and of men. *Psychology of Women Quarterly*, **5**, 402–417.

Bellah, R. N., Madsen, R., Sullivan, W.M., Swidler, A., & Tipton, S.M. (1985) *Habits of the heart: Individualism and commitment in American life*. San Francisco: Harper & Row.

Belsher, G., & Costello, C.G. (1991)   Do confidants of depressed women provide less social support that confidants of nondepressed women? *Journal of Abnormal Psychology*, **100**, 516–525.

Benjamin, L. S. (1993)   *Interpersonal diagnosis and treatment of personality disorders*. New York: Guilford.

Benjamin, L. S., & Wonderlich, S.A. (1994)   Social perceptions and borderline personality disorder: The relation to mood disorders. *Journal of Abnormal Psychology,* **103**, 610–624.

Benson, J. K. (1977)   Organizations: A dialectical view. *Administrative Science Quarterly*, **22**, 1–21.

Berg, J. H., & Derlega, V. J. (1987)   Themes in the study of self-disclosure. In V.J. Derlega & J. H. Berg (Eds) *Self-disclosure: Theory, research and therapy* (pp. 1–8). New York: Plenum.

Berger, C. R. (1988)   Uncertainty and information exchange in developing relation-ships. In S. W. Duck (Ed.) *Handbook of Personal Relationships* (pp. 239–256). Chichester: Wiley.

Berger, C. R. (1993)   Goals, plans and mutual understanding in personal relation-ships. In S. W. Duck (Ed.) *Individuals in relationships* (Understanding relationship processes 1) (pp. 30–59). Newbury Park, CA: Sage.

Berger, C. R., & Bradac, J. J. (1982)   *Language and social knowledge: Uncertainty in interpersonal relationships*. London: Edward Arnold.

Berger, P., & Kellner, H. (1964)   Marriage and the construction of reality: An exercise in the microsociology of knowledge: *Diogenes*, **46**, 1–23.

Berger, P., & Luckmann, T. (1966)   *The Social Construction of Reality*. Harmondsworth: Penguin.

Bergmann, J. R. (1993)   *Discreet indiscretions: The social organization of gossip*. New York: Aldine de Gruyter.

Berlo, D. K. (1960)   *The process of communication: An introduction to theory and practice*. New York: Holt, Reinehart and Winston.

Bernstein, B. (1964)   Elaborated and restricted codes: Their social origins and some consequences. *American Anthropologist*, **66** (2), 55–69.

Berscheid, E. (1994). Interpersonal relationships. *Annual Review of Psychology*, **45**, 79–129.

Berzon, B. (1992)   Developing a positive gay identity. In B. Berzon & R. Leighton (Eds) *Positively gay* (pp. 3–15), Milrose, CA: Celestial Arts.

Biglan, A., Hops, H., Sherman, L., Friedman, L.S., Arthur, J., & Osteen, V. (1985) Problem-solving interactions of depressed women and their husbands. *Behavior Therapy*, **16**, 431–451.

Billig, M. (1987)   *Arguing and thinking: A rhetorical approach to social psychology*. Cambridge, MA: Cambridge University Press.

Bleicher, J. (1980)   *Contemporary Hermeneutics: Hermeneutics as Method, Philosophy and Critique*. London: Routledge & Kegan Paul.

Blieszner, R., & Adams, R. G. (1992)   *Adult friendship*. Newbury Park, CA: Sage.

Block, J. D. (1980)   *Friendship*. New York: Macmillan.

Bocharov, S. (1994)   Conversations with Bakhtin. *PMLA*, **109**, 1009–1024.

Bochner, A. P. (1982)   On the efficacy of openness in closed relationships. In M. Burgoon (Ed) *Communication yearbook 5* pp. 109–142. New Brunswick, NJ, Transaction Books.

Bochner, A. P. (1984)   The functions of human communication in interpersonal bonding. In C. Arnold & J. Bowers (Eds) *Handbook of rhetorical and communication theory* (pp. 544–621). Boston: Allyn & Bacon.

Bochner, A. P. (1994)   Perspectives on inquiry II: Theories and stories. In M. Knapp & G. Miller (Eds) *Handbook of interpersonal communication, 2nd ed* pp. 21–41, Newbury Park, CA: Sage.

Bochner, A. P. (1977)   It's about time: Narrative and the divided self, *Qualitative Inquiry*, **3**, 418–438

Bochner, A. P., & Eisenberg, E. (1987)   Family process: System perspectives. In C. R. Berger & S. Chaffee (Eds) *Handbook of communication science* (pp. 540–563). Thousand Oaks, CA: Sage.

Bochner, A. P., & Ellis, C. (1992)   Personal narrative as a social approach to interpersonal communication, *Communication Theory*, **2**, 165–172.

Bochner, A. P., & Ellis, C. (1995)   Telling and living: Narrative co-construction and the practices of interpersonal relationships. In W. Leeds-Hurwitz (Ed.) *Communication as social construction: Social approaches to the study of interpersonal interaction*. New York: Guilford.

Bochner, A. P., & Waugh, J. (1995)   Talking with as a model for writing about: Implications of Rortian pragmatism for Communication Theory. In L. Langsdorf & A. Smith (eds) *Recovering Pragmatism's Voice: The Classical Tradition and the Philosophy of Communication* pp. 211–233. SUNY Press.

Bochner, A. P., Ellis, C., & Tillmann-Healy, L. (1998)   Mucking around looking for truth. In B. Montgomery & L. Baxter (Eds) *Dialectical approaches to studying personal relationships* pp. 41–62, Mahwah, NJ: Erlbaum.

Bolger, N., & Kelleher, S. (1993)   Daily life in relationships. In S. W. Duck (Ed.) *Social contexts of relationships* (Understanding Relationship Processes 3) (pp. 100–109). Newbury Park, CA Sage.

Bookwala, J., & Zdaniuk, B. (1998)   Adult attachment styles and aggressive behavior within dating relationships. *Journal of Social and Personal Relationships*, **15**, 175–190.

Booth, A., & Hess, E. (1974)   Cross-sex friendship. *Journal of Marriage and the Family*, 38–47.

Bopp, M. J., & Weeks, G. R. (1984)   Dialectical metatheory in family therapy. *Family Process*, **23**, 49–61.

Bornstein, R. F. (1992)   The dependent personality: Developmental, social, and clinical perspectives. *Psychological Bulletin,* **112**, 3–23.

Bostrom, R. & Donohew, L. (1992). The case for empiricism: clarifying fundamental issues in communication theory. *Communication Monographs,* **59**, 109–29.

Bowlby, J. (1969)   *Attachment and loss: Vol. I. Attachment.* New York: Basic Books.

Bowlby, J. (1973)   *Attachment and loss: Vol. II. Separation, anxiety, and anger.* New York: Basic Books.

Brain, R. (1976)   *Friends and lovers.* New York: Basic Books.

Braithwaite, D. O., & Baxter, L. A. (1995)   "I do" again: The relational dialectics of renewing marriage vows. *Journal of Social and Personal Relationships*, **12**, 177–198.

Bratslavsky, E., Baumeister, R. F., & Sommer, K. L. (1998)   To love or be loved in vain: The trials and tribulations of unrequited love. In B. H. Spitzberg & W. R. Cupach (Eds), *The dark side of close relationships* (pp. 307–326). Mahwah, NJ: Erlbaum.

Bridge, K., & Baxter, L. A. (1992)   Blended friendships: Friends as work associates. *Western Journal of Communication*, **56**, 200–225.

Brink, T. L., & Niemeyer, L. (1993)   Hypochondriasis, loneliness, and social functioning. *Psychological Reports,* **72**, 1241–1242.

Brody, H. (1987)   *Stories of Sickness.* New Haven, CT: Yale University Press.

Brown, B., Altman, I., & Werner, C. (1992)   Close relationships in the physical and social world: Dialectical and transactional analyses. *Communication Yearbook*, **15**, 508–521.

Brown, G. W., & Harris, T. (1978)   *Social origins of depression.* New York: Free Press.

Brown, P., & Levinson, S. (1987)   *Politeness: Some universals in language usage.* Cambridge: Cambridge University Press.

Bruess, C. J. S., & Pearson, J. C. (1993)   'Sweet pea' and 'pussy cat': An examination of idiom use and marital satisfaction over the life cycle. *Journal of Social and Personal Relationships*, **10**, 609–615.

Bruner, J. (1986)   *Actual Minds, Possible Worlds*, Cambridge, MA: Harvard University Press.

Bruner, J. (1990)   *Acts of Meaning*, Cambridge, MA: Harvard University Press.

Bryson, J. B. (1991)   Modes of response to jealousy-evoking situations. In P. Salovey (Ed.), *The psychology of jealousy and envy* (pp. 178–207). New York: Guilford.

Buber, M. (1937)   *I and thou*. New York: Scribner.

Buelow, G., McClain, M., & McIntosh, I. (1996)   A new measure for an important construct: The attachment and object relations inventory. *Journal of Personality Assessment*, **66**, 604–623.

Bukowski, W., & Hoza, B. (1989)   Popularity and friendship: Issues in theory, measurement and outcome. In T. Berndt & G. Ladd (Eds) *Peer relationships in child development* (pp. 15–45). New York: Wiley.

Bukowski, W. M., Nappi, B. J. & Hoza, B. (1987)   A test of Aristotle's model of friendship for young adults' same-sex and opposite-sex relationships. *The Journal of Social Psychology,* **127,** 595–603

Burgess, A. W., Baker, T., Greening, D., Hartman, C. R., Burgess, A. G., Douglas, J. E., & Halloran, R. (1997)   Stalking behaviors within domestic violence. *Journal of Family Violence*, **12**, 389–403.

Burgess, E. W., & Cottrell, L. S. (1939)   *Predicting success or failure in marriage*. Englewood Cliffs, NJ: Prentice-Hall.

Burleson, B. R. (1991). Review of *Studying Interpersonal Interaction. ISSPR Bulletin,* **8,** 29–31.

Burleson, B. R. (1994)   Comforting messages: Significance, approaches, and effects. In B. R. Burleson, T. L. Albrecht, & I. G. Sarason (Eds) *Communication of social support: Messages, interactions, relationships, and community*. Thousand Oaks, CA: Sage.

Burnett, R. (1984)   Thinking and communicating about personal relationships: Some sex differences. Paper presented at the Second International Conference on Personal Relationships, Madison, WI

Burns, D. D., Sayers, S.L., & Moras, K. (1994)   Intimate relationships and depression: Is there a causal connection? *Journal of Consulting and Clinical Psychology*, **62**, 1033–1043.

Burt, R. S. (1983)   Distinguishing relational contents. In R. S. Burt, M. J. Minor & Associates (Eds) *Applied network analysis: A methodological introduction* (pp. 35–74). Beverly Hills, CA: Sage.

Buss, A. R. (1979)   A dialectical psychology. New York: Irvington.

Buss, D. M. (1988)   From vigilance to violence: Tactics of mate retention in American undergraduates. *Ethology and Sociobiology*, **9**, 291–317.

Butler, S., & Rosenblum, B. (1991)   *Cancer in Two Voices*. San Francisco, CA: Spinster.

Buunk, B., & Bringle, R. G. (1987)   Jealousy in love relationships. In D. Perlman & S. W. Duck (Eds) *Intimate relationships: Development, dynamics, and deterioration* (pp. 123–147). Newbury Park, CA: Sage.

Calam, R., Waller, G., Slade, P., & Newton, T. (1990)   Eating disorders and perceived relationships with parents. *International Journal of Eating Disorders*, **9**, 479–485.

Canary, D. J., & Stafford, L. (Eds) (1994)   *Communication and relational mainte-nance*. San Diego, CA: Academic Press.

Cappella, J. N. (1985)   Production principles for turn-taking rules in social inter-action: Socially anxious vs. socially secure persons. *Journal of Language and Social Psychology*, **4**, 193–212.

Cappella, J. N., & Palmer, M. T. (1990)   Attitude similarity, relational history, and attraction: The mediating effects of kinesic and vocal behaviors. *Communication Monographs*, **57**, 161–183.

Carroll, L., Corning, F., Morgan, R., & Stevens, D. (1991)   Perceived acceptance, psychological functioning, and sex role orientation of narcissistic persons. *Journal of Social Behavior and Personality*, **6**, 943–954.

Carroll, L., Hoenigmann-Stovall, N., King, A., Wienhold, J., & Whitehead, G.I. (1998)   Interpersonal consequences of narcissistic and borderline personality disorders. *Journal of Social and Clinical Psychology*, **17**, 38–49.

Carson, C. L., & Cupach, W. R. (1999, November)   Fueling the flames of the green-eyed monster: The role of ruminative thought in reaction to perceived relationship threat. Paper presented at the National Communication Association convention, Chicago, IL.

Carson, R. C. (1983)   The social-interactional viewpoint. In M. Hersen, A.E. Kazdin, & A.S. Bellack (Eds) *The clinical psychology handbook* (pp. 143–153). New York: Pergamon.

Cartwright, D., & Harary, F. (1956)   Structural balance: A generalization of Heider's theory. *Psychological Review*, **63**, 277–293.

Carver, C. S., & Scheier, M. F. (1990)   Origins and functions of positive and negative affect: A control-process view. *Psychological Review*, **97**, 19–35.

Cass, V. C. (1979)   Homosexual identity formation: A theoretical model. *Journal of Homosexuality*, **4**, 219–235.

Cates, R. M., & Lloyd, S.A. (1992)   *Courtship*. Newbury Park, CA: Sage.

Chelune, G. J. (1979)   Measuring openness in interpersonal communication. In G. J. Chelune and Associates (eds), *Self-disclosure: Origins, patterns, and implica-tions of openness in interpersonal relationships*. (pp. 1–27), San Francisco, CA: Jossey-Bass.

Chown, S. M. (1981)   Friendship in old age. In S. Duck & R. Gilmour (Eds), *Personal relationships, Vol. 2: Developing personal relationships* (pp. 231–246). New York: Academic Press.

Cissna, K. N., Cox, D. E., & Bochner, A. P. (1990)   The dialectic of marital and parental relationships within the stepfamily. *Communication Monographs*, **57**, 44–61.

Clark, K., & Holquist, M. (1984)   Mikhail Bakhtin. Cambridge, MA: The Belknap Press of Harvard University Press.

Clark, M. S., & Reis, H. T. (1988)   Interpersonal process in close relationships. *Annual Review of Psychology*, **39**, 609–672.

Cline, R. J. (1983a)   Promising new directions for teaching and research: Self disclosure. Paper presented at the Annual Convention of the Speech Communication Association, November, Washington, D.C.

Cline, R. J. (1983b)   The acquaintance process as relational communication. In R. N. Bostrom (Ed.) *Communication Yearbook* 7 (pp. 396–413). Beverly Hills, CA, Sage.

Cline, R. J. (May, 1982)   Revealing and relating: A review of self-disclosure theory and research. Paper presented at the International Communication Association Convention.

Cline, R. J., Johnson, S. J., & Freeman, K. E. (1992)   Talk among sexual partners: Interpersonal communication for risk reduction or risk enhancement. *Health Communication, 4,* 39–56.

Cochran, M., Larner, M., Riley, D., Gunnarsson, L., & Henderson, C. R. (1990) *Extending families: The social networks of parents and their children.* Cambridge: Cambridge University Press.

Cody, M. (1982)   A typology of disengagement strategies and an examination of the role intimacy, reactions to inequity and relational problems play in strategy selection. *Communication Monographs, 49,* 148–170.

Cogan, R., & Porcerelli, J. H. (1996)   Object relations in abusive partner relationships: An empirical investigation. *Journal of Personality Assessment, 66,* 106–115.

Coleman, E. (1982)   Developmental stages of the coming out process, *Journal of Homosexuality, 7,* 31–43.

Coles, R. (1989)   *The Call of Stories: Teaching and the Moral Imagination.* Boston, MA: Houghton Mifflin.

Collins, L. (1994)   Gossip: A feminist defense. In R. F. Goodman and A. Ben-Ze'ev (Eds) *Good gossip* (pp. 106–114). Manhattan, KS: University Press of Kansas.

Collins, N. L., & Miller, L.C. (1994)   The disclosure-liking link: From meta-analysis toward a dynamic reconceptualization. *Psychological Bulletin,* **116,** 457–475.

Conville, R. L. (1983)   Second-order development in interpersonal communication. *Human Communication Research,* **9,** 195–207.

Conville, R. L. (1988)   Relational transitions: An inquiry into their structure and functions. *Journal of Social and Personal Relationships,* **5,** 423–437.

Conville, R. L. (1991)   *Relational transitions: The evolution of personal relationships.* New York: Praeger.

Cornforth, M. (1968)   *Materialism and the dialectical method.* New York: International Publishers.

Coyne, J. C. (1976a)   Toward an interactional description of depression. *Psychiatry,* **39,** 28–40.

Coyne, J. C. (1976b)   Depression and the response of others. *Journal of Abnormal Psychology,* **85,** 186–193.

Coyne, J. C., Kahn, J., & Gotlib, I.H. (1987)   Depression. In T. Jacob (Ed.), *Family interaction and psychopathology* (pp. 509–533). New York: Plenum.

Coyne, J. C., Kessler, R.C., Tal, M., Turnbull, J., Wortman, C.B., & Greden, J.F. (1987)   Living with a depressed person. *Journal of Consulting and Clinical Psychology,* **55,** 347–352.

Craig, R., Tracy, K., & Spisak, F. (1986)   The discourse of requests: Assessment of a politeness approach. *Human Communication Research, 12,* 437–468.

Cramer, R. E., Weiss, R. F., Steigleder, M. K., & Balling, S. S. (1985)   Attraction in context: Acquisition and blocking of person-directed action. *Journal of Personality and Social Psychology, 49,* 1221–1230.

Crites, S. (1971)   The narrative quality of experience. *Journal of the American Academy of Religion*, **39**, 291–311.

Crites, S. (1986)   Storytime: Recollecting the past and projecting the future. In T. Sarbin (Ed.) *Narrative Psychology: The Storied Nature of Human Conduct* (pp. 152–173), New York: Praeger.

Cupach, W. R., & Metts, S. (1990)   Remedial processes in embarrassing predicaments. In J. A. Anderson (Ed.), *Communication yearbook 13* (pp. 323–352). Newbury Park, CA: Sage.

Cupach, W. R., & Metts, S. (1993, June)   Correspondence between relationship partners on relationship beliefs and face predilections as predictors of relational quality. Paper presented at the conference of the International Network on Personal Relationships, Milwaukee, WI.

Cupach, W. R., & Metts, S. (1994)   *Facework*. Thousand Oaks, CA: Sage.

Cupach, W. R., & Spitzberg, B. H. (1997, February)   The incidence and perceived severity of obsessive relational intrusion behaviors. Paper presented at the Western States Communication Association convention, Monterey, CA.

Cupach, W. R., & Spitzberg, B. H. (1998)   Obsessive relational intrusion and stalking. In B. H. Spitzberg & W. R. Cupach (Eds) *The dark side of close relationships* (pp. 233–263). Mahwah, NJ: Erlbaum.

Cupach, W. R., & Spitzberg, B. H. (Eds) (1994)   *The dark side of interpersonal communication* . Hillsdale NJ: Erlbaum.

Daly, S. (1978)   Behavioral correlates of social anxiety. *British Journal of Social and Clinical Psychology,* **17**, 117–120.

Dare, C., Le Grange, D., Eisler, I., & Rutherford, J. (1994)   Redefining the psychosomatic family: Family process of 26 eating disorder families. *International Journal of Eating Disorders*, **16**, 211–226.

Davidson, K. P., & Pennebaker, J.W. (1996)   Social psychosomatics. In E.T. Higgins & A.W. Kruglanski (Eds) *Social psychology: Handbook of basic principles* (pp. 102–130). New York: Guilford.

Davis, J. A. (1970)   Clustering and hierarchy in interpersonal relations: Test two graph theoretical models on 742 sociomatrices. *American Sociological Review*, **35**, 843–851.

Davis, K. E., & Todd, M. J. (1985)   Assessing friendship: Prototypes, paradigm cases and relationship description. In S. W. Duck & D. Perlman (Eds) *Understanding Personal Relationships* (pp. 17–38). London: Sage.

de Becker, G. (1997)   The gift of fear: Survival signals that protect us from violence. Boston, MA: Little, Brown.

Deaux, K., & Major, B. (1987)   Putting gender into context: an interactive model of gender-related behavior. *Psychological Review*, **94**, 369–389.

Delia, J. G. (1980)   Some tentative thoughts concerning the study of interpersonal relationships and their development. *Western Journal of Speech Communication*, **44**, 97–103.

Denzin, N. (1989a)   *Interpretive Biography*. Newbury Park, CA: Sage.

Denzin, N. (1989b)   *Interpretive Interactionism*, Newbury Park, CA: Sage.

Denzin, N. (1991)   *Images of Postmodern Society: Social Theory and Contemporary Cinema*. London: Sage.

Denzin, N. (1992) *Symbolic Interactionism and Cultural Studies: The Politics of Interpretation.* Oxford: Basil Blackwell.

Denzin, N. (1993) Narrative's phenomena. Paper presented at Midwest Sociological Society, Chicago, IL.

Denzin, N. (1995) *The cinematic society: The voyeur's gaze.* London: Sage.

Denzin, N. K. (1997) *Interpretive ethnography: Ethnographic practices for the 21st century.* Thousand Oaks, CA: Sage.

Denzin, N., & Lincoln, Y. (Eds) (1994) *Handbook of qualitative research,* Thousand Oaks, CA: Sage.

DePaulo, B. M., Epstein, J.A., & LeMay, C.S. (1990) Responses of the socially anxious to the prospect of interpersonal evaluation. *Journal of Personality,* **58,** 623–640.

Derlega, V. J., & Chaikin, A. (1977) Privacy and self-disclosure in social relationships. *Journal of Social Issues,* **33,** 102–115.

Derlega, V. J., Metts, S., Petronio, S., and Margulis, S.T. (1993) *Self-disclosure.* Newbury Park, CA: Sage.

Dickens, D., & Fontana, A. (Eds) (1991). *Postmodernism & Sociology.* Chicago, IL: University of Chicago Press.

Dickson, F. C. (1995). The best is yet to be: Research on long-lasting marriages. In J. Wood & S. W. Duck (Eds) *Under-studied relationships: Off the beaten track* (pp. 22–50). Thousand Oaks, CA: Sage.

Dindia, K. (1982) Reciprocity of self-disclosure: A sequential analysis. In M. Burgoon (Ed.), *Communication yearbook* 6 (pp. 506–530). Sage, Beverly Hills, CA.

Dindia, K. (1984, May) Antecedents and consequents of self-disclosure. Paper presented at the meeting of the International Communication Association, San Francisco, CA.

Dindia, K. (1994) The intrapersonal–interpersonal dialectical process of self-disclosure. In S. W. Duck (Ed.) *Dynamics of relationships* (Understanding relationship processes 4), Thousand Oaks, CA: Sage. pp. 27–57.

Dindia, K. (1998) "Going into and coming out of the closet": The dialectics of stigma disclosure. In B.M. Montgomery & L.A. Baxter (Eds) *Dialectical approaches to studying personal relationships.*(pp. 83–108). Mahwah, NJ: Erlbaum.

Dindia, K., & Allen, M. (1992) Sex-differences in self-disclosure: A meta-analysis: *Psychological Bulletin,* **112,** 106–124.

Dindia, K., & Canary, D. J. (1993) Definitions and theoretical perspectives on maintaining relationships. *Journal of Social and Personal Relationships,* **10,** 163–173.

Dindia, K., & Tieu, T. (1996, November) The process of self-disclosure of homosexual identity. Paper presented at the Speech Communication Association Convention, San Diego, CA.

Dindia, K., Fitzpatrick, M. A., & Kenny, D. A. (1997) Self-disclosure in spouse and stranger dyads: A social relations analysis. *Human Communication Research,* **23,** 388–412.

Doane, J. A., West, K.L., Goldstein, M.J., Rodnick, E.H., & Jones, J.E. (1981) Parental communication deviance and affective style: Predictors of subsequent schizophrenia spectrum disorders. *Archives of General Psychiatry,* **38,** 679–685.

Dodge, C. S., Heimberg, R.G., Nyman, D., & O'Brian, G.T. (1987)   Daily interactions of high and low socially anxious college students: A diary study. *Behavior Therapy,* **18**, 90–96.

Downey, G., & Coyne, J.C. (1990)   Children of depressed parents: An integrative review. *Psychological Bulletin,* **108**, 50–76.

Driscoll, R., Davis, K. E., & Lipetz, M. E. (1972)   Parental interference and romantic love: The Romeo and Juliet effect. *Journal of Personality and Social Psychology,* **24**, 1–10.

Duck, S. W. (1982)   A topography of relationship disengagement and dissolution. In S. W. Duck (Ed.), *Personal relationships 4: Dissolving personal relationships* (pp. 1–30). London: Academic Press.

Duck, S. W. (1988a)   *Relating to others.* Chicago: Dorsey Press.

Duck, S. W. (1988b)   *Handbook of Personal Relationships: Theory, Research and Interventions.* Chichester: Wiley.

Duck, S. W. (1990)   Relationships as unfinished business: Out of the frying pan and into the 1990s. *Journal of Social and Personal Relationships,* **7**, 5–29.

Duck, S. W. (1993)   *Social context and relationships* (Understanding relationship processes 3). Newbury Park, CA: Sage.

Duck, S. W. (1994a)   *Meaningful relationships: Talking, sense, and relating.* Thousand Oaks, CA: Sage.

Duck, S. W. (1994b)   Stratagems, spoils, and a serpent's tooth: On the delights and dilemmas of personal relationships. In W. R. Cupach & B. H. Spitzberg (Eds) *The dark side of interpersonal communication* (pp. 3–24). Hillsdale, NJ: Erlbaum.

Duck, S. W. (Ed.) (1997)   *Handbook of Personal Relationships,* 2nd Edn. Chichester: Wiley.

Duck, S. W. & Montgomery, B. M. (1991). The interdependence among interaction substance, theory and methods. In B. M. Montgomery & S. Duck (Eds), *Studying Interpersonal Interaction* (pp. 3–15). New York: Guilford.

Duck, S. W., & Pittman, G. (1994)   Social and personal relationships. In M. Knapp & G. Miller (Eds) *Handbook of interpersonal communication,* 2nd edn.(pp. 676–695). Thousand Oaks, CA: Sage.

Duck, S. W., & Pond, K. (1989)   Friends, Romans, Countrymen; lend me your retrospective data: Rhetoric and reality in personal relationships. In C. Hendrick (Ed.) *Close relationships,* Vol. **10**, (pp. 17–38). Newbury Park, CA: Sage.

Duck, S. W., & Sants, H. K. A. (1983)   On the origin of the specious: Are personal relationships really interpersonal states? *Journal of Social and Clinical Psychology,* **1**, 27–41.

Duck, S. W., & Wood, J. T. (1995)   For better for worse, for richer for poorer: The rough and the smooth of relationships. In S. W. Duck & J. T. Wood (Eds), *Confronting relationship challenges* (Understanding relationship processes 5) (pp. 1–21). Thousand Oaks, CA: Sage.

Duck, S. W., Rutt, D. J., Hurst, M., & Strejc, H. (1991)   Some evident truths about conversations in everyday relationships: All communication is not created equal. *Human Communication Research,* **18**, 228–267.

Duck, S. W., West, L., & Acitelli, L. K. (1997)   Sewing the field: The tapestry of relationships in life and research. In S. W. Duck (Ed) *Handbook of Personal Relationships, 2nd edn.* (pp. 1–24). Chichester: Wiley.

Duranti, A. (1988)   Intentions, language, and social interaction in a Samoan context. *Journal of Pragmatics*, **12**, 13–33.

Dutton, D. G. (1998)   The abusive personality: Violence and control in intimate relationships. New York: Guilford.

Dutton, D. G., Saunders, K., Starzomski, A., & Bartholomew, K. (1994)   Intimacy anger and insecure attachment as precursors of abuse in intimate relationships. *Journal of Applied Social Psychology*, **24**, 1367–1386.

Dutton, D. G., van Ginkel, C., & Landolt, M. A. (1996)   Jealousy, intimate abusiveness, and intrusiveness. *Journal of Family Violence*, **11** (4), 411–423.

Edgar, T. (1994)   Self-disclosure behaviors of the stigmatized: Strategies and outcomes for the revelation of sexual orientation. In R.J. Ringer (Ed.) Queer words, queer images (pp. 221–237). New York: New York University Press.

Eggert, L. L., & Parks, M. R. (1987)   Communication network involvement in adolescents' friendships and romantic relationships. In M. L. McLaughlin (Ed.) *Communication yearbook 10* (pp. 283–322). Newbury Park, CA: Sage.

Eidelson, R. J. (1980)   Interpersonal satisfaction and level of involvement: A curvilinear relationship. *Journal of Personality and Social Psychology*, **39**, 460–470.

Ellis, C. (1991)   Sociological introspection and emotional experience. *Symbolic Interaction*, **14**, 23–50.

Ellis, C. (1993)   There are survivors: Telling a story of sudden death. *The Sociological Quarterly*, **34**, 711–730.

Ellis, C. (1995a)   *Final negotiations: A story of love, loss, and chronic illness.* Philadelphia. PA: Temple University Press.

Ellis, C. (1995b)   Speaking of dying: An ethnographic short story. *Symbolic Interaction*, **18**, 73–81.

Ellis, C. (1996)   On the demands of truthfulness in writing personal loss narratives. *Journal of Personal and Interpersonal Loss*, **1**, 151–178.

Ellis, C., & Bochner, A. P. (1992)   Telling and performing personal stories: The constraints of choice in abortion. In C. Ellis & M. Flaherty (Eds) *Investigating subjectivity* (pp. 79–101). Thousand Oaks, CA: Sage.

Ellis, C., & Bochner, A. P. (1996)   *Composing ethnography: Alternative forms of qualitative writing.* Walnut Creek, CA: AltaMira Press.

Ellis, C., & Bochner, A. P. (in press). Researcher as subject: Autoethnography, personal narrative, reflexivity. In N. Denzin & Y. Lincoln (Eds) *Handbook of qualitative research 2nd edn*. Thousand Oaks, CA: Sage.

Emerson, R. M., Ferris, K. O., & Gardner, C. B. (1998)   On being stalked. *Social Problems*, **45**, 289–314.

Erickson, D.H., Beiser, M., Iacono, W.G., Fleming, J.A.E., & Lin, T. (1989)   The role of social relationships in the course of first-episode schizophrenia and affective psychosis. *American Journal of Psychiatry*, **146**, 1456–1461.

Faucett, J. A., & Levine, J.D. (1991)   The contributions of interpersonal conflict to chronic pain in the presence or absence of organic pathology. *Pain*, **44**, 35–43.

Fehr, B. (1993)   How do I love thee? … Let me consult my prototype. In S. W. Duck (Ed.) *Individuals in relationships* (Understanding relationship processes 1) (pp. 87–120). Newbury Park, CA: Sage.

Felmlee, D. H. (1995)   Fatal Attractions: Affection and disaffection in intimate relationships. *Journal of Social and Personal Relationships*, **12**, 295–311.

Festinger, L., Schachter, S., & Back, K. W. (1950)   *Social pressure in informal
groups: A study of human factors in housing*. New York: Harper.

Fincham, F. D. (1992)   The account episode in close relationships. In M. L.
McLaughlin, M. J. Cody, and S. J. Read (Eds), *Explaining one's self to others:
Reason-giving in a social context* (pp. 167–182). Hillsdale, NJ: Erlbaum.

Fincham, F. D., & Bradbury, T. N. (1987)   The impact of attributions in marriage: A
longitudinal analysis. *Journal of Personality and Social Psychology*, **53**, 510–517.

Fine, M. A. & Demo, D. (2000)   Consequences of divorce. In R. M. Milardo & S. W.
Duck (Eds) *Families as relationships*. Chichester: Wiley.

Fiscella, K., Franks, P., & Shields, C.G. (1997)   Received family criticism and
primary care utilization: Psychosocial and biomedical pathways. *Family Process,*
36, 25–41.

Fischer, C. S. (1982)   *To dwell among friends*: *Personal networks in town and city*.
Chicago, IL: University of Chicago Press.

Fischer, C. S., Jackson, R. M., Stueve, C. A., Gerson, K., & Jones, L. M., with
Baldassare, M. (1977)   *Networks and places*. New York: Free Press.

Fisher, W. (1987)   *Human communication as narration: Toward a philosophy of
reason, value, and action*, Columbia, SC: University of South Carolina.

Fiske, V., & Peterson, C. (1991)   Love and depression: The nature of depressive
romantic relationships. *Journal of Social and Clinical Psychology*, **10**, 75–90.

Fitch, K. (1994). Culture, ideology, and interpersonal communication research.
Communication Yearbook, **17,** 104–35.

Fitch, K. L. (1998)   *Speaking relationally: Culture, communication, and interpersonal connection*. New York: Guilford.

Fitzpatrick, M. A. (1987)   Marriage and verbal intimacy In V.J. Derlega & J. H.
Berg (Eds) *Self-disclosure: Theory, research and therapy (pp. 131–154)*, New
York: Plenum.

Fitzpatrick, M. A. (1993). Review of *Friendship Matters. Communication Theory,* **3,**
83–5.

Fletcher, G. J. O., & Fitness, J. (1993)   Knowledge structures and explanations in
intimate relationships. In S. W. Duck (Ed.), *Understanding relationship processes
1: Individuals in relationships* (pp. 121–143). Newbury Park, CA: Sage.

Ford, C. V. (1986)   The somatizing disorders. *Psychosomatics,* **27**, 327–337.

Ford, C. V. (1995)   Dimensions of somatization and hypochondriasis. *Neurologic
Clinics,* **13**, 241–253.

Foucault, M. (1970)   *The order of things: An archaeology of the human sciences*.
New York: Random House.

Franck, D. (1993)   *Separation*, New York: Alfred A. Knop.

Frank, A, (1995)   *The Wounded Storyteller: Body, Illness, and Ethics*. Chicago, IL:
University of Chicago Press.

Frank, A. (1991)   *At the Will of the Body: Reflections on Illness*, Boston, MA:
Houghton Mifflin.

Frank, A. (1993)   The rhetoric of self-change: Illness experience as narrative. *The
Sociological Quarterly*, **34**, 39–52.

Fremouw, W. J., Westrup, D., & Pennypacker, J. (1997)   Stalking on campus: The prevalence and strategies for coping with stalking. *Journal of Forensic Sciences*, **42**, 664–667.

Freud, S. (1917/1966)   *Introductory lectures on psychoanalysis*. New York: W.W. Norton. (original work published in 1917).

Fromm-Reichmann, F. (1960)   *Principles of intensive psychotherapy*. Chicago, IL: Phoenix Books.

Furman, L. G. (1986)   Cross-gender friendships in the workplace: Factors and components. Unpublished doctoral dissertation, Fielding Institute.

Gadamer, H. (1989)   *Truth and Method (2nd edn.)*. New York: Crossroad.

Gaines, S. O. Jr. (1994)   Exchange of respect-denying behaviors among male–female friendships. *Journal of Social and Personal Relationships*, **11**, 5–24.

Gard, L. (1990)   Patient disclosure of human immunodeficiency virus (HIV) status to parents: clinical considerations. *Professional Psychology: Research and Practice*, **21**, 252–256.

Garfinkel, P. E., Garner, D.M., Rose, J., Darby, P.L., Brandes, J.S., O'Hanlon, J., & Walsh, N. (1983)   A comparison of characteristics in families of patients with anorexia nervosa and normal controls. *Psychological Medicine*, **13**, 821–828.

Geertz, C. (1973)   *The Interpretation of Cultures*. New York: Basic Books.

Georgoudi, M. (1983)   Modern dialectics in social psychology: A reappraisal. *European Journal of Social Psychology*, **13**, 77–93.

Gergen, K. J. (1973)   Social psychology as history. *Journal of Personality and Social Psychology*, **26**, 309–320.

Gergen, K. J. (1980)   Toward generative theory. *Journal of Personality and Social Psychology*, **36**, 1344–1360.

Gergen, K. J. (1982)   *Towards Transformation in Social Knowledge*, New York: Springer-Verlag.

Gergen, K. J. (1994). *Realities and Relationships: Soundings in Social Construction.* Cambridge, MA: Harvard University Press

Gergen, K. J., & Davis, K. (Eds) (1985)   *The Social Construction of the Person*, New York: Springer-Verlag.

Gergen, K. J., & Gergen, M. (1986)   Narrative form and the construction of psychological science. In T. Sarbin (Ed.) *Narrative psychology: The storied nature of human conduct* (pp. 22–44), New York: Praeger.

Gergen, K. J., & Gergen, M. (1987)   Narratives of relationship. In R. Burnett, P. McGhee & D. Clarke (Eds) *Accounting for relationships: Explanation, representation and knowledge* (pp. 269–288). London: Methuen.

Gergen, K. J., & Water, R. (1998)   Real/izing the relational. *Journal of Social and Personal Relationships,* **15**, 110–126.

Gergen, M. (1992)   Life stories: Pieces of a dream. In G.C. Rosenwald & R.L. Ochberg (Eds) *Storied lives: The cultural politics of self-understanding* (pp. 127–144), New Haven, CT: Yale University Press.

Gershman, H. (1983)   The stress of coming out. *American Journal of Psychoanalysis*, **43**, 129–138.

Giddens, A. (1979)   *Central problems in social theory: Action, structure and contradiction in social analysis*. Berkeley: University of California Press.

Gilbert, S. J., & Horenstein, D. (1975)   The communication of self-disclosure: Level versus valence. *Human Communication Research*, **1**, 316–322.

Ginsburg, G. (1988)   Rules, scripts and prototypes in personal relationships. In S. W. Duck (Ed.) *Handbook of personal relationships: Theory, research and interventions* (pp. 23–39), Chichester: Wiley.

Goffman, E. (1959)   *The presentation of self in everyday life*. New York: Anchor Books.

Goffman, E. (1957)   *Interaction ritual: Essays on face-to-face behavior.* Garden City, NY: Anchor Books.

Goffman, E. (1974)   *Stigma: Notes on the management of spoiled identity.* New York: Jason Aronson.

Goldsmith, D. (1990)   A dialectical perspective on the expression of autonomy and connection in romantic relationships. *Western Journal of Speech Communication*, **54**, 537–56.

Goldsmith, D. (1992)   Managing conflicting goals in supportive interaction: An integrative theoretical framework. *Communication Research*, **19**, 264–286.

Goldsmith, D. (1994)   The role of facework in supportive communication. In B. R. Burleson, T. L. Albrecht, & I. G. Sarason (Eds) *Communication of social support: Messages, interactions, relationships, and community* (pp. 29–49). Thousand Oaks, CA: Sage.

Goldsmith, D., & Parks, M. R. (1990)   Communication strategies for managing the dilemmas of social support. In S. W. Duck & R. C. Silver (Eds) *Personal relationships and social support* (pp. 104–121). Newbury Park, CA: Sage.

Goldstein, M. J. (1987)   Family interaction patterns that antedate the onset of schizophrenia and related disorders: A further analysis of data from a longitudinal, prospective study. In K. Hahlweg & M.J. Goldstein (Eds) *Understanding major mental disorder: The contribution of family interaction research* (pp. 11–32). New York: Family Process Press.

Goldstein, M. J., & Strachan, A.M. (1987)   The family and schizophrenia. In T. Jacob (Ed.) *Family interaction and psychopathology: Theories, methods, and findings* (pp. 481–508). New York: Plenum.

Goode, W. J. (1956)   *Women in divorce*. New York: Macmillan.

Goodstein, L., & Reinecker, V. (1974)   Factors affecting self-disclosure: A review of the literature. *Progress in Experimental Personality Research*, **7**, 49–77.

Gotlib, I. H., & Lee, C.M. (1989)   The social functioning of depressed patients: A longitudinal assessment. *Journal of Social and Clinical Psychology*, **8**, 223–237.

Gotlib, I. H., & Whiffen, V.E. (1989)   Depression and marital functioning: An examination of specificity and gender differences. *Journal of Abnormal Psychology*, **98**, 23–30.

Gottlieb, B. H. (1983)   *Social support strategies: Guidelines for mental health practice*. Beverly Hills, CA: Sage.

Gottman, J. M. (1979)   *Marital interaction: Experimental investigations*. New York: Academic Press.

Gottman, J. M. (1982)   Temporal form: Toward a new language for describing relationships. *Journal of Marriage and the Family*, **44**, 943–962.

Gottman, J. M. (1986) The world of coordinated play: Same- and cross-sex friendship in young children. In J.M. Gottman & J.G. Parker (Eds) *Conversations of friends: Speculations on affective development* (pp. 139–191). Cambridge, MA: Cambridge University Press.

Gottman, J. M. (1994) *What predicts divorce?* Hillsdale, NJ: Erlbaum.

Gray J. (1992). *My books are from Uranus.* Clarion: New York.

Grissett, N. I., & Norvell, N. K. (1992) Perceived social support, social skills, and quality of relationships in bulimic women. *Journal of Consulting and Clinical Psychology*, **60**, 293–299.

Guba, E. G. (1990). Carrying on the dialog. In E. G. Guba (Ed.), *The Paradigm Dialog* (pp. 368–78). Newbury Park: Sage

Guerrero, L. K. (1998) Attachment-style differences in the experience and expression of romantic jealousy. *Personal Relationships*, **5**, 273–291.

Guerrero, L. K., & Andersen, P. A. (1998) The dark side of jealousy and envy: Desire, delusion, desperation, and destructive communication. In B. H. Spitzberg & W. R. Cupach (Eds), *The dark side of close relationships* (pp. 33–70). Mahwah, NJ: Erlbaum.

Guerrero, L. K., Andersen, P. A., Jorgensen, P. F., Spitzberg, B. H., & Eloy, S. V. (1995) Coping with the green-eyed monster: Conceptualizing and measuring communicative responses to romantic jealousy. *Western Journal of Communication*, **59**, 270–304.

Hacker, H. M. (1981) Blabbermouths and clams: Sex differences in self-disclosure in same-sex and cross-sex friendship dyads. *Psychology of Women Quarterly*, **5**, 385–401.

Haley, J. (1963) *Strategies of psychotherapy.* New York: Grune & Stratton.

Hall, D. M. (1998) The victims of stalking. In J. R. Meloy (Ed.) *The psychology of stalking* (pp. 113–137). San Diego, CA: Academic Press.

Hammen, C. L., Gordon, D., Burge, D., Adrian, C., Janicke, C., & Hiroto, D. (1987) Communication patterns of mothers with affective disorders and their relationship to children's status and social functioning. In K. Hahlweg & M.J. Goldstein (Eds) *Understanding major mental disorder* (pp. 103–119). New York: Family Process Press.

Hammer, M. (1980) Predictability of social connections over time. *Social Networks*, **2**, 165–180.

Harré, R. (1995) Relationships as dialog. Paper presented to the Annual Conference of the International Network on Personal Relationships, Williamsburg, VA, June.

Harris, L. M., & Sadeghi, A. (1987) Realizing: How facts are created in human interaction. *Journal of Social and Personal Relationships*, **4**, 480–495.

Harvey, J. H. (Ed.) (1996) *Journal of Personal and Interpersonal Loss.* Basingstoke: Taylor & Francis.

Harvey, J. H., & Uematsu, M. (1995) Why we must develop and tell our accounts of loss. Paper presented at Applied Research in Cognition and Memory Meeting, UBC.

Harvey, J. H., Agostinelli, G., & Weber, A.L. (1989) Account-making and the formation of expectations about close relationships. *Review of Personality and Social Psychology*, **10**, 39–62.

Harvey, J. H., Flanery, R., & Morgan, M. (1986)   Vivid memories of vivid loves gone by. *Journal of Social and Personal Relationships,* **3**, 359–373.

Harvey, J. H., Hendrick, S., & Tucker, K. (1988)   Self-report methods in studying personal relationships. In S. W. Duck (Ed.) *Handbook of personal relationships: Theory, research and interventions* (pp. 99–113). Chichester: Wiley.

Harvey, J. H., Orbuch, T., & Weber, A.L. (1990)   A social psychological model of account-making in response to severe stress. *Journal of Language and Social Psychology,* **9**, 191–207.

Harvey, J. H., Orbuch, T., & Weber, A.L. (1992)   (Eds) *Attributions, Accounts, and Close Relationships.* New York: Springer- Verlag.

Harvey, J. H., Orbuch, T., Weber, A.L., Merbach, N., & Alt, R. (1992)   House of pain and hope: Accounts of loss. *Death Studies,* **16**, 99–124.

Harvey, J. H., Weber, A.L. & Orbuch, T.L. (1990)   *Interpersonal accounts: A social psychological perspective.* Oxford: Blackwell.

Harvey, J. H., Wells, G., & Alvarez, M. (1978)   Attribution in the context of conflict and separation in close relationships. In J.H. Harvey, W. Ickes, & R. Kidd (Eds) *New directions in attribution research, Vol. 2* (pp. 235–259), Hillsdale, NJ: Erlbaum.

Haskell, M. (1990)   *Love and other infectious diseases: A memoir*, New York: William Morrow.

Hays, J. C., Landerman, L.R., George, L.K., Flint, E.P., Koenig, H.G., Land, K.C., & Blazer, D.G. (1998)   Social correlates of the dimensions of depression in the elderly. *Journals of Gerontology: Psychological Sciences and Social Sciences,* **53B**, P31-P39.

Hays, R. B. (1984)   The development and maintenance of friendship. *Journal of Social and Personal Relationships*, **1**, 75–98.

Hazan, C., & Shaver, P. (1987)   Romantic love conceptualized as an attachment process. *Journal of Personality and Social Psychology*, **52**, 511–524.

Hendrick, S. S., & Hendrick, C. (1992)   *Romantic love.* Newbury Park, CA: Sage.

Hendrick, S. S., & Hendrick, C. (1993)   Lovers as friends. *Journal of Social and Personal Relationships*, **10**, 459–466.

Herdt, G., & Boxer, A. (1992)   Introduction: Culture, history, and life course of gay men In G. Herdt (Ed.) *Gay culture in America* (pp. 1–28). Boston: Beacon Press.

Herzog, D. B., Pepose, M., Norman, D.K., & Rigotti, N.A. (1985)   Eating disorders and social maladjustment in female medical students. *Journal of Nervous and Mental Disease,* **173**, 734–737.

Hewitt, J., & Stokes, R. (1975)   Disclaimers. *American Sociological Review,* **40**, 1–11.

Hinde, R. A. (1979). *Towards Understanding Relationships.* Academic Press, London.

Hinde, R. A. (1987). *Individuals, Relationships and Culture.* New York: Cambridge University Press.

Hobfoll, S. E. (1996)   Social support: Will you be there when I need you? In N. Vanzetti & S. W. Duck (Eds) *A lifetime of relationships* (pp. 46–76). Monterey, CA: Brooks/Cole.

Hoffman, L. (1981)   *Foundations of family therapy.* New York: Basic Books.

Holland, D. C., & Eisenhart, M. A. (1990)   *Educated in romance: Women, achievement, and college culture.* Chicago, IL: University of Chicago Press.

Holmes, R. M. (1993)   Stalking in America: Types and methods of criminal stalkers. *Journal of Contemporary Criminal Justice*, **9**, 317–327.

Holquist, M. (1990)   *Dialogism: Bakhtin and his world*. New York: Routledge.

Honeycutt, J. M. (1993)   Memory structures for the rise and fall of personal relationships. In S. W. Duck (Ed.) *Individuals in relationships* (Understanding relationship processes 1) (pp. 60–86). Newbury Park, CA: Sage.

Honeycutt, J. M., Woods, B. L., & Fontenot, K. (1993)   The endorsement of communication conflict rules as a function of engagement, marriage and marital ideology. *Journal of Social and Personal Relationships,* **10**, 285–304.

Hooley, J. M. (1985)   Expressed emotion: A review of the critical literature. *Clinical Psychology Review*, **5**, 119–139.

Hooley, J. M., & Hiller, J. B. (1997)   Family relationships and major mental disorder: Risk factors and preventive strategies. In S. W. Duck (Ed.), *Handbook of personal relationships: Theory, research and interventions, 2nd edn.* (pp. 621–648). Chichester: Wiley.

Hopper, R. (1981)   How to do things without words: The taken-for-granted as speech action. *Communication Quarterly*, **29**, 228–236.

Hopper, R., Knapp, M. L., & Scott, L. (1981)   Couples' personal idioms: Exploring intimate talk. *Journal of Communication,* **31**, 23–33.

Hornstein, G. A. (1985)   Intimacy in conversational style as a function of the degree of closeness between members of a dyad. *Journal of Personality and Social Psychology*, **49**, 671–681.

Hughes, A. M., Medley, I., Turner, G.N., & Bond, M.R. (1987)   Psychogenic pain: A study of marital adjustment. *Acta Psychiatrica Scandinavia,* **75**, 166–170.

Humphrey, L. L. (1986)   Family relations in bulimic-anorexic and nondistressed families. *International Journal of Eating Disorders*, **5**, 223–232.

Hupka, R. B., Jung, J., & Silverthorn, K. (1987)   Perceived acceptability of apologies, excuses and justifications in jealousy predicaments. *Journal of Social Behavior and Personality,* **2**, 303–314.

Israel, J. (1979)   The language of dialectics and the dialectics of language. Copenhagen: Munksgaard.

Jackson, M. (1989)   *Paths Toward a Clearing: Radical Empiricism and Ethnographic Inquiry*. Bloomington, IN: Indiana University Press.

Johnson, M. P. (1991a)   Commitment to personal relationships. In W. H. Jones & D. W. Perlman (Eds) *Advances in personal relationships,* Vol. 3 (pp. 117–143). London: Jessica Kingsley.

Johnson, M. P. (1991b)   Reply to Levinger and Rusbult. In W. H. Jones & D. W. Perlman (Eds) *Advances in personal relationships* Vol. 3 (pp. 171–176). London: Jessica Kingsley.

Johnson, M. P., & Milardo, R. M. (1984)   Network interference in pair relationships: A social psychological recasting of Slater's theory of social regression. *Journal of Marriage and the Family*, **46**, 893–899.

Johnson, R. L., & Glass, C.R. (1989)   Heterosocial anxiety and direction of attention in high school boys. *Cognitive Therapy and Research,* **13**, 509–526.

Joiner, T., & Coyne, J.C. (Eds) (1999)   *The interactional nature of depression: Advances in interpersonal approaches*. Washington, DC: American Psychological Association.

Jones, E., & Gallois, C. (1989)   Spouses' impressions of rules for communication in public and private marital conflicts. *Journal of Marriage and the Family,* **51,** 957–967.

Jones, W. H., Briggs, S.R., & Smith, T.G. (1986)   Shyness: Conceptualization and measurement. *Journal of Personality and Social Psychology,* **51,** 629–639.

Josselson, R., & Lieblich, A. (Eds) (1993)   *The narrative study of lives* Newbury Park, CA: Sage.

Jourard, S. M. (1971)   *Self-disclosure*: *An experimental analysis of the transparent self.* New York: Wiley.

Julien, D., & Markman, H. (1991)   Social support and *Social Networks* as determinants of individual and marital outcomes, *Journal of Social and Personal Relationships*, **8,** 549–568.

Julien, D., Begin, J. & Chartrand, P. S. (1995)   Networks' support and interference in marriage: A comparison of husbands' and wives' disclosures of marital problems to confidants. Paper presented at the Annual Convention of the International Communication Association, Albuquerque, NM, May.

Kalichman, S. C., Sarwer, D. B., Johnson, J. R., Akram, S., Early, J., & Tuten, J. T. (1993)   Sexually coercive behavior and love styles. *Journal of Psychology & Human Sexuality*, **6,** 93–106.

Kaniasty, K., & Norris, F. H. (1997)   Social support dynamics in adjustment to disasters. In S. W. Duck (Ed.), *Handbook of Personal Relationships,* 2nd edn (pp. 595–620). Chichester: Wiley.

Karpel, M. (1976)   Individuation: From fusion to dialogue. *Family Process*, **15,** 65–82.

Kelley, H. H. (1979)   *Personal relationships: Their structure and process.* Hillsdale, NJ: Erlbaum.

Kelley, H. H., & Thibaut, J. W. (1978)   *Interpersonal relations: A theory of interdependence.* New York: Wiley.

Kelley, H. H., Berscheid, E., Christensen, A., Harvey, J. H., Huston, T. L., Levinger, G., McClintock, E., Peplau, L. A., & Peterson, D. R. (1983)   *Close relationships.* New York: W. H. Freeman.

Kempler, W. (1981)   *Principles of gestalt family therapy.* Salt Lake City, UT: Deseret Press.

Kerby, A. (1991)   *Narrative and the Self.* Bloomington, IN: Indiana University Press.

Kernberg, O. F. (1974)   Mature love: Prerequisites and characteristics. *Journal of the American Psychoanalytic Association*, **22,** 743–768.

Kernberg, O. F. (1986)   Structural derivatives of object relationships. In P. Buckley (Ed.) *Essential papers on object relations* (pp. 350–384). New York: New York University Press.

Kidd, V. (1975)   Happily ever after and other relationship styles: Advice on interpersonal relations in popular magazines, 1951–1973. *Quarterly Journal of Speech*, **61,** 31–39.

Kienlen, K. K. (1998)   Developmental and social antecedents of stalking. In J. R. Meloy (Ed.) *The psychology of stalking* (pp. 51–67). San Diego, CA: Academic Press.

Kienlen, K. K., Birmingham, D. L., Solberg, K. B., O'Regan, J. T., & Meloy, J. R. (1997)   A comparative study of psychotic and nonpsychotic stalking. *Journal of the American Academy of Psychiatry and Law*, **25,** 317–334.

Kiesinger, C. (1995)   The anorexic and bulimic self. Unpublished PhD Dissertation, University of South Florida.

Killworth, P. D., Bernard, H. R., & McCarty, C. (1984)   Measuring patterns of acquaintanceship. *Current Anthropology*, **25**, 381–397.

Kim, H. J., & Stiff, J. B. (1991)   *Social Networks* and the development of close relationships. *Human Communication Research*, **18**, 70–91.

Klerman, G. L. (1986)   Historical perspectives on contemporary schools of psychopathology. In T. Millon & G.L. Klerman (Eds) *Contemporary directions in psychopathology: Toward the DSM-IV* (pp. 3–28). New York: Guilford.

Knapp, M. L., & Taylor, E. H. (1994)   Commitment and its communication in romantic relationships. In A. L. Weber & J. H. Harvey (Eds) *Perspectives on close relationships* (pp. 153–175). Boston, MA: Allyn & Bacon.

Knapp, M. L., & Vangelisti, A. (1992)   *Interpersonal communication and human relationships,* 2nd edn. Boston, MA: Allyn and Bacon.

Kon, I., & Losenkov, V. A. (1978)   Friendship in adolescence: Values and behavior. *Journal of Marriage and the Family*, **40**, 143–155.

Krain, M. (1977)   A definition of dyadic boundaries and an empirical study of boundary establishment in courtship. *International Journal of Sociology of the Family*, **7**, 107–123.

Kuhn, T. (1970)   Reflections on my critics. In E. Lakatos & A. Musgrave (Eds) *Criticism and the growth of knowledge* (pp. 231–278).Cambridge: Cambridge University Press.

L'Abate, K., & L'Abate, B. (1979)   The paradoxes of intimacy. *Family Therapy*, **6**, 175–184.

La Gaipa, J. J. (1990)   The negative effects of informal support systems. In S. W. Duck (Ed.) *Personal relationships and social support* (pp. 122–139). Newbury Park, CA: Sage.

Laing, R. (1969)   *Self and Others*. London: Penguin.

Langellier, K., & Peterson, E. (1993)   Family storytelling as a strategy of social control. In D. Mumby (Ed.) *Narrative and social control: Critical perspectives* (pp.49–76). Newbury Park, CA: Sage.

Lannamann, J. W. (1991)   Interpersonal communication research as ideological practice, *Communication Theory*, **1**, 179–203.

Lannamann, J. W. (1992)   Deconstructing the person and changing the subject of interpersonal studies. *Communication Theory*, **2**, 139–148.

Larson, L. (1974)   System and subsystem perception of family roles. *Journal of Marriage and the Family*, **36**, 123–138.

Laws, J. L., & Schwartz, P. (1981)   *Sexual scripts: The social construction of female sexuality*. Washington, DC: University Press of America.

Lazarus, R .S. (1993)   From psychological stress to the emotions: A history of changing outlooks. *Annual Review of Psychology*, **22**, 1–21.

Leary, M. R. (1983)   Social anxiousness: The construct and its measurement. *Journal of Personality Assessment,* **47**, 66–75.

Leary, M. R., & Atherton, S.C. (1986)   Self-efficacy, social anxiety, and inhibition in interpersonal encounters. *Journal of Social and Clinical Psychology,* **4**, 256–267.

Leary, M. R., & Kowalski, R. M. (1988)   Self-presentational concerns and social anxiety: The role of generalized impression expectations. *Journal of Research in Personality,* **22**, 308–321.

Leary, M. R., & Kowalski, R. M. (1995)   *Social anxiety.* New York: Guilford.

Leary, M. R., Knight, P.D., & Johnson, K.A. (1987)   Social anxiety and dyadic conversation: A verbal response mode analysis. *Journal of Social and Clinical Psychology,* **5**, 34–50.

Leary, M. R., Kowalski, R.M., & Campbell, C. (1988)   Self-presentational concerns and social anxiety: The role of generalized impression expectancies. *Journal of Research in Personality,* **22**, 308–321.

Leary, T. (1957)   *Interpersonal diagnosis of personality.* New York: Ronald.

Leichty, G., & Applegate, J. L. (1991)   Social-cognitive and situational influences on the use of face-saving persuasive strategies. *Human Communication Research,* **17**, 451–484.

Leslie, L. A. (1983)   Parental influences and premarital relationship development (Doctoral dissertation, Pennsylvania State University, 1982). *Dissertation Abstracts International,* **43**, 277A.

Leslie, L. A., Huston, T. L., & Johnson, M. P. (1986)   Parental reactions to dating relationships: Do they make a difference? *Journal of Marriage and the Family,* **48**, 57–66.

Levinger, G. (1965)   Marital cohesiveness and dissolution: An integrative review. *Journal of Marriage and the Family,* **27**, 19–28.

Levinger, G. (1979)   A social exchange view of the dissolution of pair relationships. In R. L. Burgess & T. L. Huston (Eds) *Social exchange in developing relationships* (pp. 169–193). New York: Academic Press.

Levinger, G. (1991)   Commitment vs. cohesiveness: Two complementary perspectives. In W. H. Jones & D. W. Perlman (Eds) *Advances in personal relationships* Vol. 3 (pp. 145–150). London: Jessica Kingsley.

Levinger, G., & Snoek, D. J. (1972)   *Attraction in relationship: A new look at interpersonal attraction.* Morristown, N.J: General Learning Press.

Lewinsohn, P. M. (1974)   A behavioral approach to depression. In R.J. Friedman & M.M. Katz (Eds) *The psychology of depression: Contemporary theory and research* (pp. 157–185). Washington, DC: Winston-Wiley.

Lewinsohn, P. M. (1975)   The behavioral study and treatment of depression. In M. Hersen, R. M. Eisler, & P.M. Miller (Eds) *Progress in behavior modification,* Vol 1, (pp. 19–64). New York: Academic Press.

Lewis, H .B. (1971)   *Shame and guilt in neurosis.* New York: International Universities Press.

Lewis, R. A. (1973)   Social reaction and the formation of dyads: An interactionist approach to mate selection. *Sociometry,* **36**, 409–418.

Lim, T. S. (1990)   Politeness behavior in social influence situations. In J. P. Dillard (Ed.) *Seeking compliance: The production of interpersonal influence messages* (pp. 75–86). Scottsdale, AZ: Gorsuch Scarisbrick.

Lim, T. S. (1994)   Facework and interpersonal relationships. In S. Ting-Toomey (Ed.) *The challenge of facework: Cross-cultural and interpersonal issues* (pp. 209–230). Albany: State University of New York Press.

Lim, T. S., & Bowers, J. W. (1991) Facework: Solidarity, approbation, and tact. *Human Communication Research*, **17**, 415–450.

Limandri, B. (1989) Disclosure of stigmatizing conditions: The discloser's perspective. *Archives of Psychiatric Nursing*, **III**, 69–78.

Lin, Y-H. W., & Rusbult, C.E. (1995) Commitment to dating relationships and cross-sex friendships in America and China. *Journal of Social and Personal Relationships*, **12**, 7–26.

Linde, C. (1993) *Life stories: The creation of coherence.* Oxford: Oxford University Press.

Linden, R. (1993) *Making stories, making selves: Feminist reflections on the Holocaust.* Columbus, OH:Ohio State University Press.

Lloyd, S. A., & R. M. Cate (1985) 'The developmental course of conflict in dissolution of premarital relationships.' *Journal of Social and Personal Relationships*, **2**, 179–194.

Locke, H. J. (1951) *Predicting adjustment in marriage.* New York: Holt.

Lucas, A. R., Beard, C.M., O'Fallon, W.M., & Kurland, L.T. (1988) Anorexia nervosa in Rochester, Minnesota: A 45-year study. *Mayo Clinic Proceedings*, **63**, 433–442.

Lyotard, J. (1984) *The postmodern condition: A report on knowledge*, Minneapolis, MN: University of Minnesota Press.

Maccoby, E. (1988) Gender as a social category. *Developmental Psychology*, **24**, 755–765.

MacFarlane, I., & Krebs, S. (1986) Techniques for interviewing and evidence gathering. In K. MacFarlane & J. Waterman (Eds) *Sexual abuse of young children* (pp. 67–100). New York: Guilford.

Mahler, M. S. (1986) On the first three subphases of the separation-individuation process. In P. Buckley (Ed.) *Essential papers on object relations* (pp. 222–232). New York: New York University Press.

Mahoney, J., & Heretick, D.M.L. (1979) Factor-specific dimensions in person perception for same- and opposite- sex friendship dyads. *Journal of Social Psychology*, **107**, 219–225.

Maines, D. (1993) Narrative's moment and sociology's phenomena: Toward a narrative sociology. *Sociological Quarterly*, **34**, 17–38.

Mairs, N. (1989) *Remembering the bone house: An erotics of place and space.* New York: Harper & Row.

Malone, J. W. (1980) *Straight women/gay men.* New York: Dial Press.

Malow, R. M., & Olson, R.E. (1984) Family characteristics of myofascial pain dysfunction syndrome patients. *Family Systems Medicine,* **2**, 428–431.

Mao, T. (1965) *On contradiction.* Beijing: Foreign Languages Press.

Marks, G., Bundek, N., Richardson, J., Ruiz, M., Maldonado, N., & Mason, J. (1992) Self-disclosure of HIV infection: Preliminary results from a sample of Hispanic men. *Health Psychology*, **11**, 300–306.

Martin, L. L., & Tesser, A. (1989) Toward a motivational and structural theory of ruminative thought. In J .S. Uleman & J. A. Bargh (Eds) *Unintended thought* (pp. 306–326). New York: Guilford.

Martin, L. L., & Tesser, A. (1996a) Clarifying our thoughts. In R. S. Wyer (Ed.) *Ruminative thoughts* (pp. 189–208). Mahwah, NJ: Erlbaum.

Martin, L. L., & Tesser, A. (1996b)   Some ruminative thoughts. In R .S. Wyer (Ed.) *Ruminative thoughts* (pp. 1–47). Mahwah, NJ: Erlbaum.

Martin, L. L., Tesser, A., & McIntosh, W. D. (1993)   Wanting but not having: The effects of unattained goals on thoughts and feelings. In D. M. Wegner & J. W. Pennebaker (Eds) *Handbook of mental control* (pp. 552–572). Englewood Cliffs, NJ: Prentice-Hall.

Masheter, C. (1991)   Postdivorce relationships between ex-spouses: The roles of attachment and interpersonal conflict. *Journal of Marriage and the Family*, **53**, 103–110.

Masheter, C. (1994)   Dialogues between ex-spouses: Evidence of dialectic relationship development. In R. Conville (Ed.) *Structure in communication study* (pp. 83–102). New York: Praeger.

Masheter, C., & Harris, L. (1986)   From divorce to friendship: A study of dialectic relationship development. *Journal of Social and Personal Relationships*, **3**, 177–190.

Maturana, H. (1991)   Science and daily life: The ontology of scientific explanations. In F. Steier (Ed.) *Research and reflexivity* (pp. 30–52), London: Sage.

Maynard, D. W., & Zimmerman, D. H. (1984)   Topical talk, ritual and the social organization of relationships. *Social Psychology Quarterly*, **47**, 301–316.

Mazanec, M. J. (1995, November)   Border work by gays, lesbians, and bisexuals: Coming out on the borders of experience. Paper presented at the Speech Communication Association Convention, San Antonio.

McCabe, A. (Ed.) (1993)   *Journal of Narrative and Life History*. Erlbaum, Hillsdale, NJ.

McCabe, S. B., & Gotlib, I.H. (1993)   Interactions of couples with and without a depressed spouse: Self-report and observations of problems-solving interactions. *Journal of Social and Personal Relationships*, **10**, 589–599.

McCall, G. J. (1982)   Becoming unrelated: The management of bond dissolution. In S. W. Duck (Ed.) *Personal relationships 4: Dissolving personal relationships* (pp. 211–231). London: Academic Press.

McCall, G. J. (1988)   The organizational life cycle of relationships. In S. W. Duck (Ed.) *Handbook of personal Relationships* (pp. 467–486). Chichester: Wiley.

McCann, J. T. (1998)   Subtypes of stalking (obsessional following) in adolescents. *Journal of Adolescence*, **21**, 667–675.

McIntosh, W. D. (1996)   When does goal nonattainment lead to negative emotional reactions, and when doesn't it?: The role of linking and rumination. In L. L. Martin & A. Tesser (Eds) *Striving and feeling: Interactions among goals, affect, and self-regulation* (pp. 53–77). Mahwah, NJ: Erlbaum.

McIntosh, W. D., & Martin, L. L. (1992)   The cybernetics of happiness: The relation of goal attainment, rumination, and affect. In M. S. Clark (Ed.) *Emotion and social behavior* (pp. 222–246). Newbury Park, CA: Sage.

McIntosh, W. D., Harlow, T. F., & Martin, L. L. (1995)   Linkers and nonlinkers: Goal beliefs as a moderator of the effects of everyday hassles on rumination, depression, and physical complaints. *Journal of Applied Social Psychology*, **25**(14), 1231–1244.

McIntyre, A. (1981)   *After virtue: A study in moral theory*, London: Duckworth.

McLaughlin, M. L., Cody, M. J., & O'Hair, H. D. (1983) The management of failure events: Some contextual determinants of accounting behavior. *Human Communication Research, 9*, 208–224.

Mead, G. H. (1934) *Mind, self, and society.* Chicago, IL: Cambridge University Press.

Meloy, J. R. (1992) *Violent attachments.* Northvale, NJ: Jason Aronson.

Meloy, J. R. (1996) Stalking (obsessional following): A review of some preliminary studies. *Aggression and Violent Behavior, 1*, 147–162.

Meloy, J. R. (1998) The psychology of stalking. In J. R. Meloy (Ed.) *The psychology of stalking* (pp. 2–24). San Diego, CA: Academic Press.

Meloy, J. R., & Gothard, S. (1995) Demographic and clinical comparison of obsessional followers and offenders with mental disorders. *American Journal of Psychiatry, 152*, 258–263.

Metts, S. (1992) The language of disengagement: A face-management perspective. In T. L. Orbuch (Ed.) *Close relationship loss* (pp. 111–127). New York: Springer-Verlag.

Metts, S. (1994) Relational transgressions. In B. R. Cupach & B. H. Spitzberg (Eds) *The dark side of interpersonal communication* (pp. 217–240). Hillsdale, NJ: Erlbaum.

Metts, S., & Cupach, W. R. (1989) Situational influence on the use of remedial strategies in embarrassing predicaments. *Communication Monographs, 56*, 151–162.

Metts, S., & Mongeau, P. (1994, July) The management of critical events in continuing and noncontinuing relationships. Paper presented at the annual meeting of the Speech Communication Association, Atlanta, GA.

Metts, S., & Spitzberg, B. H. (1996) Sexual communication: A script-based approach. In B. R. Burleson (Ed.), *Communication Yearbook* 19 (pp. 49–92). Thousand Oaks, CA: Sage.

Metts, S., Backaus, S., & Kazoleas, D. (1995, February) Social support as problematic communication. Paper presented at the annual meeting of the Western States Speech Communication Association Convention, Portland, OR.

Metts, S., Cupach, W. R., & Bejlovec, R. A. (1989) "I love you too much to ever start liking you": Redefining romantic relationships. *Journal of Social and Personal Relationships, 6*, 259–274.

Miell, D. E. (1984) Cognitive and communicative strategies in developing relationships. Unpublished doctoral dissertation, University of Lancaster.

Miell, D. E., & Duck, S. W. (1986) Strategies in developing friendships. In V.J. Derlega & B.A. Winstead (Eds) *Friends and social interaction* (pp. 129–143), New York: Springer Verlag.

Miklowitz, D. J. (1994) Family risk indicators in schizophrenia. *Schizophrenia Bulletin, 20*, 137–149.

Miklowitz, D. J., Goldstein, M.J., & Neuchterlein, K.H. (1995) Verbal interactions in the families of schizophrenic and bipolar affective patients. *Journal of Abnormal Psychology, 104*, 268–276.

Miklowitz, D. J., Stracham, A.M., Goldstein, M.J., Doane, J.A., Snyder, K.S., Hogarty, G.E., & Falloon, I.R. (1986) Expressed emotion and communication deviance in the families of schizophrenics. *Journal of Abnormal Psychology, 95*, 60–66.

Miklowitz, D. J., Velligan, D.I., Goldstein, M.J., Nuechterlein, K.H., Gitlin, M.J., Ranlett, G., & Doane, J.A. (1991)   Communication deviance in families of schizophrenic and manic patients. *Journal of Abnormal Psychology*, **100**, 163–173.

Milardo, R. M. (1982)   Friendship networks in developing relations: Converging and diverging environments. *Social Psychology Quarterly*, **45**, 162–172.

Milardo, R. M. (1984)   Theoretical and methodological issues in the identification of the *Social Networks* of spouses. *Journal of Marriage and the Family*, **51**, 165–174.

Milardo, R. M. (1987)   Changes in *Social Networks* of women and men following divorce. *Journal of Family Issues*, **8**, 78–96.

Milardo, R. M. (1988)   Families and *Social Networks*: An overview of theory and methodology. In R. M. Milardo (Ed.), *Families and social networks* (pp. 13–47). Newbury Park, CA: Sage.

Milardo, R. M. (1989)   Theoretical and methodological issues in identifying the *Social Networks* of spouses. *Journal of Marriage and the Family*, **51**, 165–174.

Milardo, R. M., & Lewis, R. A. (1985)   *Social Networks*, families, and mate selection: A transactional analysis. In L. L'Abate (Ed.) *Handbook of family psychology and therapy*, Vol. 1 (pp. 258–283). Homewood, IL: Dorsey.

Milardo, R. M., & Wellman, B. (1992)   The personal is social. *Journal of Social and Personal Relationships*, **9**, 339–342.

Milgram, S. (1967)   The small world problem. *Psychology Today*, **1**, 60–67.

Millar, K. U., Tesser, A., & Millar, M. (1988)   The effects of a threatening life event on behavior sequences and intrusive thought: A self-disruption explanation. *Cognitive Therapy and Research*, **12**, 441–457.

Miller, G. R. (1989). Paradigm dialogues: brief thoughts on an unexplored theme. In B. Dervin, L. Grossberg, B. O'Keefe & E. Wartella (Eds), *Rethinking Communication, Vol. 1: Paradigm Issues* (pp. 187–91). Newbury Park, CA: Sage.

Miller, R. S. (1996)   *Embarrassment: Poise and peril in everyday life*. New York: Guilford.

Millon, T. (1981)   *Disorders of personality: DSM-III, Axis II*. New York: Wiley-Interscience.

Millon, T. (1990)   The disorders of personality. In L.A. Pervin (Ed.) *Handbook of Personality Theory and Research* (pp. 339–370). New York: Guilford.

Mills, C. (1963)   *Power, Politics and People: The Collected Essays of C. Wright Mills* In I. Horowitz (Ed.) New York: Ballantine.

Mink, L. (1969–1970)   History and fiction as modes of comprehension. *New Literary History*, **1**.

Minuchin, P. (1974)   *Families and family therapy*. Cambridge, MA: Harvard University Press.

Mirkovic, D. (1980)   *Dialectic and sociological thought*. St. Catherines. Ontario, Canada: Diliton Publications.

Mishler, E. (1986)   The analysis of interview-narratives. In T. Sarbin (Ed.*)* *Narrative psychology: The storied nature of human conduct* (pp. 233–255) New York: Praeger.

Mishler, E. (1995)   Models of narrative analysis: A typology. *Journal of Narrative and Life History*, **5**, 87–123.

Mitchell, J. C. (1969)   The concept and use of *Social Networks*. In J. C. Mitchell (Ed) *Social networks in urban situations: Analyses of personal relationships in central African towns* (pp. 1–50). Manchester: Manchester University Press.

Monsour, M. (1992)   Meanings of intimacy in cross- and same-sex friendships. *Journal of Social and Personal Relationships*, **9**, 277–295.

Monsour, M. (1994)   Challenges confronting cross-sex friendships: "Much ado about nothing?". *Sex Roles*, **31**, 55–77.

Monsour, M., Betty, S., & Kurzweil, N. (1993)   Levels of perspectives and the perception of intimacy in cross-sex friendships: A balance theory explanation of shared perceptual reality. *Journal of Social and Personal Relationships*, **10**, 529–550.

Montgomery, B. M. (1984)   Communication in intimate relationships: A research challenge. *Communication Quarterly*, **32**, 233–240.

Montgomery, B. M. (1988)   Quality communication in personal relationships. In S. W. Duck (Ed.) *Handbook of personal relationships: Theory, research, and interventions* (pp. 343–359) Chichester: Wiley.

Montgomery, B. M. (1992)   Communication as the interface between couples and culture. *Communication Yearbook,* **15**, 475–507

Montgomery, B. M. (1993)   Relationship maintenance versus relationship change: A dialectical dilemma. *Journal of Social and Personal Relationships*, **10**, 205–224.

Montgomery, B. M., & Baxter, L. A. (Eds) (1998)   *Dialectical approaches to studying personal relationships*. Mahwah, NJ: Erlbaum.

Morrison, H. L. (Ed.) (1983). *Children of depressed parents: Risk, identification, and intervention.* New York: Grune & Stratton.

Morson, G., & Emerson, C. (1990)   *Mikhail Bakhtin: Creation of a prosaics.* Palo Alto, FL:: Stanford University Press.

Mukaia, T. (1989)   A call for our language: Anorexia from within. *Women's Studies International Forum*, **12**, 613–638.

Murphy, R. (1971)   *The dialectics of social life.* New York: Basic Books.

Myerhoff, B. (1978)   *Number our days.* New York: Simon & Schuster.

Nardi, P. M. (1992)   Sex, friendship, and gender roles among gay men. In P. Nardi (Ed.) *Men's friendships* (pp. 173–185). Newbury Park: Sage.

Nestle, J., & Preston, J. (1994)   *Sister and brother: Lesbians and gay men write about their lives together.* San Francisco, CA: Harper Collins.

Neugeboren, J. (1997)   *Imagining Robert: My brother, madness, and survival.* New York: William Morrow.

Nezlek, J. B., Imbrie, M., & Shean, G.D. (1994)   Depression and everyday social interaction. *Journal of Personality and Social Psychology*, **67**, 1101–1111.

Nordahl, H. M., & Stiles, T.C. (1997)   Perceptions of parental bonding in patients with various personality disorders, lifetime depressive disorders, and healthy controls. *Journal of Personality Disorders*, **11**, 391–402.

Norton, R. W. (1988)   Communicator style theory in marital interaction: persistent challenges. In S. W. Duck (Ed.) *Handbook of Personal Relationships* (pp. 307–324). Chichester: Wiley.

Nussbaum, J.F. (1989)   Life-span communication: An introduction. In J.F. Nussbaum (Ed.) *Life-span communication: Normative processes* (pp. 1–4), Hillsdale, NJ: Erlbaum.

O'Mahony, J. F., & Hollwey, S. (1995)   Eating problems and interpersonal functioning among several groups of women. *Journal of Clinical Psychology*, **51**,
345–351.

O'Meara, J. D. (1989)   Cross-sex friendship: Four basic challenges of an ignored
relationship. *Sex Roles*, **21**, 525–543.

O'Meara, J. D. (1994)   Cross-sex friendship's opportunity challenge: Uncharted
terrain for exploration. *Personal Relationship Issues*, **2**, 4–7.

Ohbuchi, K., Kameda, M., & Agarie, N. (1989)   Apology as aggression control: Its
role in mediating appraisal of and response to harm. *Journal of Personality and
Social Psychology*, **56**, 219–227.

Oliker, S. J. (1989)   *Best friends and marriage*: *Exchange among women*. Berkeley,
CA: University of California Press.

Olson, D. H. (1993)   Circumplex model of marital and family systems: Assessing
family functioning. In F. Walsh (Ed.) *Normal family processes*, 2nd edn (pp.
104–137). New York: Guilford.

Overholser, J. C. (1996)   The dependent personality and interpersonal problems.
Journal of Nervous and Mental Disease, **184**, 8–16.

Owen, W. F. (1987)   Mutual interaction of discourse structures and relational pragmatics in conversational influence attempts. *Southern Journal of Speech
Communication*, **52**, 103–127.

Paget, M. (ed. by M.L. DeVault) (1993)   A *Complex Sorrow: Reflections on Cancer
and an Abbreviated Life*. Philadelphia, PA: Temple University Press.

Paine, R. (1974)   An exploratory analysis in 'middle-class' culture. In E. Leylon
(Ed.) *The compact: Selected dimensions of friendship* (pp. 117–137). St. John's:
Institute of Social and Economic Research.

Palmer, R. L., Oppenheimer, R., & Marshall, P.D. (1988)   Eating-disordered
patients remember their parents: A study using the parental bonding instrument.
International Journal of Eating Disorders, **7**, 101–106.

Paradis, B. A. (1991)   Seeking intimacy and integration: Gay men in the era of
AIDS. *Smith College Studies in Social Work*, **61**, 260–274.

Parks, M. R. (1982)   Ideology in interpersonal communication: Off the couch and
into the world. In M. Burgoon (Ed). *Communication Yearbook* 5 (pp. 79–108),
New Brunswick, NJ: Transaction Books.

Parks, M. R. (1995)   Webs of influence in interpersonal relationships. In C. R.
Burger & M. E. Burgoon (Eds) *Communication and social influence processes* (pp.
155–178). East Lansing, MI: Michigan State University Press.

Parks, M. R., & Adelman, M. B. (1983)   Communication networks and the development of romantic relationships: An expansion of uncertainty reduction theory.
Human Communication Research, **10**, 55–79.

Parks, M. R., & Barnes, K. J. (1988)   With a little help from my friends: The role
of third parties in the initiation of interpersonal relationships. Paper presented at
the Annual Convention of the Speech Communication Association, New
Orleans, LA.

Parks, M. R., & Eggert, L. (1991)   The role of social context in the dynamics of
personal relationships in W. Jones and D. Perlman (Eds), *Advances in Personal
Relationships, Vol.2*. London: Jessica Kingsley. (pp. 1–34).

Parks, M. R., & Floyd, K. (1995)   Friends in cyberspace: Exploring personal relationships formed through the Internet. Paper presented at the annual convention of
the International Communication Association, Albuquerque, NM, May.

Parks, M. R., & Riveland, L. (1987)   On dealing with disliked friends of friends: A
study of the occurrence and management of imbalanced relationships. Paper
presented at the annual conventionof the International Communication
Association. Montreal, Quebec, May.

Parks, M. R., Stan, C., & Eggert, L. L. (1983)   Romantic involvement and social
network involvement. *Social Psychology Quarterly*, **46**, 116–130.

Parry, A. (1991)   A universe of stories. *Family Process*, **30**, 37–54.

Parry, A., & Doan, R. (1994)   *Story Re-Visions: Narrative Therapy in the
Postmodern World*. New York: Guilford.

Pathé, M., & Mullen, P. E. (1997)   The impact of stalkers on their victims. *British
Journal of Psychiatry*, **170**, 12–17.

Pearce, W. B. (1989)   *Communication and the human condition*. Carbondale, IL:
Southern Illinois University Press.

Pearce, W. B., & Cronen, V. (1980)   *Communication, action and meaning: The
creation of social realities*. New York: Prager.

Pearce, W. B., & Sharp, S. M. (1973)   Self-disclosing communication. *Journal of
Communication*, **23**, 409–425.

Penman, R. (1994)   Facework in communication: Conceptual and moral challenges.
In S. Ting-Toomey (Ed.) *The challenge of facework* (pp. 15–46). New York: State
University of New York Press.

Petronio, S. (1988)   The dissemination of private information: The use of a
boundary control system as an alternative perspective to the study of disclosures.
Paper presented at the Speech Communication Association Convention, New
Orlean, LA, November.

Petronio, S. (1991)   Communication boundary management: A theoretical model of
managing disclosure of private information between marital couples.
Communication Theory, **1**, 311–335.

Pike, K. M., & Rodin, J. (1991)   Mothers, daughters, and disordered eating. *Journal
of Abnormal Psychology*, **100**, 198–204.

Pinto, R. P., & Hollandsworth, J. G. (1984)   A measure of possessiveness in intimate
relationships. *Journal of Social and Clinical Psychology*, **2**(3), 273–279.

Planalp, S., & Garvin-Doxas, K. (1994)   Using mutual knowledge in conversation:
Friends as experts in each other. In S. W. Duck (Ed.) *The dynamics of relationship*
(Understanding relationship processes 4) (pp. 1–26). Thousand Oaks, CA: Sage

Plummer, K. (1975)   *Sexual stigma: An interactionist account*. London: Routledge
and Kegan Paul..

Polkinghorne, D. (1988)   *Narrative knowing and the human sciences*, Albany:
SUNY Press.

Prusank, D., Duran, R., & DeLillo, D. A. (1993)   Interpersonal relationships in
women's magazines: Dating and relating in the 1970s and 1980s. *Journal of Social
and Personal Relationships*, **10**, 307–320.

Pyszczynski, T., & Greenberg, J. (1987)   Self-regulatory perseveration and the
depressive self-focusing style: A self-awareness theory of reactive depression.
Psychological Bulletin, **102**, 122–138.

Rabinow, P., & Sullivan, W. (1987) *Interpretive social science: A second look*, Berkeley, CA: University of California Press.

Rachman, S. (1997) A cognitive theory of obsessions. *Behaviour Research and Therapy*, **35**, 793–802.

Rands, M. (1988) Changes in *Social Networks* following marital separation and divorce. In R. M. Milardo (Ed.) *Families and social networks* (pp. 127–146). Newbury Park, CA: Sage.

Rawlins, W. K. (1981) Friendship as a communicative achievement: A theory and an interpretive analysis of verbal reports. Unpublished doctoral dissertation, Temple University.

Rawlins, W. K. (1982) Cross-sex friendship and the communicative management of sex-role expectations. *Communication Quarterly*, **30**, 343–352.

Rawlins, W. K. (1983a) Negotiating close friendship: The dialectic of conjunctive freedoms. *Human Communication Research*, **9**, 255–266.

Rawlins, W. K. (1983b) Openness as problematic in ongoing friendships: Two conversational dilemmas. *Communication Monographs*, **50**, 1–13.

Rawlins, W. K. (1989) A dialectical analysis of the tensions, functions, and strategic challenges of communication in young adult friendships. *Communication Yearbook,* **12**, 157–189.

Rawlins, W. K. (1992) *Friendship matters: Communication, dialectics, and the life course*. New York: Aldine de Gruyter.

Rawlins, W. K. (1993) Communication in cross-sex friendships. In L.P. Arliss & D.J. Borisoff (Eds) *Women and men communicating* (pp. 51–70). Orlando, FL: Holt, Rinehart and Winston, Inc.

Rawlins, W. K. (1994) Being there and growing apart: Sustaining friendships during adulthood. In D. J. Canary & L. Stafford (Eds) *Communication and relational maintenance* (pp. 275–296). New York: Academic Press.

Rawlins, W. K., & Holl, M. R. (1987) The communicative achievement of friendship during adolescence: Predicaments of trust and violation. *Western Journal of Speech Communication*, **51**, 345–363.

Rawlins, W. K., & Holl, M. R. (1988) Adolescents' interaction with parents and friends: Dialectics of temporal perspective and evaluation. *Journal of Social and Personal Relationships*, **5**, 27–46.

Retzinger, S. M. (1991) *Violent emotions: Shame and rage in marital quarrels*. Newbury Park, CA: Sage.

Retzinger, S. M. (1995) Shame and anger in personal relationships. In S. W. Duck & J. T. Wood (Eds) *Relationship challenges:* (Understanding relationship processes 5) (pp. 22–42). Thousand Oaks, CA: Sage.

Rhodes, B., & Kroger, J. (1992) Parental bonding and separation-individuation difficulties among late-adolescent eating disordered women. *Child Psychiatry and Human Development*, **22**, 249–263.

Rhodewalt, F., & Morf, C.C. (1995) Self and interpersonal correlates of the narcissistic personality inventory: A review and new findings. *Journal of Research in Personality*, **29**, 1–23.

Richardson, L. (1990) Narrative and sociology. *Journal of Contemporary Ethnography*, **19**, 116–135.

Richardson, L. (1994)   Writing as a method of inquiry. In N. Denzin & Y. Lincoln (Eds) *Handbook of qualitative research*. Thousand Oaks, CA: Sage.

Ricoeur, P. (1983)   *Hermeneutics and the human sciences: Essays on language, action and interpretation* (Trans. J. Thompson). New York: Cambridge University Press.

Riegel, K. (1976)   The dialectics of human development. *American Psychologist*, **31**, 689–700.

Riessman, C. (1990)   *Divorce talk: Men and women make sense of personal relationships*. New Brunswick, NJ: Rutgers University Press.

Riessman, C. (1992)   Making sense of marital violence: One woman's narrative. In G.C. Rosenwald & R.L. Ochberg (Eds) *Storied lives: The cultural politics of self-understanding* (pp. 231–249). New Haven, CT: Yale University Press.

Roberts, A. R., & Dziegielewski, S. F. (1996)   Assessment typology and intervention with the survivors of stalking. *Aggression and Violent Behavior*, **1**, 359–368.

Roberts, M. K. (1982)   Men and women: Partners, lovers, friends. In K. E. Davis & T. Mitchell (Eds), *Advances in descriptive psychology*, **2**, 57–78.

Roloff, M. E. (1987)   Communication and reciprocity within intimate relationships. In M. R. Roloff & G. R. Miller (Eds) *Interpersonal processes: New directions in communication research* (pp. 11–38). Newbury Park, CA: Sage.

Roloff, M. E., & Janiszewski, C. A. (1989)   Overcoming obstacles to interpersonal compliance: A principle of message construction. *Human Communication Research,* **16**, 33–61.

Roloff, M. E., Janiszewski, C. A., McGrath, M. A., Burns, C. S., Manrai, L. A. (1988) Acquiring resources from intimates: When obligation substitutes for persuasion. *Human Communication Research,* **14**, 364–396.

Romans, J. S. C., Hays, J. R., & White, T. K. (1996)   Stalking and related behaviors experienced by counseling center staff members from current or former clients. *Professional Psychology: Research and Practice*, **27**, 595–599.

Ronai, C. R. (1992)   The reflexive self through narrative: A night in the life of an erotic dancer/researcher. In C. Ellis & M. Flaherty (Eds) *Investigating subjectivity: Research on lived experience* (pp. 102–124. Newbury Park, CA: Sage.

Ronai, C. R. (1994)   Multiple reflections on child sex abuse: An argument for a layered account. *Journal of Contemporary Ethnography*, **23**, 395–426.

Rorty, R. (1967)   *The linguistic turn: Recent essays in philosophical method*, Chicago, IL: University of Chicago Press.

Rorty, R. (1979)   *Philosophy and the mirror of nature*, Princeton, NJ: Princeton University Press.

Rorty, R. (1982)   *Consequences of pragmatism (essays 1972–1980)*, Minneapolis, MN: University of Minnesota Press.

Rorty, R. (1989)   *Contingency, irony, solidarity*, Cambridge: Cambridge University Press.

Rosaldo, R. (1984)   Grief and a headhunter's rage: On the cultural force of the emotions. In E. Bruner (Ed.) *Text, play, and story: The construction and reconstruction of self and society: Proceedings of the American Ethnological Society* (pp. 178–195). Washington, DC: American Ethnological Society.

Rose, S. M. (1985)   Same- and cross-sex friendships and the psychology of homosociality. *Sex Roles*, **12**, 63–74.

Rosenau, P. (1992)   *Postmodernism and the social sciences: Insights, inroads, and intrusions*. Princeton, NJ: Princeton University Press.

Rosenberg, S., Rosenberg, H., & Farrell, M. (1992)   In the name of the father. In G.C. Rosenwald & R.L. Ochberg (eds) *Storied lives: The cultural politics of self-understanding* (pp. 41–59). New Haven, CT: Yale University Press.

Rosenberger, N. R. (1989). Dialectic balance in the polar model of self: the Japan case. *Ethos*, **17**, 88–113.

Rosenfarb, I. S., Goldstein, M.J., Mintz, J., & Nuechterlein, K.H. (1995)   Expressed emotion and subclinical psychopathology observable with the transactions between schizophrenic patients and their family members. *Journal of Abnormal Psychology*, **104**, 259–267.

Rosenwald, G. C. (1992)   Conclusion: Reflections on narrative understanding. In G.C. Rosenwald & R.L. Ochberg (Eds) *Storied lives: The cultural politics of self-understanding* (pp. 265–289). New Haven, CT: Yale University Press.

Rosenwald, G. C. & Ochberg, R.L. (Eds) (1992)   *Storied lives: The cultural politics of self-understanding*. New Haven, CT: Yale University Press.

Rotenberg, K. J., & Hamel, J. (1988)   Social interaction and depression in elderly individuals. *International Journal of Aging and Human Development*, **27**, 305–318.

Roth, P. (1991)   *Patrimony: A true story*. New York: Simon & Schuster.

Rounsaville, B. J., Weissman, M.M., Prusoff, B.A., & Herceg-Baron, R.L. (1979). Marital disputes and treatment outcome in depressed women. *Comprehensive Psychiatry*, **20**, 483–490.

Rubin, L. B. (1985)   *Just friends: The role of friendship in our everyday lives*. New York: Harper & Row.

Rubin, Z. (1973)   *Liking and loving*. New York: Holt, Rinehart & Winston.

Rusbult, C. E. (1980)   Commitment and satisfaction in romantic associations: A test of the investment model. *Journal of Experimental Social Psychology*, **16**, 172–186.

Rusbult, C. E. (1991)   Comment on Johnson's "Commitment to personal relationships": What's interesting, and what's new? In W. H. Jones & D. Perlman (Eds) *Advances in personal relationships*, Vol. 3 (pp. 151–169). London: Jessica Kingsley.

Ruscher, S. M., & Gotlib, I.H. (1988)   Marital interaction patterns of couples with and without a depressed partner. *Behavior Therapy*, **19**, 455–470.

Russek, L. G., Schwartz, G.E., Bell, I.R., & Baldwin, C.M. (1998)   Positive perceptions of parental caring are associated with reduced psychiatric and somatic symptoms. *Psychosomatic Medicine*, **60**, 654–657.

Rychlak, J. F. (1988)   *The psychology of rigorous humanism*, 2nd edn.. New York: New York University Press.

Rychlak, J. F. (1976)   (Ed) Dialectic: Humanistic rational for behavior and development. New York: Karger.

Ryder, R. G., & Bartle, S. (1991)   Boundaries as distance regulators in personal relationships. *Family Process*, **30**, 393–406.

Sabini, J., & Silver, M. (1982)   *Moralities of everyday life*. Oxford: Oxford University Press.

Sacks, H. (1972)   An initial investigation of the usability of conversational data for doing sociology. In D. Sudnow (Ed) *Studies in social interaction* (pp. 31–75). New York: Free Press.

Salzinger, L. L. (1982)   The ties that bind: The effects of clustering on dyadic relationships. *Social Networks*, **4**, 117–145.

Sandler, J., & Sandler, A-M. (1986)   On the development of object relationships and affects. In P. Buckley (Ed) *Essential papers on object relations* (pp. 272–292). New York: New York University Press.

Sapadin, L. A. (1988)   Friendship and gender: Perspectives of professional men and women. *Journal of Social and Personal Relationships*, **5**, 387–403.

Sarbin, T. (ed) (1986)   *Narrative psychology: The storied nature of human conduct.* New York: Praeger.

Schlenker, B.R., & Leary, M.R. (1982)   Social anxiety and self-presentation: A conceptualization and model. *Psychological Bulletin*, **92**, 641–669.

Schonbach, P. (1980)   A category system for account phases. *European Journal of Social Psychology*, **10**, 195–200.

Schonbach, P., & Kleibaumhuter, P. (1990)   Severity of reproach and defensiveness of accounts. In M. J. Cody & M. L. McLaughlin (Eds) *The psychology of tactical communication* (pp. 229–243). Clevedon: Multilingual Matters.

Schutz, A. (1971)   In M Natanson (Ed.) *Collected Papers: Volume I: The Problems of Social Reality.* The Hague: Matinus Nijoff.

Schutz, W. C. (1958)   *FIRO: A three-dimension theory of interpersonal behavior.* New York: Holt, Rinehart, & Winston.

Schwenzer, M. (1996)   Social fears in hypochondriasis. *Psychological Reports,* **78**, 971–975.

Scott, M. B., & Lyman, S. M. (1968)   Accounts, *American Sociological Review*, **33**, 46–62.

Searle, J. (1969)   *Speech acts: An essay in the philosophy of language.* Cambridge: Cambridge University Press.

Seattle Times (1994)   They met at a wedding and later had their own. *Seattle Times*, p. G2, March 29.

Segrin, C. (1990)   A meta-analytic review of social skill deficits in depression. *Communication Monographs*, **57**, 292–308.

Segrin, C. (1992)   Specifying the nature of social skill deficits associated with depression. *Human Communication Research*, **19**, 89–123.

Segrin, C. (1993)   Interpersonal reactions to depression: The role of relationship with partner and perceptions of rejection. *Journal of Social and Personal Relationships*, **10**, 83–97.

Segrin, C. (1996)   The relationship between social skills deficits and psychosocial problems: A test of a vulnerability model. *Communication Research*, **23**, 425–450.

Segrin, C. (1999)   Social skills, stressful life events, and the development of psychosocial problems. *Journal of Social and Clinical Psychology,* **18**, 14–34.

Segrin, C. (in press). Social skills deficits associated with depression. *Clinical Psychology Review.*

Segrin, C., & Dillard, J.P. (1991)   (Non)depressed persons' cognitive and affective reactions to (un)successful interpersonal influence. *Communication Monographs*, **58**, 115–134.

Segrin, C., & Dillard, J.P. (1992)   The interactional theory of depression: A meta-analysis of the research literature. *Journal of Social and Clinical Psychology*, **11**, 43–70.

Segrin, C., & Fitzpatrick, M. A. (1992)   Depression and verbal aggressiveness in different marital couple types. *Communication Studies*, **43**, 79–91.

Segrin, C., & Flora, J. (in press). Poor social skills are a vulnerability factor in the development of psychosocial problems. *Human Communication Research.*

Segrin, C., & Kinney, T. (1995)   Social skills deficits among the socially anxious: Loneliness and rejection from others. *Motivation and Emotion*, **19**, 1–24.

Selvini-Palazzoli, M., Boscola, L., Cecchin, G., & Prata, G. (1978)   *Paradox and counterparadox*. New York: Jason Aronson.

Semin, G. R., & Manstead, A. S. R. (1983)   *The accountability of conduct: A social psychological analysis*. London: Academic Press.

Sexton, L. G. (1994)   *Searching for Mercy Street: My journey back to my mother, Anne Sexton*. Boston, MA: Little, Brown.

Sherwood, S., Smith, P., & Alexander, J. (1993)   The British are coming … again! The hidden agenda of "cultural studies." *Cultural Studies*, **22**, 370–375.

Shotter, J. (1987)   The social construction of an (us): Problems of accountability and narratology. In R. Burnett, P. McGee, & D. Clarke (eds) *Accounting for relationships: Explanation, representation, and knowledge* (pp. 225–247). London; Methuen.

Shotter, J. (1992)   What is a "personal" relationship? A rhetorical-responsive account of "unfinished business". In J. H. Harvey, T. L. Orbuch, & A. Weber (Eds) *Attributions, accounts and close relationships* (pp. 19–39). New York: Springer-Verlag.

Shotter, J. (1993)   *Conversational realities: Constructing life through language*. Thousand Oaks, CA: Sage.

Shotter, J., & Gergen, K. (Eds) (1989). *Texts of identity*. London: Sage.

Siegel, K., & Krauss, B.J. (1991)   Living with HIV infection: Adaptive tasks of seropositive gay men. *Journal of Health and Social Behavior*, **32**, 17–32.

Sights, J. R., & Richards, H.C. (1984)   Parents of bulimic women. *International Journal of Eating Disorders*, **3**, 3–13.

Sigman, S. J. (1991)   Handling the discontinuous aspects of continuous social relationships: Toward research on the persistence of social forms. *Communication Theory*, **1**, 106–127.

Singer, M., Wynne, L., & Toohey, M. (1978)   Communication disorders and the families of schizophrenics. In L.C. Wynne, R.L. Cromwell, & S. Matthysse (Eds) *The nature of schizophrenia: New approaches to research and treatment* (pp. 499–511). New York: Wiley.

Snyder, M., Berscheid, E., & Glick, P. (1985)   Focusing on the exterior and the interior: Two investigations of the initiation of personal relationships. *Journal of Personality and Social Psychology*, **48**, 1427–1439.

Sorensen, T., & Snow, B. (1991)   How children tell: The process of disclosure of child sexual abuse. *Journal of the Child Welfare League of America*, **LXX**, 3–15.

Spanier, G. B., & Casto, R. F. (1979)   Adjustment to separation and divorce: A qualitative analysis. In G. Levinger & O. Moles (Eds) *Divorce and separation* (pp. 211–227). New York: Basic Books.

Spence, D. (1982) *Narrative Truth and Historical Truth*. New York: W.W. Norton.

Spencer, E. E. (1994) Transforming relationships through ordinary talk. In S. W. Duck (Ed) (pp. 58–85). *Dynamics of relationships,* (Understanding relationship processes 4): (pp. 58–85). Newbury Park: Sage.

Spencer, T. (1993a) A new approach to assessing self-disclosure. Paper presented at the annual meeting of the Western States Communication Association, Albuquerque, NM, February.

Spencer, T. (1993b) The use of a turning point conversation task to stimulate nearly natural conversation. Paper presented at the Fourth International Network Conference on Personal Relationships, Milwaukee, WI, June.

Spencer, T. (1993c) Testing the self-disclosure reciprocity hypothesis within the context of conversational sequences in family interaction. Paper presented at the annual meeting of the Speech Communication Association, Miami, FL, November.

Spencer, T. (1994) Transforming relationships through ordinary talk. In S. W. Duck (Ed), *Dynamics of relationships* (Understanding relationship processes 4) (pp. 58–85). Thousand Oaks, CA: Sage.

Spencer, T., & Derlega, V.J. (1995) Important self-disclosure decisions: Coming out to family and HIV-positive disclosures. Paper presented at the Western States Communication Association convention, Portland, OR, February.

Sperling, M. B., & Berman, W. H. (1991) An attachment classification of desperate love. *Journal of Personality Assessment*, **56**, 45–55.

Spitzberg, B. H., & Cupach, W. R. (1996) Obsessive relational intrusion: Victimization and coping. Paper presented at the International Society for the Study of Personal Relationships Conference, Banff, Canada, August.

Spitzberg, B. H., & Cupach, W. R. (1998) Dusk, detritus, and delusion: A prolegomenon to *The dark side of close relationships*. In B. H. Spitzberg & W. R. Cupach (Eds) *The dark side of close relationships* (pp. xi–xxii). Mahwah, NJ: Erlbaum.

Spitzberg, B. H., & Cupach, W. R. (1999) Jealousy, suspicion, possessiveness and obsession as predictors of obsessive relational intrusion. Paper presented at the International Communication Association convention, San Francisco, CA, May.

Spitzberg, B. H., & Rhea, J. (1999) Obsessive relational intrusion and sexual coercion victimization. *Journal of Interpersonal Violence*, **14**, 3–20.

Stacey, J. (1990) *Brave new families*. New York: Basic Books.

Stafford, L. (1994) Tracing the threads of spider webs. In D. J. Canary & L. Stafford (Eds) *Communication and relational maintenance* (pp. 297–305). New York: Academic Press.

Stamp, G. H., & Banski, M. A. (1992) The communicative management of constrained autonomy during the transition to parenthood. *Western Journal of Communication*, **56**, 281–300.

Steedman, P. (1991) On the relations between seeing, interpreting, and knowing. In F. Steier (Ed.) *Research and reflexivity* (pp. 53–62). London: Sage.

Steier, F. (Ed.) (1991) *Research and reflexivity*. London: Sage.

Stern, M. I., Herron, W. G., Primavera, L. H., & Kakuma, T. (1997) Interpersonal perceptions of depressed and borderline inpatients. *Journal of Clinical Psychology,* **53**, 41–49.

Stewart, J. (1995) *Bridges not walls: A book about interpersonal communication,* 6th edn. New York: McGraw-Hill.

Stillwell, A. M., & Baumeister, R. F. (1997)   The construction of victim and perpetrator memories: Accuracy and distortion in role-based accounts. *Personality and Social Psychology Bulletin*, **23**, 1157–1172.

Stone, E. (1988)   *Black sheep and kissing cousins: How our family stories shape us*, New York: Penguin.

Sugarman, D. B., & Hotaling, G. T. (1989)   Dating violence: Prevalence, context, and risk markers. In M. A. Pirog-Good & J. E. Stets (Eds) *Violence in dating relationships: Emerging social issues* (pp. 3–32). New York: Praeger.

Sullivan, H. S. (1953)   *The interpersonal theory of psychiatry*. New York: Norton.

Summit, R.C. (1983)   The child sexual abuse accommodation syndrome. *Child Abuse and Neglect*, **7**, 177–193.

Sunnafrank, M. (1984)   A communication-based perspective on attitude similarity and interpersonal attraction in early acquaintance. *Communication Monographs*, **51**, 372–380.

Surra, C. A., & Milardo, R. (1991)   The social psychological context of developing relationships: Psychological and interactive networks. In D. Perlman & W. Jones (Eds), *Advances in personal relationships, Vol. 3* (pp. 1–36). London: Jessica Kingsley.

Surra, C. A., & Ridley, C. (1991). Multiple perspectives on interaction: Participants, peers and observers. In B. M. Montgomery & S. W. Duck (Eds) *Studying interpersonal interaction* (pp. 35–55). New York: Guilford.

Swados, E. (1991)   *The Four of Us*. New York: Farrar, Straus & Giroux.

Swain, S. O. (1992)   Men's friendships with women: Intimacy, sexual boundaries, and the informant role. In P. Nardi (Ed) *Men's friendships* (pp. 153–171). Newbury Park, CA: Sage.

Tangney, J. P. (1995)   Recent advances in the empirical study of shame and guilt. *American Behavioral Scientist*, **38**, 1132–1145.

Tangney, J. P., Wagner, P. E., Hill-Barlow, D., Marschall, D. E., & Gramzow, R. (1996)   Relation of shame and guilt to constructive versus destructive responses to anger across the lifespan. *Journal of Personality and Social Psychology*, **70**, 797–809.

Tangney, J. P., Wagner, P., Fletcher, C., & Gramzow, R. (1992)   Shamed into anger? The relation of shame and guilt to anger and self-reported aggression. *Journal of Personality and Social Psychology*, **62**, 669–675.

Tannen, D. (1990)   *You just don't understand: Women and men in conversation*. New York: Morrow.

Taylor, C. (1977)   Interpretation and the sciences of man. In F. Dallmayr & T. McCarthy (Eds) *Understanding and social inquiry* (pp. 101–131). Notre Dame: University of Notre Dame Press.

Taylor, D. A. (1968)   Some aspects of the development of interpersonal relationships: Social penetration processes. *Journal of Social Psychology*, **75**, 79–90.

Taylor, D.A., & Altman, I. (1987)   Communication in interpersonal relationships: Social penetration processes. In M.E. Roloff and G.R. Miller (Eds) Interpersonal processes: New directions in communication research (pp. 257–277). Newbury Park, CA: Sage.

Tennov, D. (1979)   *Love and limerance*. New York: Stein and Day.

Tesser, A. (1978)   Self-generated attitude change. In L. Berkowitz (Ed.) *Advances in experimental social psychology,* Vol. **11** (pp. 289–338). New York: Academic Press.

Thompson, J.M., Whiffen, V.E., & Blain, M.D. (1995)   Depressive symptoms, sex, and perceptions of intimate relationships. *Journal of Social and Personal Relationships,* **12**, 49–66.

Thompson, L., & Walker, A. J. (1982)   The dyad as the unit of analysis: Conceptual and methodological issues. *Journal of Marriage and the Family,* **44**, 889–900.

Thornes, B., & Collard, J. (1979)   *Who divorces?* London: Routledge & Kegan Paul.

Tillmann-Healy, L. (1998)   Life projects: A narrative ethnography of gay–straight friendship. Unpublished PhD Dissertation, University of South Florida.

Titus, S. L. (1980)   A function of friendship: Social comparisons as a frame of reference for marriage. *Human Relations,* **33**, 409–431.

Tjaden, P., & Thoennes, N. (1998)   *Stalking in America: Findings from the National Violence Against Women Survey.* Washington DC: National Institute of Justice and Centers for Disease Control and Prevention (NCJ 169592).

Todorov, T. (1984)   *Mikhail Bakhtin: The dialogic principle* (Trans, W. Godzich). Minneapolis, MN: University of Minnesota Press (original work published 1981).

Tolhuizen, J. H. (1989)   Communication strategies for intensifying dating relationships: Identification, use and structure, *Journal of Social and Personal Relationships,* **6**, 413–434.

Tracy, K. (1990)   The many faces of facework. In H. Giles and W. P. Robinson (Eds), *Handbook of language and social psychology* (pp. 209–226). New York: Wiley.

Trull, T. J., Useda, D., Conforti, K., & Doan, B. (1997)   Borderline personality disorder features in nonclinical young adults: 2. Two-year outcome. *Journal of Abnormal Psychology,* **106**, 307–314.

Uematsu, M. (1996) Giving voice to the account: The healing power of writing about loss, *Journal of Personal and Interpersonal Loss.* **1**, 17–28.

van Furth, E. F., van Strien, D.C., Martina, L.M.L., van Son, M.J.M., Hendrickx, J.J.P., & van Engeland, H. (1996)   Expressed emotion and the prediction of outcome in adolescent eating disorders. *International Journal of Eating Disorders,* **20**, 19–31.

Vandereycken, W., Kog, E., & Vanderlinden, J. (Eds) (1989)   *The family approach to eating disorders.* New York: PMA Publishing.

Vangelisti, A. L. (1994)   Family secrets: Forms, functions and correlates. *Journal of Social and Personal Relationships,* **11**, 113–135.

Vangelisti, A.L., & Banski, M.A. (1993)   Couples' debriefing conversations: the impact of gender, occupation, and demographic characteristics. *Family Relations,* **42**, 149–157.

Van Lear, C. A. (1987)   The formation of social relationships: A longitudinal study of social penetration, *Journal of Social and Personal Relationships,* **13**, 299–322.

Van Lear, C. A. (1991)   Testing a cyclical model of communicative openness in relationship development: Two longitudinal studies. *Communication Monographs,* **58**, 337–361.

Vaughn, C., & Leff, J.P. (1976)   The measurement of expressed emotion in the families of psychiatric patients. *British Journal of Clinical and Social Psychology,* **15**, 157–165.

Vernberg, E. M., Abwender, D.A., Ewell, K.K., & Beery, S.H. (1992) Social anxiety and peer relationships in early adolescence: A prospective analysis. *Journal of Clinical Child Psychology,* **21**, 189–196.

Veroff, J., Sutherland, L., Chaidla, L., & Ortega, R. M. (1993) Newly weds tell their stories: A narrative method for assessing marital experience. *Journal of Social and Personal Relationships*, **10**, 437–457.

Veroff, J., Young, A. M., & Coon, H. M. (1997) The early years of marriage. In S. W. Duck (Ed) *Handbook of personal relationships,* 2nd edn (pp. 431–450). Chichester: Wiley.

Voloshinov, V. N./Bakhtin, M. M. (1973) *Marxism and the philosophy of language* (Trans. L. Matejks & I. R. Titunik). Cambridge, MA: Harvard University Press.

Vygotsky, L. S. (1986) *Thought and language* (Trans. A. Kozulin). Cambridge, MA: MIT Press.

Walkover, B. (1992) The family as an overwrought object of desire. In G.C. Rosenwald & R.L. Oshberg (Eds) *Storied lives: The cultural politics of self-understanding* (pp. 178–191). New Haven, CT: Yale University Press.

Waller, G., & Calam, R. (1994) Parenting and family factors in eating problems. In L. Alexander-Mott & D.B. Lumsden (Eds) *Understanding eating disorders: Anorexia nervosa, bulimia nervosa, and obesity* (pp. 61–76). Philadelphia, PA: Taylor & Francis.

Waller, G., Slade, P., & Calam, R. (1990) Family adaptability and cohesion: Relation to eating attitudes and disorders. *International Journal of Eating Disorders*, **9**, 225–228.

Watzlawick, P., Beavin, J. H. & Jackson, D. D. (1967) *Pragmatics of human communication: A study of interactional patterns, pathologies, and paradoxes.* New York: W.W. Norton.

Watzlawick, P., Weakland, J. H., & Fisch, R. (1974) *Change: Principles of problem formation and resolution.* New York: Norton.

Weber, A. L., & Harvey, J. H. (1994) Accounts in coping with relationship loss. In A.L. Weber & J.H. Harvey (Eds) *Perspectives on close relationships.* Needham Heights, MA: Allyn & Bacon.

Weber, A. L., Harvey, J. H. & Stanley, M. (1987) The nature and motivations of accounts for failed relationships. In R. Burnett, P. McGhee, & D. Clarke (Eds) *Accounting for Relationships* (pp. 114–135). London: Methuen.

Weinstein, A. (1988) *The fiction of relationship.* Princeton, NJ: Princeton University Press.

Weiss, R. (1975) *Marital separation,* New York: Basic Books.

Wellman, B. (1979) The community question: The intimate networks of East Yorkers. *American Journal of Sociology*, **84**, 1201–1231.

Wellman, B., Carrington, P., & Hall, A. (1988) Networks as personal communities. In B. Wellman and S. D. Berkowitz (Eds) *Social structures: A network approach* (pp. 130–184). Cambridge: Cambridge University Press.

Wells, J. W., & Kline, W. B. (1987) Self-disclosure and homosexual orientation, *Journal of Social Psychology*, **127**, 191–197.

Werking, K. J. (1992) The communicative management of cross-sex friendship. Unpublished doctoral dissertation, Purdue University.

Werking, K. J. (1994a)   Barriers to the formation of cross-sex friendship. Paper presented at the INPR Annual Conference (Professional Development), Iowa City, IA, May.

Werking, K. J. (1994b)   Topics of talk and the activities of close cross-sex friends. Unpublished manuscript.

Werking, K. J. (1994c)   Dissolving cross-sex friendships. Paper presented at the Speech Communication Association conference, New Orleans, LA, November.

Werking, K. J. (1995)   "We're just good friends": Women and men in friendship. Unpublished manuscript.

Werner, C. M., & Baxter, L. A. (1994)   Temporal qualities of relationships: Organismic, transactional and dialectical views. In M. L. Knapp & G. R. Miller (Eds) *Handbook of interpersonal communication*, 2nd edn (pp. 323–379). Newbury Park: Sage.

Werner, C. M., Altman, I., & Oxley, D. (1985)   Temporal aspects of homes: A transactional perspective. In I. Altman & C. M. Werner (Eds) *Human behavior and environment: Advances in theory and research* (pp. 1–32). Beverly Hills, CA: Sage.

Werner, C. M., Altman, I., Brown, B., & Ginat, J. (1993)   Celebrations in personal relationships: A transactional/dialectical perspective. In S. W. Duck (Ed.) *Social context and relationships* (pp. 109–138). Newbury Park, CA: Sage.

Werner, C. M., Altman, I., Oxley, D., & Haggard, L. M. (1987)   People, place and time: A transactional analysis of neighborhoods. In W. Jones & D. Perlman (Eds) *Advances in personal relationships*, Vol. 1 (pp. 243–275). Greenwich, CT: JAI.

Werner, C. M., Brown, B., Altman, I., & Staples, J. (1992)   Close relationships in their physical and social contexts: A transactional perspective. *Journal of Social and Personal Relationships*, **9**, 411–431.

Werner, C. M., Haggard, L. M., Altman, I., & Oxley, D. (1988)   Temporal qualities of rituals and celebrations: A comparison of Christmas Street and Zuni Shalako. In J. E. McGrath (Ed) *The social psychology of time: New perspectives* (pp. 203–231). Newbury Park, CA: Sage.

West, C., & Fenstermaker, S. (1995)   Doing difference. *Gender & Society*, **9**, 8–37.

West, C., & Zimmerman, D.H. (1987)   Doing gender. *Gender & Society*, **1**, 125–151.

White, H. (1980)   The value of narrativity in the representation of reality. *Critical Inquiry*, **7**, 5–27.

Whitney, C. (1990)   *Uncommon lives: Gay men and straight women*. New York: New American Library.

Wiggins, J. S. (1982)   Circumplex models of interpersonal behavior in clinical psychology. In P.C. Kendall & J.N. Butcher (Eds) *Handbook of research methods in clinical psychology* (pp. 183–221). New York: Wiley.

Wilmot, W. W., Carbaugh, D. A., & Baxter, L. A. (1985)   Communicative strategies used to terminate romantic relationships. *Western Journal of Speech Communication*, **49**, 204–216.

Wilson, S. R. (1992)   Face and facework in negotiation. In L. L. Putnam & M. E. Roloff (Eds) *Communication and negotiation* (pp. 176–205). Newbury Park, CA: Sage.

Winters, A. M., & Duck, S. W. (2000). You ****!!! Swearing as an aversive and a relational activity. In R Kowalski (Ed.) *The underbelly of social interaction: Aversive interpersonal behaviors.* Washington, DC: APA Books.

Wiseman, J. P. (1986) Friendship: Bonds and binds in a voluntary relationship. *Journal of Social and Personal Relationships*, **3**, 191–211.

Wonderlich, S. (1992) Relationship of family and personality factors in bulimia. In J.H. Crowther, D.L. Tennenbaum, S.E. Hobfoll, & M.A.P. Stephens (Eds) *The etiology of bulimia nervosa: The individual and familial context* (pp. 103–126). Washington, DC: Hemisphere.

Wonderlich, S., Ukestad, L., & Perzacki, R. (1994) Perceptions of nonshared childhood environment in bulimia nervosa. *Journal of the American Academy of Child and Adolescent Psychiatry*, **33**, 740–747.

Wood, J. T. (1993) Engendered relations: Interaction, caring, power and responsibility in intimacy. In S. W. Duck (Ed.) *Social context and relationships* (pp. 26–54). Newbury Park, CA: Sage.

Wood, J. T. (1995) Feminist scholarship and the study of relationships. *Journal of Social and Personal Relationships*, **12**, 103–120.

Wood, J. T., Dendy, L. L., Dordek, E., Germany, M., & Varallo, S. M. (1994) Dialectic of difference: An interpretive study of intimates' meanings for difference. In K. Carter & M. Presnell (Eds) *Interpretive approaches to interpersonal communication* (pp. 115–136). New York: SUNY Press.

Wood, L. A., & |Kroger, R. O. (1994). The analysis of facework in discourse: Review and proposal. *Journal of Language and Social Psychology,* **13**, 248–277.

Wright, J. A., Burgess, A. G., Burgess, A. W., Laszlo, A. T., McCrary, G. O., & Douglas, J. E. (1996) A typology of interpersonal stalking. *Journal of Interpersonal Violence*, **11**, 487–502.

Wright, P. H. (1989) Gender differences in adults' same- and cross-gender friendships. In R.G. Adams & R. Blieszner (Eds) *Older adult friendship* (pp. 197- 221). Newbury Park, CA: Sage.

Wynne, L. (1984) The epigenesis of relational systems: A model for understanding family development. *Family Process*, **23**, 297–318.

Wynne, L. C. (1981) Current concepts about schizophrenics and family relationships. *Journal of Nervous and Mental Disease*, **169**, 82–89.

Yalom, I. (1989) *Love's Executioner. and other tales of psychotherapy*, New York: Harper Perennial.

Yalom, I., & Elkin, G. (1974) *Every day gets a little closer: A twice-told therapy.* New York: Basic Books.

Yerby, J., Buerkel-Rothfuss, N., & Bochner, A.P. (1995) *Understanding family communication*, Scottsdale, AZ: Gorsuch Scarisbrick.

Zelditch, M. (1964) Family, marriage and kinship. In R. E. L. Faris (Ed) *Handbook of modern sociology* (pp. 680–733). Chicago: Rand McNally.

Zicklin, G. (1969) A conversation concerning face-to-face interaction. *Psychiatry*, **August**, 236–249.

Zola, I. (1982a) *Missing pieces: A chronicle of living with a disability*, Philadelphia; PA: Temple University Press.

Zola, I. (1982b) (Ed.) *Ordinary lives: Voices of disability and disease*. Cambridge: Apple-wood Books.

AUTHOR INDEX

SUBJECT INDEX